C1 *for* *Wholeness*

The Science, Religion, and Astrology of Knowing
Yourself and Living in Harmony

Andrew Benedict Acheampong, PhD

PROMONTORY
P R E S S

CREATED FOR WHOLENESS
The Science, Religion, and Astrology of Knowing
Yourself and Living in Harmony

Promontory Press
www.promontorypress.com

ISBN: 978-1-927559-48-2

First Edition: May 2014

Typeset by Arlene Littler Design in ITC Veijovic

Cover by McCorkle Creations

Printed in Canada

DEDICATION

To the memory of my mother, Mary Adu Acheampong
(1930-2007)

ACKNOWLEDGEMENTS

I am deeply thankful to Alfreda Acheampong, my wife, and Peter Abe, my son by marriage, for their love, compassion and support in my life. I would like to thank members of my extended family, my friends and partners for their support over the years in my religious expression, spiritual journey, graduate education and scientific careers.

I would also like to express my gratitude to Matthew Adu Acheampong, Peter Abe, Georgina Adubofuor, Felicity Acquah, Theresa Kyerematen, Alex Doku, Paul Banahene, George Piprah, Sahara Ohene Karikari, Moses Oduro, David Faraday Agyeman, and Ernest Quansah for their advice on living a life of wholeness.

I am grateful to the editor, Mary Rosenblum, for her review, corrections and optimally improving the quality of the manuscript. I am indebted to Mary for her kindness and good heart in guiding me in the revision process. Special thanks goes to Heather McCorkle for the layout and design of the book. I am also appreciative of the artistic suggestions provided to me by Gyedu Adomako.

I am also thankful to those who inspired and encouraged me when I began to develop the concept for this book, including Madam Agatha Appiagyei, Madam Margaret Simons, Anthony Osei Tutu, Diane Tang-Liu, Myrlene Chapman and Rose Brempong.

TABLE OF CONTENTS

INTRODUCTION

Motives for This Book

Life presents us with numerous mysteries that draw our attention to the creative Mind of God. One of them is how each one of us is created with uniqueness and purpose. The Bible tells us that God knew us before we were born (Jeremiah 1:5). *Who are you? If you think you know who you are, how much do you know about yourself?* If someone were to ask you informally or in a date to describe yourself, without talking about your origins and what you do for a living, what would you say? Your answer may describe your personal characteristics or qualities. I am strongly convinced that knowledge of myself and law of wholeness made a huge difference for me in overcoming huge challenges and obstacles in my life.

Webster's dictionary defines wholeness as *"being healthy, at ease, in abundance with creation, and complete."* A whole soul is a person who is full of life, integrity, unbroken, complete, unified, well integrated, well-aligned, all rounded, well balanced, concurred, self-harmonized, or not conflicted. The person of wholeness is also disciplined, self-controlled, content, adaptable and emotionally stable.

> *Fernando Pessoa in Poems of Fernando Pessoe wrote:*
> *To be great, be whole*
> *Exclude nothing, exaggerate nothing that is not you*
> *Be whole in everything.*
> *Put all you are into the smallest thing you do*
> *So, in each lake, the moon shines with splendor*
> *Because it blooms above*

You may ask *"How is understanding myself going to help me to be satisfied, happy or less worried with my life?"* Your self-image is a mental image of your physical body and individuality. There is more to you than your self-image or your genetic make-up. For starters, your personality reveals your feelings, thinking, behaviors, and actions. Secondly, each one of us is a divided self who is evolving into wholeness. Thirdly, there are your Body self, Personality self, Conscious self (Ego-mind), Subconscious self (habits, motivations, memories), Unconscious self (hidden self), Executive self (soul) and Higher self (spirit). So, which self is running your life? Is it your body self or your soul? Is each part of yourself whole? The Tao Te Ching v.1 explains that to be whole, each part of the total self has to be whole and the total self has to be whole in each part.

My aim in writing this book is to share my experience as I found out who I am and what my purpose is as a human being. And equally important, I want to share my personal story about my search for my soul, amidst struggle and the process of learning how to be a whole person. Once you know your strengths, weaknesses, and bad habits, you will have a strong motivation to live a purposeful and fulfilled life. To become whole and happy, you have to know who you are and accept who you are and make necessary improvements to achieve self-harmony and harmony with your neighbors and the Spirit of your Creator.

I found out early in my life that I am a seeker of knowledge of the self, God, and spiritual practices for achieving wholeness of my soul. I want to share my spiritual knowledge and experiences that I have accumulated over the years. This understanding of spirituality has strengthened my faith and trust in myself and my Creator. I also want to share with you what I learned in the discovery of new dimensions in personalities, religion, astrology, and meditation. Regarding meditation, the Tao Te Ching says in v.37, *"Returning to silence is returning to peace. Returning to peace the world reharmonizes itself."*

ANDREW BENEDICT ACHEAMPONG

My experience with Christianity, the science of yoga, meditation, and astrology make this book unique, compared to other books on self-knowledge. I point out what I think are common threads or differences in a variety of spiritual practices and religious belief systems. I have integrated these ideas based on my understanding of religious scriptures and my spiritual experiences. The Bible says in Proverbs 18: 14-15:

The strong spirit of a man sustains him in a bodily pain or trouble, but a weak and broken spirit who can raise up or bear? The mind of the prudent man is ever getting knowledge and the ear of the wise is ever seeking knowledge.

In terms of self-knowledge, there is also a text in the Islamic Hadith that says, *"He who knows himself knows the Lord."*

This book is for those of you who are also seeking knowledge of the self and want to validate who you are and your experiences of yourself. It is for those of you who want to increase your consciousness of your soul's personalities, work on your weaknesses, renew your mind, make changes to escape from bad habits and wrong beliefs, and re-awaken the spirit of God within you.

My approach is to simply present the realities on self-knowledge and wholeness of the soul. I decided to be real and not couch the message in fairy tales, fantasy or mythic forms. I have to apologize if the message sounds like I am preaching, moralizing, or pontificating. I included many quotations of key ideas from well-known spiritual teachers and religious scriptures. I am a realist and I want to know who I am, not who others want me to be. As a realist, I also want to be an idealist to encourage those who need the message of self-knowledge and wholeness to liberate them from ignorance of the self, self-pity or self-doubt. My intention is to lay out what I know and share my experience with others.

This is a book not only about self-knowledge, but also about one's purpose in life and the struggle to be an integrated, whole self. It is not just about self-growth or self-help but also repairing your life with power of your reborn spirit. I am sharing my lifelong search of what is achievable in wholeness. I am sure different folks have the idea of what wholeness means and how they will go about achieving wholeness. Hopefully, those who are struggling to know themselves and stay whole (rather than seeking to be holier than thou) will find this material useful.

I am writing with knowledge of principles of those who appeared on Earth before me and from what knowledge I have accumulated over the years. I was unsure about some of the personal information I have in the book, but then I am a realist. I hope I don't sound like I am being holier than thou. I am just telling it like it is, from my heart and soul, to avoid hypocrisy. The Bible says, *"Be on your guard against the leaven of the Pharisees, which is hypocrisy. Nothing is covered up that it will not be revealed, hidden that it will not be known"* (Luke 12: 1-2).

Soul Searching for Identity and Wholeness

I believe God has created us to be stewards of this glorious universe. We begin life with the insecurity of a baby and become creative and whole, as God is the source of creativity and perfection. However, if we don't know ourselves, our creative potential, and what our contribution to this world will be, we may live our lives below par. So we all need to do some soul searching and talk to friends, family and professionals to help us know ourselves.

We are all imperfect souls seeking to be happy and become whole in body, mind and soul. We all struggle with bad habits. Unconscious decisions, behavior and actions that lead to bad habits sometimes come to haunt us. Self-inquiry is one good way to approach things and to discover what we are all struggling for in terms of self-knowledge and wholeness. I can think of the following questions for you to think about in order to know yourself, your purpose, faith, personality, and astrological profile.

In terms of self-knowledge:

- Do you know your true strengths and weaknesses?

- Do you know your bad habits and dysfunctional behaviors?

- Does who you say you are match what others say you are?

Purpose in life:

- Do you feel that you are living up to your creative potential?

- Are you certain of your purpose and priorities in life?

Personality-type:

- How well do you know your personality?

- Have you taken a personality assessment test to know your personality type?

- Are you are a thinking, emotional, sensational, or intuitive type?

Astrological profile:

- Are you aware of your Astrological Sun sign and Ascendant?

- In relationships, what signs are you compatible or incompatible with?

Passion in life:

- Do you spend too much time on your job and less on what you love to do?

Religion:

- Do you lose faith in religion because of some beliefs you disagree with?

- Do you know the rationale of the beliefs systems in your religion?

- Do you read your religious scriptures regularly for insight and inspiration?

- Have you learned how to pray and meditate effectively?

Spirituality:

- Do you know what your spiritual path is?

- Do you try too much to fix yourself with your ego-mind?

- Do you awaken your spirit to get things done effortlessly?

- Are your body, mind, and soul aligned with spirit in harmony and purpose?

Journey to wholeness:

- Have you ever experienced major challenges and crises in your life?

- Have you learned any soul lessons from major difficulties in your life?

- Are you having difficulty in overcoming addictions and destructive habits?

Different Names of God but There is One God

Many Holy Scriptures tell us that there is one God. I subscribe to the spiritual law of one God. There is an eternal One who is the Ultimate Reality and Creator of the universe and human beings. We were created out of His Love. God is Pure Consciousness. He is revealed to us through our consciousness and from reading the Holy Scriptures. I am open to finding the truth in myself, the truth in God and in the spiritual laws of God. Since Pure Consciousness is wholeness and godliness, our consciousness is enhanced when we live a life of wholeness.

Since God is called Lord, Yahweh, Allah, Brahman, Krishna, Tao, Cosmic Intelligence, Ground of Being, Ultimate Reality, Great Integrity, Great Web of Life, Sky God or Pure Consciousness in different religions, schools and cultures, I will use the word God in most of this book to represent the Creator of the universe and Ultimate Reality. The Tao Te Ching v. 40 says, *"The movement of the Great Integrity is infinite yet its characteristics is passive. Being defines every form of life, yet all originate in and return to non-being."*

Since God is both a personal God and an impersonal God, I hope that people of different religions will find the word 'God' acceptable in this book to represent the Creator of the universe. For those who prefer a personal God, the personal God is the part of God who is in every human being. For those who favor the impersonal God, the impersonal God is the God that is eternal, unchanging and infinite.

Mysteries of the Self and Universe

There are some people who need proof that God exists before they will believe in God. To me, the mysteries of life, the mysteries of the infinite universe, the mystery of the human brain and mind, and the physical, scientific and spiritual laws of the world are sufficient for me as proof to accept the existence of God.

The Tao Te Ching v. 25 says, *"What preceded life? The earth. What preceded the earth? The Universe. What preceded the universe? The soundless and shapeless origin of origins, ever transforming and having no beginning and end."*

There are numerous mysteries in the universe that God has created. We do not know why we are created the way we are, where we came from before our incarnation on Earth and where we are going after we pass away. The Islamic poet, Hazret Al said, *"You thought you are a part, small, whereas in you there is a universe, the greatest."* Expressed in another way, Dane Rudhyar said in the Astrology of Personality that the individual soul is a microcosm of the macrocosm of the universe.

At least, the mysteries of the subconscious mind, unconscious mind, and dreams should remind you that you are more than your body and that your Creator is impeccable and has amazing creativity. Ralph Emerson said, *"God enters by a private door into every individual. Long prior to the age of reflection is the thinking of the mind. Out of darkness, it came insensibly into the marvelous light of today. Whatever your mind does or says is after a law and this nature law remains over it after it has come to reflection and conscious thought."*

A lot of new discoveries have emerged as we strive to understand the mysteries of the self, mind, soul, and spirit through religion, spirituality, philosophy, science, and astrology. Humans have discovered and developed mystical philosophies, such as astrology, numerology and palmistry. I know a lot of religious folks who do not want to hear anything about science, astrology, and evolution these days. I have met scientists who are skeptical about astrology and religion, but I feel the wave of popularity of religion on the television and in neighborhoods, as well as the popularity of astrology in magazines, newspapers, and on the internet.

Albert Einstein said that *"Science without religion is lame and religion without science is blind."* He also said in *"The World As I See It"* that *"coincidence is God's way of remaining anonymous."* My life-long pursuit is to find out how much I can know myself from evolution, psychology, brain science, spirituality, religion, and astrology to understand the self, mind, soul, and spirit.

Law of Created Being Evolution to Wholeness

Knowledge of wholeness. I am a pharmaceutical scientist who is interested in chemistry, pharmacology, drug safety and application of chemistry and pharmacokinetics to the discovery and development of drugs that heal the body and restore the patient to wellness, without any significant adverse effects from the drug.

As a scientist, yoga practitioner and a Christian, I have devoted considerable time to seeking knowledge and presence of God. I am building my theories on existing ideas of wholeness, studied by philosophers, spiritual teachers and scientists, for testing in the lives of people that I come into contact with. Everybody struggles to become whole, whether you are rich or poor, black or white, weak or strong, Muslim or Jewish, Christian or Buddhist, and Hindu or Taoist. The founding Fathers of the major religions, such as Jesus, Buddha, Lao Tzu, St Paul and scholars, such as Socrates, Carl Jung, and Dane Rudhyar, all taught about self-knowledge, wholeness of self, way of life and way of God. The prerequisite for a life of holiness, godliness or righteousness is to achieve a life of wholeness.

The concept of self-knowledge tends to be related to knowing one's character and purpose. In John 8:14, Jesus responded to the Pharisees, *"Even if I do bear witness about myself, my testimony is true for I know where I came from and where I am going."* The Bible also tells us to commit ourselves "as a living sacrifice, holy and well pleasing to God, which is your reasonable service and spiritual worship" (Roman 12:1).

What is a theory? A theory is a rational model or principle that has been developed to explain a law of nature or nature of human behavior. It is developed by testing the hypothesis of the theory to see if the theory agrees with observations from the test. A hypothesis that is unproven is just a speculation without observations and predictability. An unproven theory goes back to being a hypothesis. When the theory agrees with the test observations, the proven theory can move up to become a principle or law of nature based on its ability to predict future outcomes.

Defining the Problem of human struggle. God created humans with the potential for wholeness. Psalm 82:6 says, *"I said, you are gods. Indeed all of you are children of the most High God."* We are children of God and made in the image of God (Genesis 1:26). If we are made in God's image, according to his likeness, we should behave like God. The American scholar, Ralph Waldo Emerson said, *"Man is God playing the fool."* It seems human beings have followed their own desires and struggled for over thousands of years. These struggles have created various kinds of personalities, which are the karma of different types of souls.

What causes a human to continue to struggle in life? The law of sinful nature requires us to avoid desires of the flesh. If we act on our desires, we create karma. The law of karma is the law of action and reaction. We use our free will to choose good or evil action, and the law of karma warns that we reap what we sow. Whenever you behave badly towards others, you get a response automatically. Our brain and mind record everything we do and think about. Most religions, including Hinduism, Buddhism, Muslim and Christianity, believe that God has knowledge of everything humans do and think about. So, we need to make good choices in life. Each time that we choose evil deeds, we move further and further away from our potential for wholeness. For the human soul to evolve to wholeness and restore the original nature, we need faith to be born again. The Bible says that, with faith in God as our partner, all things are possible.

What do we want out of this world? In various cultures, most people want to be somebody significant, learn some skills and know something in life to have a nice job and live a life of happiness. The problem facing us is that we have to decide to choose a life of material success and pleasure or a life of being like God. Hinduism says we should live a life of wholeness where the self realizes itself as *"Sat, Chit, Ananda."* Thus, the self wants to be God-like and achieve infinite existence (sat), infinite knowledge (chit) and infinite bliss (ananda).

Wholeness is not perfection, but the destination you

achieve before reaching perfection. Christ Jesus is said to have possessed the perfect personality and spiritual consciousness while on Earth. He came to tell the poor, who are struggling in the material world, not to worry, by proclaiming, *"Blessed are the poor (who are) in spirit, for theirs is the kingdom of God"* (Matt 6:10). Those who stay in the awakened spirit will be blessed with peace and joy.

Psychology is the study of human mind and behavior. Knowledge of who you are is important so that you can correct the weaknesses or deficiencies in your personality. Some people don't care to know who they are and don't do the soul work needed for wholeness. There are others who think they individually came up with their personality and therefore they can change their personality at will.

Test observations: I observed my life and the lives of individuals that I have interacted with all these years. As I analyzed the information gathered which is categorized into personality type, soul type, spiritual inclinations, mental type and other personal characteristics, I have come to recognize the different types of struggles for wholeness that we all face. We all recognize that the challenges we encounter in life shape our character and that there is no gain for anyone without pain, including hard work. Suffering provides opportunity for us to grow, mature and experience the joy of being. By overcoming challenges and adversity, we strengthen our faith and accumulate power for turning painful experiences into positive ones.

From these observations, I developed a theory for the soul's journey based on the lives of individuals I know and the operations of at least four key spiritual laws:

- law of sinful nature
- law of karma
- law of faith and reason
- law of love
- law of divine potentialities

Theories on wholeness: As a scientist, I described the theories of the evolution of the soul to wholeness as follows:

- **We are created with divine potentialities to evolve from struggle to wholeness.** Achieving wholeness is the key to an extraordinary life. We have to achieve wholeness within ourselves before we can achieve holiness or union with God or Christ (John 10:30, John 15:4). A person of holiness is a person of godliness, perfect in goodness and a person of righteousness. The Bible says no one is perfect, except God. Only a very, very small number of people can attain holiness. However, the majority of human beings have the creative potential to attain wholeness. We are indeed created for wholeness. To achieve permanent holiness, one has to be in permanent union with God.

- Life is a journey from innocence to sinful nature to wholeness. Evolution signifies progressive changes in behavior for personal growth and spiritual development. God formed each human being to fight a good fight between the forces of good and evil, ignorance and knowledge, lower self and higher self and between love and hate. We are formed to take advantage of the abundance of nature for everything we need in our lives. The Bible says in 2 Peter 3, *"For His divine power has given us everything we need for a life of godliness through our knowledge of God who called us by His own glory and goodness."*

- **Each person is formed with a unique soul, unique personality, unique purpose and role in god's plan on earth** (Psalm 139:16, Jeremiah 1:5).

- There is no one like you. Each one of us has to learn our soul lessons in life, find out their purpose and destiny, and work on the karma of their soul to be born again and have their soul and life restored in wholeness and godliness. God loves everyone that he has created. The Bible says in 1 Cor. 1:28, *"God chose what is low and despised, what is regarded as nothing to set aside what is regarded as something."*

- **Each person has to know his or her essence, faith, strengths and weaknesses.** Everyone has to know who they are and understand their personality, religious faith, spiritual path and spiritual goals for wholeness. As an imperfect being, each person has to know his or her strengths and weaknesses. Do not be tempted by your weaknesses to act in a destructive manner. We have to use our divine potentialities to go beyond temptations.

- Lack of self-knowledge and knowledge of God can be an impediment to knowing your strengths and weaknesses, understanding your self-knowledge and wholeness, our lives can be a life of struggle, difficulties, disappointments, chaos, and unhappiness.

- **The goal of your life's karma is for you to become an integrated or whole self.** We grow into wholeness by being born again, prepared to follow God's spiritual laws. Judgment comes to each person because of the way we live our lives, through the law of sinful nature and law of karma. It comes to everyone so that we can overcome evil and strive towards wholeness.

- Challenges in life reveal our character and what we are made of. If the choices we take are destructive to us, our body, mind and soul will feel the pain and suffering. We build up our faith, wisdom and power by choosing compassion and right action on the way to wholeness.

- **Wholeness is achieved when your body, mind and soul are aligned with your awakened spirit through your faith in god consciousness or spirit**. When you achieve wholeness with alignment of your body, mind, and soul to your spirit, you are filled with the fruits of the spirit, which includes love, joy of being, wisdom and peace of God. What demonstrates one's greatness in life is not in one's material possessions, but how whole you are in your soul and your contribution to building a better world with love, unity, peace, and joy. Love is the most important spiritual gift that we must cultivate and commit our life to. The Bible says, *"And so faith, hope, love abide; these three; but the greatest is love."* (Cor. 13:13).

How I Started in Self-Knowledge and Religion

My quest for self-knowledge began in Ghana, West Africa, in the 1960s and continues as I make daily efforts towards the wholeness of my soul in the blessed country of United States of America. I was born in Kumasi, Ghana, a great country in the western part of Africa. I am the oldest son of my mother in a family with two brothers and three sisters. My mother was a powerful woman, an expert midwife, and a very devout Catholic. I was raised as a Catholic and I have been rooted in my Christian faith since the age of about 10 when I was confirmed as a Catholic. My interest in yoga exercises, yoga, astrology, and meditation came at the age of about 14 when I was in high school. Later on, I got into transcendental meditation at the age of about 19, when I was in college.

The spiritual teachers and experts who motivated and spurred me into an intense study of knowing myself, exploring the science of being, understanding scriptures, meditation, and wholeness in the western and eastern wisdom traditions include: George Gurdjieff, P. D. Ouspensky, Swami Sivananda,

Maharishi Mahesh Yogi, Thomas Merton, Father John Main, Dane Rudhyar and Pastor Frederick K. C. Price. I had to do some research to broaden my knowledge and understanding of self-knowledge and wholeness with respect to psychology, philosophy, religion and astrology. If there were important concepts that I had to understand, I was able to find some of the experts in a particular area of discipline.

Thomas Merton was a Catholic priest and mystic, who wrote extensively about spirituality, contemplation, meditation, faith, reason, love, interfaith cooperation and social justice. I feel that my path as a Catholic and Christian is taking me on a similar path to that taken by Thomas Merton. Although he was committed to Christianity as I am, he studied Buddhism and Taoism as I have done. As a Catholic, he practiced contemplation and meditation, just as I, as a Catholic, practice meditation.

I learned about the Science of Yoga from two great gurus, Swami Sivananda and Maharishi Mahesh Yogi. In his book on the *"Mind, its Mysteries and Control"*, Swami Sivananda taught me about the mind and its mysteries from Vedanta theory. He said, *"Mind and matter are two aspects of subject and object, of one and the same all-full Brahman (God), who is neither and yet includes both ... Mind is the subtle form of matter ... The soul is the only source of Intelligence, it is self-evident, and it shines by its own light."*

In his books on Transcendental Meditation and the Bhagavad Gita, Maharishi Mahesh Yogi really gave me a very good understanding of what meditation is all about, how to meditate effectively, and how meditation works. I started to practice transcendental meditation at the age of about 19. In his book on Transcendental Meditation, Maharishi explained clearly to me how bad habits and behavior put us in bondage to karma. He explained that the actions we take *"create a deep impression which comes to the surface as a is the seed to action. Action in turn produces an impression and thus the cycle of impression, desire and action continues, keeping a person bound to the cycle of cause and effect."*

P. D. Ouspensky is a spiritual teacher who first made me understand why it is so important that we seek wholeness and increase our body, mental, and spiritual consciousness. In his book, *"The Fourth Way"*, he expounded on the problem of identification or attachment, and the techniques of self-observation and self-remembering. According to Ouspensky, identification or attachment is everywhere in our lives. It leads us to bad habits, negative emotions and destructive addiction. He says in *"The Fourth Way" that "in a state of identification you cannot feel right, see right or judge right."*

Reverend K. C. Price is the Bishop of Ever Increasing Faith Ministries in the USA. He is among the early TV evangelists who based his preaching on providing extensive teaching of Biblical texts concerning faith, obedience to God's laws, healing and prosperity. I learned a lot about interpretation of the Bible texts from his TV ministry in the 1990s. He encouraged his members to develop a strong faith in God and walk by faith.

Integration of Science, Religion and Astrology

What may be missing in books that have opened our minds to how we can know ourselves is the lack of integration of self-knowledge from the three areas of religion, science, and astrology. Integration of these three factors appears to provide the clues you need to move from imperfection to wholeness. The important lesson for me and the message I keep repeating in this book is that you can know yourself through science, religion, spirituality, and astrology. I found out that correcting one's weaknesses for wholeness is a difficult thing to do, but we have no choice but to do it with love and tenderness, if we want to achieve the fruits of the spirit, which the Bible says in Gal. 5:22-23 are *"love, joy, peace, kindness, patience, faithfulness, goodness, gentleness and self-control."* Understanding yourself and moving towards wholeness provides alignment of the soul's transformation with spirit.

We live in an imperfect world where there are conflicts, wars, strife, racism, corruption, poverty, and evil. Religion helps us to know our spirit and influence our soul's behavior. When religion tries to dominate us with its belief systems, dogma and doctrines, we may suffer from an absence of reason in religious doctrines and sermons. Therefore, we may be unable to understand our body-mind-soul-spirit connection. Astrology reveals knowledge about our soul's challenges based on our Sun signs, ascendants, and other planetary influences. When astrology dominates us with predictions and psychic readings, it loses its influence on the reason for investigations of the body-mind-soul-spirit connection. It turns out we need religion, science, and astrology in order to know and improve ourselves and to create a better world for our children.

Science is the greatest achievement for mankind. Without science, we will have problems understanding and restoring our body, brain, and personality for wholesome living. Science dominates in helping us to know our body, brain, and mind, how they work, and their connection with our behavior. Science has been able to use biology, genetics, paleoanthropology, and geography to provide reasonable theories on human evolution and the movement of humans from Africa to the Middle East, Europe, Americas and Asia. Genetics also showed that Homo sapiens (not Homo erectus) evolved into modern humans. Science has therefore shown that modern humans, black, white, brown, red, and yellow, have a common ancestry.

These scientific advances have led to understanding of the evolutionary changes that have produced the color of our skin and racial features as a result of heat, cold, environment, climate changes, and other factors. The genetic changes reflect the adaptation of the different races to changes in their environment. Racial, tribal, and cultural differences influence our pursuit of happiness and wholeness as people in various communities organize themselves to support one another in moving towards survival, creating wealth, or creating wholeness of the soul.

It is the philosophers, astrologers, religious and spiritual teachers, not scientists, who have helped us most in understanding the soul and spirit. Your soul or the essence of your personality or temperament is visible early in your childhood and therefore not related to your race, skin color, or tribe. It appears to be from your creator and karma in life. Therefore, your path to wholeness does not appear to be dependent on your skin color, race, and tribe, as God is goodness and impartial to the color of one's skin or one's race. With the absence of scientific research on the relationship between the soul or spirit and personality, the realm of the soul and spirit seem to lie in the domain of religion and astrology.

Can You Change Who You Are?

What would you do if you think your personality is in the way of your path to your purpose and dreams? Should you accept who you are or change yourself to a different character? There have been philosophical debates on whether we are capable of fundamental change in who we are in essence, whether we control our personalities or whether there are forces in the universe that have predetermined how we are going to behave.

It is better to accept who you are, let everyone be who they are and understand that we are all created for wholeness. If you were to know yourself, you will be in a better position to find out what you can change and what you cannot change.

It may appear insurmountable to change the nature of the soul, but the scriptures and spiritual experience tell us that it is doable. We start by liberating our souls from negative emotions and weaknesses of personality. I have strong faith in love that moves us towards wholeness; love of oneself, love of neighbor, and love of God. I am sure some of you have heard about the Serenity Prayer:

> "God, grant me the serenity to accept the things I cannot change, the courage to change the things I can, and the wisdom to know the difference."

Why do people start from life in a more challenging or less challenging condition, only God knows? The rich person

should not assume that he is blessed because he is very affluent. Likewise, the poor person ought not to despair because
he may have started out as poor. The Bible says it is difficult
for the rich to serve both God and money. The Bible also says
"blessed are the poor in spirit." The poor are challenged to stay
in the spirit for joy and peace or seek for financial security.
Follow the laws of life and God and do the soul work to achieve
happiness and wholeness.

In this book, we will explore seven areas of self-knowledge; knowing your strengths and weaknesses, knowing human nature, knowing your psychological personality, knowing
your Western astrological profile, knowing your Chinese astrological profile, knowing your spiritual self, and knowing your
religious self.

The book also examines various approaches to wholeness,
compatibility of you and other souls in relationships and your
astrological path to well-being in your astrological profile. Your
spiritual self also seeks understanding of your body-soul-spirit
connection and needs for higher consciousness and purification of your ego-mind for wholeness. Your religious beliefs and
religious scriptures are covered under religious self. Alright, it
is time to move on to Chapter 1. I hope you enjoy reading this
book to understand yourself and others!

PART ONE

Know Your Uniqueness, Strengths, and Weaknesses

CHAPTER ONE

Building Self-awareness,
Knowledge and Wholeness

Self-Knowledge is The Foundation of Wisdom

Greek philosophers in the ancient times came out with the expression, *"Know Thyself"*, because they reasoned that knowledge of yourself is the foundation of wisdom. Life is more meaningful if you know yourself, your purpose and direction. Socrates believed that the best way to live a wholesome life is to focus on self-development, instead of material possessions. A wholesome life allows you to cultivate good habits, conscious awareness, knowledge, wisdom, creativity and a sense of balance and completeness in your life. Sometimes people are not comfortable if they do not know who you are. Once they get to know you, they may react to you in a more positive way.

The first thing you want to find out in life is who you are and what your purpose is. Then, you will know your strengths, talents, weaknesses, negative emotions, and vulnerabilities. We tend to be limited in our ability to achieve our goals because of our weaknesses and lack of awareness. Ralph Emerson said in his essays on the intellect, mind, and the soul that *"Every man beholds his human condition with a degree of melancholy. As a ship aground is battered by the waves, so man imprisoned in mortal life lies open to the mercy of coming events."* He goes on to say, *"What am I? What has my will done to make me that I am? Nothing."*

Jesus asked his disciples, *"Who do they say I am?"* (Mark 8:27). He said in the Gospel of John, *"I know where I came from and I know where I am going. You do not know what you are and where you are going."* (John 8:14). Jesus said his purpose was to save those who were lost. It is a blessing to start out early in life with a great knowledge of oneself, maximizing your strengths, minimizing the weaknesses in your personality, leveraging your skills for a well-designed professional career, knowing your purpose in life and knowing what spiritual path to take in order to nourish your soul. As Jesus Christ did, if you are convinced that you know who you are, why you are here on Earth, what you came to do on Earth, and how you can serve man and God, you will be far ahead of most people in meeting your purpose in life.

The better you know yourself, the stronger your opinion of yourself is, and the more assertive you are. The key to your future may lie in knowing what you did in your past. You want to know yourself for personal growth and spiritual development.

Jesus said, *"Be perfect, therefore, just as your heavenly Father is perfect."* (Matthew 5:48).

The soul's journey ought to move from imperfection towards wholeness. In the journey to wholeness, negative emotions tend to stop us from making progress. These negative emotions include fear, anger, hatred, guilt, shame, criticism, jealousy, envy, and depression. Avoiding negative emotions is important for wholeness. When you know yourself and the traps of negative emotions, you avoid going through the same negative emotions repeatedly.

Taoism is a religion that says that transformation of everyone into their opposite character is the nature of God, its rebirth, and way of natural processes. In the religious book, Tao the Ching vs. 32, Lao Tzu writes that:

Nothing remains itself.

Each prepares the path of its opposites

To be ready for wholeness, first be fragmented.

To be ready for rightness, first be wronged.

To be ready for fullness, first be empty.

To be ready for renewal, first be worn out.

To be ready for success, first fail.

To be ready for doubt, first be certain.

Personal Weaknesses and Failings

Displeased with himself, Apostle Paul tells us in the Bible (Rom. 7:15) that, *"I do not understand my own actions. I do not accomplish what I want to do, but then I do the very thing that I do not want to do."* Because you are three in one being, namely body, mind (soul) and spirit, you have a lot to learn if you yield to temptations and do not do what you need to do for wholeness.

When you stumble and fall and find yourself in a precarious situation, you do not give up faith in yourself and in God. As you restore faith in yourself, the spirit picks you up onto the right road of opportunity and it shows you that what you fear will pass. You do not give up in life because if you are patient, your spirit will show you a new purpose for living and your time will come for you to take advantage of the next opportunities for success. If you cannot change some of your personality deficiencies, then you accept the things that you cannot change and pray for compassion and healing.

Development of yourself should bring meaning for your body, mind, soul, and spiritual life. The Bible says in 3 John 2, *"behold I pray that you may prosper in all things and be in health, just as your soul prospers."* St. Paul said in Eph. 4:22, *"Renew yourself in the spirit of your mind."* Why should you renew your mind and spirit? Mind renewal and spiritual awakening are need-ed because the mind of the spirit is where your thoughts and actions start from. Swami Sivananda aptly puts it as follows: "What separates you from God is your mind." In essence, when you renew your mind, you are able to change your behavior and the course of your life. You renew your mind by aligning your mind and soul with the reawakened Spirit of God.

J. D. Ouspensky said in *"The Fourth Way"* that *"There are two things that are keeping us back – ignorance and weakness; we do not know enough and we are not strong enough. The question is how do you know more? By self-study – that is the only method. Then comes the struggle with identification and imagination, the chief causes of weakness."* Ouspensky wrote that identification is everywhere at every moment of ordinary life. He explained that when you identify too much with something in your life, you lose yourself and that does not bode well for you.

When you lose yourself in bad habits, addictions, and neg-ative emotions, you are no longer your true self. For example, when you get addicted to smoking or alcohol, you lose yourself because you can't do anything unless you smoke or drink al-cohol. Ouspensky tells us that *"in a state of identification, you cannot feel right, see right and judge right."*

Overcoming Weaknesses in Your Personality

Thomas Merton said in *"Ascent of Truth"* that, *"The highest forti-tude is that in which we overcome obstacles without any apprecia-ble feeling of satisfaction. The bravest man is not the one who never feels fear, but the one who overcomes the greatest fear and goes through danger cool in the presence of terror."*

We all have strengths and weaknesses in our personal-ities. Most people try to be strong so that their weakness will not be seen. However, we have to be careful with contrived appearances that may mask how we feel on the inside. Each individual is already divided into different identities, so if one identity of yourself is suffering, then you need to find out what it is. We need to focus our attention on whatever causes us to be weak, broken-hearted, or desperate during our journey to wholeness.

When you address a weakness in one aspect or identity of yourself, you recover your wholeness and unify the various identities of yourself. Being a whole person means that your multiple identities of yourself are unified into a whole so that you are decisive, unwavering and confident about what decisions or choices you are taking for the individual parts of yourself and your whole self. Being whole means you are not broken in your life or fragmented in your thinking or emotion.

Getting Rid of Addictions and Bad Habits

According to Swami Sivanada in the *"Mind, Its Mysteries and Control"*, *"Desire is the cause of restlessness of the mind. Eradicate desire to eradicate habits."* His prescription was to destroy desire with the Intellect. Peace of mind is attained when our desires don't control the person. He explains by saying that *"You gain peace and will power by giving up one thing. If you give up 15 things, your peace of mind will be still greater and the will still more powerful."* In the end, you are giving up something for something greater, your peace of mind and will-power.

The hardest part of addiction and bad habits is admitting that you have a problem that needs to be fixed. The reason why some people do not overcome their bad habits or weaknesses may be that they refuse to acknowledge their addiction or bad habits.

We are taught in life to do everything in moderation so that we do not hurt ourselves. The Tao Te Ching says in v.3, *"The natural person desires without craving and acts without excess. By not doing, everything is done."* Bad habits, especially addictions, affect our ability to expand our consciousness. Some of the major disabling addictions that we have in modern life include the following:

- Overeating leading to obesity

- Excessive drinking of alcohol, leading to alcoholism

- Addiction to smoking

- Sex addiction

- Chronic gambling

- Addiction to negative emotions, such as hatred and anger

- Addiction to power and the control of others

When you are addicted to food, smoking, or alcohol, you become upset, irritated, and angry if what you are addicted to is taken from you or someone interferes with your addiction. Thus, addiction becomes a cause for unhappiness and unwholesome behavior.

How does one overcome bad habits and addictions? That is what psychologists, priests, and family members are trying to discover in order to help each one of us who succumb to bad habits or addictions. This book focuses on a formula for change that requires one to know oneself well, including your strengths and weaknesses, and do the best you can to improve yourself towards wholeness.

Whatever you do to change your bad habits, you want to

- Know yourself and find your purpose in life.

- Do the hard work required to make changes, with support by family and friends.

- Understand your weaknesses so that you don't let them control you.

- Overcome your weaknesses with love of yourself, love of God for your healing, and love of others affected by your weaknesses.

- Cultivate good habits, even in the midst of your weakness.

A bad habit can lead easily to an addiction, which is repetitive and uncontrollable behavior. Once you get addicted to repetitive behaviors, such as excessive drinking, sex, drugs, or gambling, that gives you pleasure, you lose control of yourself and who you are. Basically, you train your mind to get used to the memory of the behavior, and your mind reacts in a reflex way if you try to deprive it of the addictive behavior. We can change from bad habits to good habits and change from addictions to freedom from cravings through the following actions:

- Power of intention

- Mindfulness and self-observation

- Self-remembering or self-awareness

- Self-control

- Meditation

- Avoiding identification and choosing to be authentic.

To change one's bad habits and addictions, you have to be highly conscious and show your intention to do what is right for yourself. Intention is an important key to change one's behavior. Several spiritual teachers have written books on the power of intention to change our habits, such as *"Power of Intention"* by Wayne Dyer, *"The Seat of the Soul"* by Gary Zukav and *"The Seven Spiritual Laws of Success"* by Deepak Chopra. No one can change your bad habits, except that you consciously intend to choose right behavior. If you slip from active awareness to passive awareness, you are vulnerable to making bad choices in your moments of transition to change your bad habits or addictions. Meditation also helps people to heal from addictive behaviors, such as alcoholism and smoking.

Mindfulness and self-observation turns our attention to our inner and outer self. Practicing mindfulness and self-observation allows you to increase your awareness and know your bad habits so that you can change your behavior. If you observe yourself you learn from your tendencies and past mistakes and you become aware of moments of negative emotions, such as sadness, depression and anger that lead you to engage in destructive habits, so that you can choose between your addiction and self-control. It is better to accept your momentarily sadness than to choose a destructive habit to ease your sadness.

Self-remembering is awareness of your true self. Self-remembering helps us to know that we are spiritual beings, so that we can choose healing actions over destructive behaviors. Self-control is one of the fruits of the spirit.

> James 3:2 says, *"For we all often stumble and fall and offend in many things. And if anyone does not offend in speech, he is a fully developed character and a perfect man, able to control his whole body and curb his entire nature.*
>
> 2 Peter 1:6 says, *"And in knowledge, self-control and in self-control steadfastness, and in steadfastness godliness."*

J. D. Ouspensky explained in his book *"The Fourth Way"* that addiction and bad habits are states of identification where we identify with the bad habit. He says, *"When one is identified, one does not exist, only the thing exists is which one is identified."* In addictions, we lose ourselves and we cannot think right and see what a terrible thing we are doing to ourselves. To change your bad habits and addictions, he recommends that you *"just turn your attention to something more important. You must learn to distinguish the important from the less important and as you turn your attention to more important things you become less identified with unimportant things."*

How I Started My Journey of Self-knowledge

My first exposure to knowledge of the self, yoga, and God came from reading two books by Swami Sivananda in the 1960s. One is titled *Bliss Divine* and the other is *"Mind, Mysteries and its Con-*

trol". The second wave of insight into self-knowledge came from reading books by George Gurdjieff (Kathleen Riordan Speeth *The Gurdjieff Work*) and P. D. Ouspensky's *"The Fourth Way"* in the late 1970s. Gurdjieff proposed in the early 1920s that each human being has several personas or 'I' within the individual and so we do not know ourselves. Instead, we behave like machines, without the ability to integrate the self and transform ourselves towards wholeness. In his book on the *"The Science of Being and Art of Living"*, Maharishi Mahesh Yogi also instructed his disciples to bring their mind from the field of multiplicity to the field of unity of transcendental consciousness. This led me into a study of different religions, spiritual practices, astrology, psychology, and brain science.

According to Wikipedia, the 2010 World Religion database had about 7 billion people in the world, with 33% Christians, 23% Muslims, 14% Hindus, 7% Buddhists, 12% Other Religions, and 11% Non-Religious people. In a Harris poll in 2008-2009, 31% of Americans believed in astrology and 45% believed in evolution.

We seek knowledge of ourselves through religion, science, spirituality, and astrology to become a better person or a more matured personality. A spiritually mature individual is one who tackles his or her weaknesses, bad habits, and the sinful nature in humans in order to effect positive changes for wholeness. Each of the four areas of religion, science, spirituality, and astrology seek the truth about humans and the universe.

Organized religion tells us who we are in God, the creator of the universe, and how we ought to behave, pray, treat each other, and serve God. Science informs us about the body, brain, mind, Universe, and how they work. Spirituality tells us about the spirit, soul, and how we can make progress from the lower self to higher levels of spiritual consciousness. Astrology helps individuals to understand the nature of their souls and the lessons they have to learn in order to overcome their weaknesses and evolve towards wholeness.

Growing Up as a Capricorn

Astrology helped me to know my strengths and weaknesses and get over being too serious, materialistic, and socially anxious. My personality as a child matched Linda Goodman's characterization in her book, *"Linda Goodman's Sun Signs"*. She says in the book:

> *"The Capricorn child is quiet, sober and more centered than the other kids in the neighborhood. He will do anything to feel secure. He knows how to survive. School is not a problem for the Capricorn kid. He tends to be an introverted bookworm and he does not throw temper tantrums. What he needs to combat pessimism and being gloomy is outdoor exercises and developing an outgoing personality."*

Linda Goodman's description of the Capricorn's personality in adulthood also matches mine. She describes the adult Capricorn as easy to recognize. *"He is not a carefree party type, but a social climber. He tends to be strong-willed and show deliberate actions. He looks harmless, but he is tough as a nail. He tends to be gloomy and pessimistic, yet he admires and courts success. He is careful, cautious to avoid obstacles, such as anger, frivolity, jealousy, gossip and impulsive actions. As they grow up, the Capricorn develops a more positive spirit."* This description is a good characterization of a Capricorn like me.

What saved me from being too quiet and serious is that I loved outdoor sports activities and competitions. I was a good soccer player and was selected to play on my elementary, high school, and university teams. Sports also helped me to become more outgoing and improve my leadership abilities as captain of my neighborhood teams. I continue to play soccer and other outdoor sports activities to this day.

Know the Key Obstacles in Your Life

As Linda Goodman pointed out in her description of the flaws of Capricorns, one of the key obstacles in my life was being too serious or less emotionally expressive and at times, gloomy. I became aware of these flaws early in my life and did my best to develop a more positive attitude through my spiritual practices, including meditation on the Spirit of God twice a day, and spending time with friends who know how to have fun.

With inspiration from my mentors, teachers and friends, I have learned a lot about the importance of self-knowledge over the years as I dealt with struggles and crises in my life. One important lesson that I learned in life is that if you know yourself well and make a conscious effort to align your body, soul, and mind with your awakened spirit and move towards wholeness, good things will happen for you through the love and grace of God, our Creator.

The Art and Science of Knowing Yourself

The ancient Greek philosophers knew the art and science of self-knowledge and the wisdom you gain from it. You have to know yourself to be yourself and not be somebody else. If you don't want to know yourself, how can you know if others are right when they say they know who you are? Your concept of yourself can affect your self-confidence, your assertiveness, and your self-esteem.

We do not know why God created us the way we are, but each one of us has to accept the way we were created. It is for you to unravel the mystery for yourself. Did you start out in life as a white, yellow, black or brown person? Were you ushered into this world as the child of a poor, middle class, or rich person? Why is it that we start out in life as imperfect souls? Only God knows. In addition to being imperfect souls, some of us may begin life seriously ill, disabled, or without parents during childhood, well before we begin to pursue material possessions, happiness, and wholeness.

There is an art and a science of knowing yourself. The art of knowing yourself is through education, culture immersion, relationships, religion, philosophy, societal standards and feedback from family members and astrologers. There is also the science of knowing yourself through genetics, biology, psychology, brain science, sociology, physiology and chemistry. There is also great knowledge that you can acquire from your spiritual teachers, advisers and mentors.

Who Do They Say I Am?

Jesus asked his followers, *"Who do they say I am?"* (Matthew 16:13-15) Do you know who Jesus is? What if someone asks you who he is? How do you find out who people are if you do not take time to get to know them, hear what they say about themselves and see what they do or how they treat others. Jesus also urged his followers to know who they are. Those followers got to know him from his sermons, social gatherings, and preaching.

All Christians need to know who they are in order to behave in a Christ-like manner. Paul said, *"I am united with God and I am one spirit with Him"* (I Cor. 6:17). Do you know how God sees you as his child? Paul said in Rom.

> 8:17, *"As a child of God, I am His heir and a fellow heir of Christ."*

Some of the spiritual teachers who practice Buddhism and Hinduism have also taught their followers to be aware and ask self-inquiring questions such as *"who am I"*. Being aware or mindful of who you are goes a long way toward the acquisition of self-knowledge and necessary corrections for personal and spiritual growth.

One of the spiritual teachers in the 20th century, who provoked my thoughts about who I am, is George Gurdjieff. He taught that when we are children we are closer to our essence, but as we get older, we become so mechanical that people are no longer aware of themselves or present in their daily activities. His perception is that people go through the motions and are not in control of their lives.

Gurdjieff taught people how to become more conscious, complete, and whole. He went on to describe how we should practice self-observation and self-remembering in order to know ourselves. Gurdjieff also believed in astrology as he suggested that there are planetary forces in the universe that seem to affect our lives. He believed strongly that self-knowledge and self-consciousness can move us from ordinary consciousness to a higher level of consciousness.

You Are a Spirit with a Soul

Human beings are spiritual beings living in a physical body on Earth. How did the ancient, indigenous people in Africa, India, Asia, Middle East, Europe and the Americas know that they were spirits who possessed a soul? They were probably able to figure out because they are not as distracted in their spiritual connection, as we are today. They could not see God, but they felt that there was a Creator of the universe through their observations of nature. Some observed the position of the stars and planets in order to come up with Middle Eastern astrology, Indian astrology, Chinese Astrology, Jewish astrology, and Mayan astrology.

Socrates, the eminent Greek philosopher and his disciple, Plato, made significant contributions to developing the concept of the immortal soul. They strove to clarify the relationship between the soul and body at about 400 years before the birth of Jesus. They believed that the soul is the home of will, desires, and reason. This concept helped religions such as Christianity, Judaism, and Hinduism develop an interpretation of the soul in their religious scriptures. Socrates also understood the concept of wholeness in terms of cultivating virtues to become a rightly ordered person.

Philosophers were able to understand that you can see your body, but not the intangible areas of your being, which include your soul and spirit consciousness. The first layer of yourself is you, the spiritual being. Without the body and soul, you will exist as a spirit. The second layer is a soul that is hidden from view. The third layer is your body, which is the vehicle for your soul and spirit.

The soul is the real you, where your personality resides, and personality is the karma of your soul. Since your personality includes your character, attitudes, thoughts, and desires, your soul is therefore made up of your desires, thoughts and actions. Consequently, your soul is the choice maker or decision-maker for your desires and actions. However, your soul is hidden and so it observes what goes on in your mind and body. Your ego mind is your false self, which competes with your soul. Every decision you want to make originates from your soul or your ego and is then carried forth by the process of the mind and the body. You have the responsibility for wholeness of your soul, however. Otherwise, your ego will take over your soul.

A spirit is who we are before our incarnation on Earth. The Bible says Jesus is a spirit of God who was incarnated on Earth. Swami Sivananda described Jesus as an Avatar who was incarnated on Earth. We may also be spirits, but we are not at the level of Jesus or Avatars.

The current understanding of spirituality from religion, astrology, and metaphysics is that humans are spiritual beings who live in a body on Earth and acquire experiences in the soul through interactions with matter, mind, and spirit. We are aware of the solid body and subtle mind, but need a higher consciousness to become aware of the more subtle soul and spirit. The spirit is eternal and comes from God. Our soul is our true self on Earth and our soul is the part of ourselves that is embarking on the journey to wholeness. The soul is the decider about who is in control of which direction to take in life. A mind of wholeness is connectable to the mind of God, but an unwholesome mind is separated from the mind of God. As the person of wholeness progresses to person of godliness or the transcendent level of consciousness, he enters into unity with God where his mind is the Mind of God.

Spiritual writers and teachers tell us that the soul is limited by the personality, unless the soul attains wholeness. Our ego, the false self, motivates us and helps us to survive in a life of competition and survival of the fittest. However, if we are not mindful of the well-being of our soul, the egoist mind will take over control from the soul. In his book, *"The Mind, Its Mysteries and Control"*, Swami Sivananda says that the ego-mind is what separates the individual from God. When there is pain or crisis from egoistic behaviors, the soul has to learn to move away from the ego and toward the spirit of God within us.

Knowledge of your strengths, weaknesses, good habits, and bad habits is the starting point for the road to wholeness. It is the soul that experiences good and bad habits, good and evil, struggle and deliverance, sin and forgiveness, and ignorance and knowledge. Our mind is the wall separating us from God. Our mind can work for us to help us achieve happiness or work against us when the ego-mind takes over the soul. Negative feelings tend to come from wrong thinking and can cause us to regress in life, away from the goal of wholeness.

Can You Feel The Soul of Another Person?

Although your soul is not a physical body, your soul vibrates and can be felt by others, revealing your outlook, thoughts, actions, feelings, desires and disposition. It is said that your eye is the window to your soul. If you see someone peering into your eyes, you know he is trying to read your soul. Sometimes, we read other people's body language and eyes to realize that something is bothering their mind or irking their soul. You have probably heard people say that this so-and-so person has a good soul because the person is kind, helpful, honest, and wholesome. You may have met children who looked to be old souls, because they looked too composed or wise for their age.

Self-knowledge is Limited by Your Level of Consciousness

My search for self-knowledge was intensified about 30 years ago, when a friend gave me a copy of the book by J. D. Ouspensky entitled, *"The Fourth Way"*. Ouspensky, a disciple of George Gurdjieff, talked about the necessity for human beings to study themselves and raise their consciousness to higher levels. Ouspensky and Gurdjieff, both Russians, taught that man is like a factory with machines. We behave in a mechanical way because each person has several identities ('I's) within the individual self and we do not know how to be fully conscious and control ourselves effectively. We operate, therefore, in a limited consciousness that leads to unwholesome behaviors and choices. When we expand our consciousness, we learn not to act on every thought that pops into our mind. Instead, we act on what will bring wholeness to our soul.

You have probably heard from somewhere that you cannot change what you are not aware of. So if you don't know your weakness, you don't what behavior to change positively. Ouspensky stated in the *"The Fourth Way"* that, *"The first thing necessary in a serious study of oneself is to understand that consciousness has several degrees. You must understand that you do not pass from one state of consciousness to another, but that they are added to one another."*

When you increase your consciousness, then you are more awake to acquire more knowledge, understand yourself better and change your bad behavior.

Ouspensky goes on to say that *"The second thing necessary in a serious study of oneself is the study of functions by observing, then learning to divide the functions in the right way, learning to recognize each function separately."*

In the early 1900s, Gurdjieff taught his disciples that the four centers in each person are the instinctive center, the moving center, the emotional center, and the intellectual center. This concept can be compared or contrasted with Plato's tripartite of the soul's personality which consists of reason, emotions, and desires or Freud's concept of id (instinctive desires), ego (regulator or mediator) and superego (moral conscience). In the *"Mind, its Mysteries and Control"*, Swami Sivananda also says, *"The four sources of knowledge are instinct, reason, intuition, and super-intuition. Reason is higher than instinct. Intuition is direct perception of truth or immediate knowledge. Intuition transcends reason, but it does not contradict it."*

Living Beyond Limitations

Do we behave as who we are or who we can be? We all face this question. Of course, it is important not to be somebody else. We want to be the best of who we truly are. A popular proverb says that it is not the cards we are dealt in life, it is how we play the game. To avoid suffering, we try to go beyond our lower self, which wants us to gratify ourselves with pleasures and desires that lead us to addictions or suffering. The journey towards wholeness involves changing our focus in life from our lower self to our higher self by expanding our awareness of our inner and outer world.

What do we have to do to expand our consciousness? We must do the following soul work:

- acquire knowledge of human nature and awareness of ourselves and others

- stay alert and live in the present moment,

- practice mindfulness or self-observation.

Mindfulness and self-observation involve increasing one's awareness of what is going on in one's body, feelings, thoughts, and intentions, with both detachment and alertness. The degree to which we improve ourselves, make good choices, and solve personal problems says a lot about our level of conscious awareness.

There are some who say that we have to live within our abilities to survive in a dog-eat-dog world. Others say we have to live up to our highest potential and break through the wall of limitations and weaknesses. Gurdjieff taught his disciples that man is not conscious enough to do anything effectively, because man is like an automatic machine that responds unconsciously. Understanding what it takes to achieve wholeness is more important now than ever. Poverty, insecurities, fears, addictions, fraud, corruption, corporate greed, high divorce rate, drug abuse, sectarian conflicts, religious conflicts, racial hatred and other conflicts have increased gun ownerships and the gap between rich and poor in the developed and developing world.

Evan Pavlov, an eminent Russian physiologist, who lived in the early 1900s in the St. Petersburg area around the same time as Ouspensky and Gurdjieff, coined the term, *'conditioned reflexes'* to refer to the ability of humans to undergo conditioned reactions to changes or stimuli. We do not react well to the stimuli or actions of other people, unless we go through an experience that creates a conditioned response. This brings forth the idea of humans behaving like automated machines, as conditioning is an automated form of learning. The acquired or conditioned response originates from the cerebral cortex, the part of the brain involved in thinking, memory, and consciousness.

Human beings have the free will and capability to expand their consciousness to change their social, cultural, racial, and tribal conditioning to alter their beliefs and produce actions that will transform their souls towards wholeness. Despite our limitations, the Bible tells us that we are made in the image of God, who is a being of pure consciousness. Human beings have conscious, subconscious and unconscious minds. Can you imagine what humans can accomplish with expanded consciousness to access the subconscious and unconscious minds? Even with only limited consciousness and scientific knowledge, humans have created a world with advanced structures, organizations, and technologies.

Functions of the Brain

It is important that we all know how our brain works. Our brain uses fear, emotions and desire to draw our attention. It also helps us in seeking pleasure from bad habits. So, we continuously struggle to break away from dysfunctional behaviors and addictions stemming from desires of our body, brain and mind.

Brain imaging technologies, human studies and animal studies have allowed scientists to obtain valuable information on brain functions and the relationship between behavior and brain types. Rita Carter, a leading science writer, has written books to help the average person to understand the basic functions, anatomy and networks of the brain. Her books titled *"Brain Book"* cover functions of different areas of the brain.

The brain is like a highly advanced computer that receives sensory input from the senses, processes them and transmits information to the various parts of the body. The brain is the seat of the mind on earth. The brain is the bridge between the gross body and the subtle mind. Your brain and your mind keep your records for your soul's journey back to God. Both brain and mind record everything you think about and do.

However, there is one important difference between the brain and the mind. When you pass away, your brain decays, but your mind, soul and spirit go back to your Creator.

The mind is made up of the conscious mind, subconscious mind and unconscious mind. The conscious mind is what we normally use to experience life in the waking state. The organizer and regulator of our conscious mind is the Ego.

The subconscious mind is the storehouse of our memories, past thoughts, habits and experiences. It is where we store past and present knowledge and memories. Once we have learned something by heart with the conscious mind or intellect, such as repetition of good or bad habits, the experience is passed on to the subconscious so that the activity can be done automatically through the subconscious mind. Therefore, elimination of bad habits requires us to use the power of our intellect, consciousness and will-power.

The unconscious mind is the part of our mind that we are not deeply aware of, either about its contents or organization. Our consciousness can be expanded greatly if we can gain access to our subconscious and unconscious minds. Our intuition is not part of our conscious process. It comes from our ability to increase our consciousness and access information in our unconscious mind and spirit.

The brain is largely made up of six areas; the forebrain, mid-brain, hind brain (brain stem), cerebellum, limbic system and basal ganglia to support the intellectual, emotional, movement, and instinctive functions of the self.

The forebrain is the largest portion of the brain and it is mainly made up of the cerebrum, the intellectual part of the brain. The cerebrum consists largely of the cerebral cortex, the outer layer of the brain. The cerebral cortex controls attention, consciousness, memory, imagination and conscious activities, including thinking, reasoning, and planning. The cerebral cortex is the seat of consciousness and it provides information for the conscious mind to be aware and understand what is going on.

The cerebrum is divided into two sections; the right and left hemispheres. Each cerebral hemisphere consists of four lobes; frontal, parietal, temporal and occipital lobes. The frontal lobe or prefrontal cortex plays a role in conscious thought or executive functions involving making decisions, choosing between good and bad actions, and consequences of actions.

The frontal lobe is also implicated in critical thinking, attention, planning, motivation and memory. The temporal lobe is involved with language, consciousness, memory storage, and mood stability. In temporal lobe epilepsy, where the sensory memories and consciousness of the temporal lobe are affected, the experience of consciousness may be altered. The parietal lobe is implicated in sensory processes, spatial abilities, and directions. The occipital lobe is the visual processing unit of the brain.

The cerebellum is below the cerebrum and beside the mid-brain. The cerebellum is the moving center of the brain. The cerebellum is involved in coordination, posture and balance. It also helps in anticipating actions of people you interact with.

The mid-brain consists of the hypothalamus, thalamus and sub thalamus. The midbrain controls the autonomic nervous system which regulates heartbeat, blood pressure and sleep patterns. The thalamus sends preprocessed sensory and motor signals to the cerebral cortex to regulate consciousness, attention and sleep.

The limbic system is the emotional center of the brain, involved in feeling and emotions. The limbic system is below the cerebrum and includes the hippocampus, amygdala, and septum. The limbic system sets the emotional nature of the individual and supports behavior, nurturing, motivation and memory. The hippocampus is involved in learning, memory and navigation. The amygdala is considered to play a key role in consciousness and instincts, such as fight or flight mechanism. The amygdala is also involved in processing fear and angry behavior. The septum may be involved in experience of pleasure.

The basal ganglia (striatum, substantial nigra, globus palladium, nucleus accumens and subthalmic nucleus) is also involved in movements and selection of behavioral actions to take in coordination with the prefrontal cortex. It sets the individual's anxiety level. The basal ganglia is described as the reptilian brain as it evolved from fear of others in one's environment. It is involved in trembling and disorders, such as obsessive-compulsive disorders and movement disorders, such as Parkinson's disease.

The brain stem is the instinctive center of the brain. The brain stem is the posterior portion of the brain and ends at the spinal cord. It is made up of medulla oblongata, pons and mid brain. The brain stem is responsible for sensory functions and instinctive movements, such as breathing, digestion, blood circulation and blood pressure monitoring. The reticular formation system is part of the mid brain and is involved in arousal, alertness and consciousness.

Brain-Mind Connection

The perplexing question is whether the mind is connected to the brain? The answer is that the mind can affect the body and the body can influence the mind. The connection between your mind and your body is observed when your thoughts influence your physical reactions. Certain types of emotional expressions can make your body tremble or shake. If your body is showing unhealthy signs, your mind may lose its ability to concentrate. When a person imagines a sexual encounter, the sexual organs get aroused. A person whose mind is at peace, hopeful, optimistic, joyous and free from worries is likely to have a harmonious mind and healthy body.

Your brain is the central command system of your body and probably the most complex organ in the body. The brain will be overwhelmed were it not for the presence of the mind. The French philosopher, Rene Descartes is considered the Father of modern philosophy on the body-mind connection. He developed the concept that your thoughts are part of who you are and that the source of your thoughts, the mind, is immaterial.

The physical world and the body are material and are separate from the immaterial mind. Your mind cannot be located in space and time, but your body is.

The concept of duality of the mind and body suggested that the mind controls the body and the body influences the mind. Mental activities affect your brain. When the mind thinks, feels, desires, and acts, there is activity in the brain areas of thinking, emotion, and desire and action centers. Physical activities in the brain also correlate with activities in the mind. Since your mind is connected to your brain, your mind is therefore experienced as your thoughts, attention, emotions, awareness, consciousness, intellect, ego, memories, desires, and instincts.

Are you your mind, body or soul? The current view these days seems that your true self is your soul, not your mind or body. Your soul is the decider or the one who make choices for action and behavior. Your soul includes your personality, mind, and desires. Your mind has to be trained to expand and go beyond limitations of the brain and senses to interpret and understand the body's interactions with its environment. Transformation of your mind involves developing your awareness and attention.

Unlike the brain, the contents of your mind cannot be located in space and time. According to Maharishi Mahesh Yogi in *"The Science of Being and the Art of Living"*, the mind's basic nature is being. The mind has thoughts, emotions, intelligence, desires, and memory. The brain also has areas that control thinking, emotions, pleasure, and memory. If the mind is a being, then the human person has a three-fold being; a body being, a mind or soul being, and a spiritual being.

Maharishi explained the brain-mind connection in a way that allows the experience of God through the mind. He says that *"knowledge in the nervous system has revealed that when a man sees, a particular part of the brain functions in a particular manner. Likewise, when he hears, thinks or smells, different parts of the brain functions for each activity. So, according to the activity in the mind, a corresponding activity is set up in the nervous system. Thus in order to produce a particular experience of the mind, the nervous system has to be brought to a state of specific activity."* This notion of brain-mind correlation brings up what some have proposed that the brain is hardwired to know the Mind of God. Thomas Merton says in *"The Ascent to Truth,"* the *"mind of man is by its very nature a participation in the intelligence of God."*

Maharishi expounded that a thought could be experienced in two ways; either the mind starts the process of thinking and correspondingly stimulates the nervous system (brain) or if such activity were produced in the brain physiologically and the mind experiences the thought. He goes on to say that *"Since a thought could be experienced in two ways, it shows that an experience could be had in two ways. Either the mind starts on the process and stimulates the nervous system for a particular experience or the nervous system is stimulated in a particular fashion to create an activity which would naturally enable the mind to experience the desired object. Thus the experience of transcendental reality would establish the nervous system in a particular state because for any experience it is necessary that the nervous system be brought to a specific type of activity."*

Right-Brained, Left-Brained, and Whole-Brained Relationships

The right brain is occupied with the present moment, present feelings, intuition and big picture. The left brain is the logical side, realistic, methodical and action-oriented. The left brain is concerned about the past memories and what is going to happen in the future based on the past memories. As a result there is a lot of chatter and incessant thinking in the left brain. The left brain is ego-oriented and it separates your identity from my identity.

To be a complete human being, one needs to integrate the right brain and left brain to produce a whole-brain thinking or holistic thinking and harmonize the functions of the left and right brain to be both a doer and a feeler or intuitive and logical thinker. The Bible says in Ephesians 5:31 that the *"man will leave his father and mother and join his wife and the two shall become one flesh"*. The relationship between a husband and a wife is supposed to help the wife and husband learn to be a whole-brain thinking person as they mature in love.

Gender Differences in Behavior

The Tao Te Ching says in verse 28, *"To know the masculine and be true to the female is to be the waterway of the world. The world is made up of opposites, masculine and feminine, yang and yin and day and night."*

Studies have shown that there are significant differences in brain structure, function and hormones between males and females. As we look at personality types from psychology, astrology, spiritual paths, and religious beliefs, we have to consider significant variations between males and females of similar personality type.

Differences in the brain structure, functions, and hormones appear to explain differences between males and females in values, emotional well-being, decision-making, and other sex-specific behaviors. Gender differences in the brain has been well documented, especially in the role of the right and left brain hemispheres. Your right brain hemisphere controls your ability for awareness, observation of others, and intuition.

Women are said to be more emotional and right-brained than men. Women appear to have strong sensibilities that they may taste, smell, see, listen, and touch better than men. Your left brain hemisphere controls your ability to think logically or rationally and act out your ego. Men are supposed to more left-brained than women. Men are therefore more ego-driven, action-oriented and single-minded than women. Men tend to value power, toughness and independence. However, wholeness does not depend on whether you are male or female, rich or poor, and black or white.

Old age causes problems in human memory and behavior. Menopause causes challenges in human behavior. Menopause effects include hot flashes and mood changes, such as anger and grouchy moods. In terms of physiology, we can get insight into the hormonal structure of men and women who are struggling to deal with their behavior, moods, and emotional well-being. Monitoring the blood or serum levels of testosterone, progesterone, and estrogen may provide some clues to the moods, anger, and the aggressive nature of some individual men and women.

The differences between men and women are of interest in the purpose and destiny of human beings. Being born male or female is like being born black or white, there is a path of life that one goes through because of the category of identity you fall into and the lessons you have to learn. As a woman, the various hormones and life of raising children and supporting the family may tax emotions and strength of women, but the blessings of Mother God can bring a lot of smiles and inner joy, when a woman carries on the creativity of life and raises children on the path to wholeness. Also, women need their friends close by to give them good company and keep them on the road to wholeness.

Men also need to connect with others and loved ones to keep them motivated in their quest for success to take care of the family and move towards wholeness of self and others. They say a virtuous woman is a gem to be treasured, and a good and caring man is hard to find. A life of isolation is a life of incompleteness with the individual missing the joys of love, service and kindness to others.

Body-Personality-Soul Connection

Your soul is said to be what brings life to the body. Plato considered the soul to be your essence or who you truly are. The soul appears to have its own being, which is different from the being of the body and being of the mind. Any action that an individual takes leaves an impression on the soul. Your personality, habits and tendencies are part of your soul. Your personality is your stored impressions of your attitude, actions, and character. Your personality is the karma of your soul. The low of karma, or cause and effect, starts with your actions which then cause the impression or effect.

Your soul is produced by your karma and your karma is produced by your soul. This is what Maharishi described as the law of the cycle of karma. If there is no karma for an individual, there is no soul. This individual without a soul has attained transcendental consciousness, where karma no longer operates and therefore one reaches enlightenment or bliss. Just as your body changes, your personality changes, and your soul changes with time. Your soul is the seat of your will, intelligence and personality.

How Much Do You Know About Yourself?

What do you have to do to move from a position of weakness in yourself to one of strength and wholeness? Knowing yourself requires asking yourself the right questions.

What type of person are you?

What knowledge do you need in order to know yourself?

Are you a thinking type, feeling person, doer, or talker? Who are you in your strengths?

Who are you in your weaknesses?

What do you need to do to overcome weaknesses in your personality? What is the bad habit that is difficult for you to change for wholeness? What type of professional career will fit you?

What skills and talents do you need to have a good career? Are you kind, loving, and easy to be with?

Are you calm, funny, optimistic, pessimistic, cautious, a frowner, open, or trusting?

Who in your life sparks your interest in living and enjoying life? What religion should you join for spiritual fulfillment?

Do you practice religion as a devotee of God through constant prayer? Is your practice in religion to serve others in need?

Are you one who studies the scriptures and preaches the Word of God? Are you a seeker of spiritual knowledge and spiritual practices?

CHAPTER TWO

You Are a Unique Soul
With a Unique Personality

You Are A Unique Creation

We come here on Earth to enable God's creation to continue its evolution, its beauty, and its splendor. We are fortunate to be born on Earth to experience the vast spaces, wonderful sights, melodious sounds, sweet tastes, aromatic smells, and the touch of love. What sets you apart from everyone and everything in the universe is your uniqueness. The Bible says in Jeremiah 1:5, *"Before you were born, I knew you. Before I formed you in the womb, I knew you."* There is no one and nothing in the universe like you.

How unique are you? Our uniqueness comes from various factors. We know our body is unique, with unique face and fingerprints. Also unique is your mind and soul. We are different from each other in our physical characteristics, way of thinking, and purpose in life. There is no one with those same features. Even your palms have unique lines that practitioners of palmistry use to describe who you are and where you are going in life. On the other hand, we can see from genetics that your physical features may be like your parents. The type of nose, eyes, or skin color may tell us which race or tribe we belong to.

Why were you born in this unique way? This is the mystery that we want to solve in the processing of knowing ourselves. Only God knows how he created you this way. However, the shape of our body can tell us about our body type. The way you think and behave can tell us about your personality. By understanding yourself based on your body type, mind type, and soul type, you may be able to find why you are who you are. It may be because of your purpose in life and the resources, talents, and qualities you need on your journey to wholeness.

Why were you born as an imperfect soul? Would it not be better if we were born perfect, like Adam and Eve were in the mythic Bible story of the first human on Earth? Rabbi David Aaron, a teacher of Torah and Kabbalah, wrote in *"The Secret Life of God"* that *"God needs us for his creation to manifest possibility of striving toward perfection. Jewish teachings teach that the work of humanity is of lofty necessity to God. Kabbalah reveals that God chooses to need us in our humanity. Our imperfection and struggle towards becoming perfect are necessary and meaningful to God, as part of God's design to express and participate in the fad of perfection."*

You Are Created for Wholeness

You are a unique person with a unique personality, strengths, weaknesses, purpose, and destiny in life. Pastors, psychologists, counselors, mentors, and astrologists try to help individuals come to know who they are through their counseling. Who you are, along with your evolution, results in your psychological personality type, spirituality, religiosity, and astrological personality.

We are all children of the Almighty God, Creator of heaven and earth. You are a spirit, you have a soul and you live in a body. Several spiritual teachers have revealed that everyone's unique personality is the result of the karma (action) of their soul. Therefore, each person's soul is not whole because each individual has weaknesses. So, we seek wholeness or completeness of our soul by overcoming our weaknesses and by increasing our level of consciousness. We focus on the soul for wholeness because the soul is our true self and it is eternal. Our body has a finite existence. In II Cor. 4: 18, the Bible reminds us that our body may perish, but our soul and spirit are eternal:

"Therefore, we do not lose heart. For though our outward man perishes, yet the inward man is being renewed day and night. For our high affliction, which is but a moment, is working for us a far more exceeding and eternal weight of glory. While we do not look at the things which are seen, but at the things which are not seen. For the things we see are temporary, but the things which are not seen are eternal."

You Have a Unique Soul and Personality

To know someone really well, you have to know their story, strengths, weaknesses and personality traits, when and where the person was born, what culture they grew up in, what education and religious beliefs did they receive, and who are their friends and family. They would have to tell you what their plans and goals are in life in order for you to know whether or not they are interested in healthy living and wholeness.

When someone asks you for your identity, they are most likely looking for a passport or driver's license to see if your face matches the photo. We are more than a body. Who you are is a bundle of identities, with each identity layered one over the other in the self. This means that there is no one who has the same self with same identity as yourself. You can identify the individual according to his or her level of spirituality, psychological type, and astrological type, level of religiousness, genetic type, upbringing, cultural influences, gender type, racial category, and energy.

Since everyone has a date of birth (month, day and year) at a specific place with specific parents, everyone is a unique individual. Your individual soul is also unique because you have a unique purpose for your soul. Our purpose in this life leads us to the areas where we can learn vital lessons for our soul's transformation towards wholeness. Your unique body type, mental attitude, emotional energy, and character will also help you navigate through your life.

Your mind is made up of your conscious mind, subconscious mind, and unconscious mind. You experience your conscious mind in the waking state. The center of your conscious mind is your ego, which is the voice in your mind that does not stop thinking until you are asleep. Your ego rules your body and tells it what to do and what it does not want to do.

You ego has a useful purpose. It helps you survive in times of danger and it motivates you to compete for a successful life. Your self-awareness and mindfulness are thus important. You need to monitor your ego and make conscious and wise choices in your actions.

Factors Influencing Your Unique Soul and Personality

Like the classic argument of 'nature or nurture,' you have your true or natural self and your acquired or nurtured self. Your true self plus your acquired self make up your total personality. Your unique body, mind, soul, spirit and personality make up who you are. However, you are in constant flux. You keep changing as you grow and develop. Many factors may influence who you are, to varying degrees.

A number of factors cause changes in your behavior or influence your soul and personality to create your unique individuality:

spiritual consciousness

Psychological personality type

astrological sun sign (Birth day and month) chinese astrology sign (Year of birth) childhood upbringing

culture environment

genetics (hereditary) religious faith and beliefs education and knowledge gender

race destiny Purpose in life

energy (aura of your soul) Body type

generational influence national origin

Your multiplicity of identities means that you experience your personal life through the filter of your unique and complex personality. Personality psychology uses personality assessments to find personality types. In addition, there are other means to know your body traits, soul traits, and spiritual traits.

Your true self or essence (natural self) is made up of your:

- **spiritual consciousness (spirit)**
- **Psychological type (mind)**
- **astrological signs (soul's date of birth)**
- **spiritual path**
- **Purpose and destiny**
- **Body type**
- **energy**
- **genetics and hereditary**
- **gender**
- **race**

You cannot change your psychological type, astrological sign, energy, gender, race, and genetics. You can expand your spiritual consciousness, choose a different spiritual path, find a new purpose and destiny, modify your faith, and change your body type systematically. Your acquired self is what you add to your true self.

Your acquired self (nurtured self) is made up of your:

- **religious beliefs**
- **spiritual knowledge**

- **childhood upbringing**

- **culture**

- **environment**

- **academic and Professional education**

- **generational influence**

- **national origin**

Losing Yourself and Your Connection to God

We tend to lose consciousness of the spirit of God within us, when we are distracted by problems in life. When this happens, we separate ourselves from God, the source of goodness, protection, and love, and replace God with something that occupies our time.

When I was in Opoku Ware high school, a Catholic boys' boarding school in Kumasi, Ghana, my half-brother, Kwasi, came to visit me one day. I was surprised to see him because that was his first time to visit me. We chatted for a while, but I did not read him to see whether he was in despair or not. Two days after his visit, my mother informed me that Kwasi had passed away. He died too young.

Once I heard about this tragedy, I wept. He was the senior brother that I was really close to and I had looked up to him to show me the ways of the outside world in our childhood. As children, we did not know the pain that my half-brother was experiencing in his life, until after his death. You see, his mother passed away when he was about 4 years old. My father did not have time to take care of him. In the old days, the men had multiple wives and several kids. However, there is an old saying that the more wives you have, the more problems you can expect to have. My father was not an exception to a host of problems.

We loved our older half-brother. He was a good student, sociable, and funny. When he turned 18, he found a job in a factory that my father's brother owned in a small town. We were excited for him because he was going to be an adult and make good money. He took me to the movies a couple of times. We thought he was enjoying life after high school, but it turned out that he was not happy with his life. My father was not spending sufficient time with him to help and advise him. It made him bitter and he thought he was alone in the world. To lose faith in yourself when you are so young is devastating.

All these years in childhood, I did not know that my half-brother was suffering from the absence of his mother. It seems he felt life was an uphill battle. Did he know his true self? Where was the love he needed in order to feel that he was loved? The Bible says in 1 Cor. 8, *"We know that we all have knowledge. Knowledge puffs up and love edifies. And if anyone thinks he knows anything, he knows nothing yet as he ought to know that well. But if anyone loves God, this one is known by Him."*

I did not know how it felt to be a motherless half-brother as a child or adolescent. I wish I had reassured him that he was a child of God, a unique person with a wonderful personality, and that the spirit of God was within him. He was too young to give up on life, considering the friends and family that he had, and the opportunities that awaited him to fulfill his needs. The lack of interest of fathers in their sons is a major problem in society. It adversely affects the journey of children on their path to wholeness.

Upbringing and Cultural Influences

Parents who are ignorant, religious extremists, domineering, dictators, racists, drug addicts, and isolationists can set their children back on the road to wholeness by their unwholesome living. The culture or environment in which a child grows up is also important to their education, personal growth, and spiritual development. If the culture is uncivilized, corrupt, regressive, oppressive, tribal, racist, or degenerative, the journey to wholeness becomes more difficult, especially if you are forced to live in a dysfunctional way in an unwholesome culture. Children are enriched by the love of the people around them, the standards that the society sets, and the care provided by institutions of learning, religion, sports, entertainment, government, and civil societies.

What children and young people need is the education and training that will strengthen their confidence and turn the weaknesses of their soul into strengths. A young person may be withdrawn, shy, promiscuous, restless, anxious, hostile, hypersensitive, less attentive, disagreeable, rebellious, eccentric, lonesome, angry, or destructive. If, however, he or she is influenced by evolved souls who are open-minded, progressive, or enlightened, they could make an impact the child's transformation to wholeness. Otherwise, their journey to wholeness could be delayed by several years, as compared to their peers.

What kids need is the good care of both parents to become well-balanced and rounded so that they can be diligent, loving, and live a life of goodness that is free from debilitating fears, bad company, and drug addicts. Those of us who had an absent father or mother know what we missed in our childhood. Parents ought to spend time in building confidence in their kids and making sure they are on the right path to wholeness.

Energy and Vibration

Energy is real. Everything in this life is energy. Energy is vibration. Energy can be formed from matter. Light, colors and sound are forms of energy. The universal electromagnetic spectrum is almost infinite, covering a wide range of energy. Energy may appear visible, like the visible spectrum. Although some energy may appear invisible to us, humans can feel certain types of energy, except the subtlest form of energy. Our energy level provides clues to what is going on with our inner and outer self. You have to know your energy level or aura, which is the energy of vibration of your being. Everything in the world is made up of vibrations. When you see someone, you can sense that person's energy. Is the person introverted, extraverted, restless, lethargic, boisterous, energetic, spirited, or calm?

Our experience of life is mediated through energy. We

experience energy of sound, love, hate and so on. We seek the right energy that allows us to communicate with a fellow human being, our spirit or the Spirit of God. We meditate to merge with the mysterious silence of God consciousness.

If you change your energy to copy the energy of someone else, you will be a different person, but not your authentic self. If you are an introvert like me, you want to be careful trying to show off as an extrovert, because you may sound inauthentic or not genuine and honest. However, if you are on the cusp between two Sun signs, one's nature can be a mix of extraversion and introversion. For example, a Sagittarius born close to December 21, may show introversion of a Capricorn or extraversion of a Sagittarius or a combination of the two.

Energy Centers or Chakras in a Person

According to Hindu metaphysical tradition, chakras are locations in the human body that are centers of life force and energy. There are seven chakras and each represents an energy center and a type of power within the body, mind, soul, and spirit of a person. The chakras start from the root chakra and end up with the crown chakra at the top of the head. The energy chakras and their symbolic colors of vibration or energy are as follows:

- Root chakra *(red)* is near the base of spine and it represents energy of fight-flight response, passion, survival, and anger. This first chakra is cultivated by paying attention to your survival and fears.

- Sacral chakra *(orange)* is near your sacrum and sexual organs. It is the seat of the energy of sex, creation, inspiration, and addictions. This second chakra is cultivated by paying attention to your sexual and creative powers.

- Solar plexus chakra *(yellow)* is at your gut or solar plexus which is where a complex collection of nerves meet near your digestive system. The third chakra is the seat of your personal power, emotions, and confidence. You control this energy by paying attention to your emotional power.

- Heart chakra *(green)* or fourth chakra is the seat of the energy of love, compassion, growth, well-being, and balance. You channel this energy by paying attention to the power of your love and compassion towards others.

- Throat chakra *(blue)* or fifth chakra is the seat of the energy of communication, self-expression, and fluency. This energy chakra is nurtured by paying attention to the power of your communication with others, your body, mind, spirit, and Spirit of God.

- Third eye chakra *(deep blue)* is near the area between your two eyebrows. This sixth chakra is seat of the energy of vision, balance between low and high self, wholeness, and intuition. This energy is developed by paying attention to wholeness of your body, mind, soul, and spirit.

- Crown chakra *(violet)* is near your brain's cerebrum, at top of your head. The seventh chakra is the seat of energy of your spiritual power, spiritual consciousness, and psychic abilities. This power is garnered by paying attention to your spiritual power, and unity with God consciousness.

The evolution of the soul to consciousness of wholeness starts with the ordinary consciousness of the human mind. According to the science of yoga, the process of evolution of the mind starts from awakening of the kundalini in the root chakra and the powerful energy moves upwards until it unites with pure consciousness in the crown chakra.

Energy and Vibration of Names

Our thoughts send out vibrations or thought waves for others to feel. It is said that the soul is hidden but the eyes are the window to your soul. Even our names have vibrations. When your name is called so many times in your life, the effect of the vibration of the name on your soul and your behavior is significant. It is not surprising that people change their names sometimes to find a name that fits their renewed self.

Creation of the World from Energy

According to the Science of Yoga, God is Pure Spirit or Pure Consciousness, from which mind and matter came from. Pure consciousness is whole and unchanging, without division. Humans are spirits who live in a body made up of matter and energy. Creation of this world cannot be explained in terms of time. Swami Sivananda writes in *"Bliss Divine"* that *"The universe is a mystery. No one can say how it came to be."* He says about the source of the world, *"Something cannot come out of nothing. Something can only come out of something only."*

The theories of the process of creation of the World are described in the Bible, Hinduism and Evolutionary Science. All three theories are similar or comparable, in that the elements of creation are similar or comparable, but they are very different when one looks at time taken for creation of human beings. It shows that God cannot be known in terms of space and time.

The Bible account in Genesis 1:1-27 is that *"In the beginning God created the heaven and earth. The earth was without form and an empty waste, and darkness was upon the face of the very great depth (SPACE). The Spirit of God was moving (VIBRATION) over the face (AIR, TOUCH) of the waters (WATER). And God said (SOUND, WORD), Let there be light (LIGHT) and there was light ... God called the dry land earth (EARTH) ... Then God made two great lights – the sun and the moon. He also made the stars ... Let the earth put forth vegetation ... Let the waters bring forth abundantly and swarm with creatures and let the birds fly over the earth ... So God created man in His own image and likeness of God. He created them, male and female."*

The ancient Hindu theory of the creation of the world is that the universe was created from the five great elements (bhutas), which are space, air, fire, water, and earth. The process started with the eternal and infinite God of pure consciousness, residing in silence. The first element to evolve was ethereal space (SPACE). Without space nothing can exist. Then came a vibration (SOUND, WORD) from God. The vibration in space caused wind (AIR) to form, as motion is the quality of air or wind. The friction of air in motion through space caused heat or fire (FIRE). When there is heat, there is water formed (WATER). So, water is formed from fire. Water cooled to form solid earth (EARTH). Whenever there is water on Earth, there are plants and then food. Therefore, earth was born out of water.

The earth provided a solid foundation or structure that with water produced vegetation, fish, animals and humans. Humans could live on earth as the earth had space, light, air, and water. Humans were formed from the earth so they have the five elements of space, air, water, fire (energy) and earth. From the five elements, humans have five senses of hearing, touch, sight, taste and smell, corresponding to space, air, fire (light), water and earth, respectively. Four of the five elements are used in astrology. Astrology has air signs (Gemini, Libra, Aquarius), fire signs (Aries, Leo, Sagittarius), water signs (Cancer, Scorpio, Pisces), and earth signs (Capricorn, Taurus, Virgo).

In the Bible, John 1 v.1 says, *"In the beginning was the Word and the Word was with God and the Word was God."* Considering the creation theory of ancient Hinduism, some practitioners of Hinduism interpret the verse *"In the beginning was the Word"* in John 1 v.1 as consistent with the Hinduism theory of creation. Thus the Word in John 1 v.1 was the sounds or vibration of God that initiated the creation of the universe.

Charles Darwin is well-known for his theory of evolution of fish, animals and humans from a common ancestor. In his book, titled, *"The magic of reality, how we know what's really true",* Richard Dawkins presents a fascinating case to support evolutionary science of creation. There are several evolutionary theories on the history of life on earth and oceans that span about a billion years.

One of the theories of evolutionary science is that the world began with collision of subatomic particles in SPACE which caused a huge explosion (SOUND and VIBRATION) that led to formation of elements, such as helium, nitrogen, carbon, silicon and compounds such as oxygen (AIR) and water (WATER). Water collected together from rain to form the ocean. The first life came from the ocean, starting from bacteria and evolving into fish. The initial elements formed reacted with oxygen and ocean water in the presence of heat (FIRE) to form iron and other substances, like silica, leading to formation of the earth (EARTH). The creatures in the ocean evolved from simple to complex ones. The earth then became covered with vegetation, which released sufficient oxygen in the environment for evolved sea creatures, such as reptiles to move to land. From four-legged reptiles came birds and four-legged mammals, from which two-legged non-human primates (apes, chimpanzees, and gorrillas) and two-legged humans evolved. Evolutionary scientists have provided some evidence to demonstrate a separation of the line of primitive relatives of humans from the line of apes.

Energy, Matter and Spirit

The relationship between matter and energy can be understood in terms of vibration. The first law of thermodynamics states that total energy of a system remains constant, as heat or matter is transferred into and out of the system. When matter is destroyed, it turns into heat or energy. Matter is gross, so your body is dense and occupies limited space and time. The brain is also physical and has a location in space and time. The mind, soul, and spirit are subtle and without location in space or time. The energy spectrum ranges from extremely low to very high frequency of energy. The highest state of spiritual consciousness produces near-zero energy or silence of the mind, as the language of God is silence.

Energy, Meditation and Brain Waves

Science tells us that there are vibrations that we cannot see with our naked eyes, such as the vibrations of brain waves, radio waves, infrared, ultraviolet, and electromagnetic forces. Brain waves have a range of frequencies. The human brain wave goes from the waking beta waves with the lowest amplitude and highest frequency to the alpha wave of wakeful relaxation, to the theta wave of daydreaming, and then to delta brain waves with the highest amplitude and lowest frequency. Meditation renews the spirit of the mind. It is associated with wakeful relaxation alpha waves and theta waves. When one reaches silence, there is no vibrational activity in the mind, except the spirit self in the mind.

PART TWO

Know Your Nature and Purpose

CHAPTER THREE

Understanding Human Nature

The History of Humans

Human beings (Homo sapiens) began their journey about 100,000 years ago in primitive societies and advanced to the present time of global civilization, while making improvements, along the way, in culture, religion, astrology, and science. Scientists have obtained important data in prehistoric times and recorded history based on paleontology, archeology, anthropology, and geology records. We have evolved physically, mentally, intellectually, religiously and spiritually over the past 30,000 years. Karen Armstrong is one of the acclaimed scholars of comparative religion that I admire for her passion to seek God and help us understand the history of religion. She really motivated me to research the history of mankind and religion in the world. Her research went back as far as 10,000 years of the religious and cultural life of humans. Table I shows a rough summary of the history of humans on earth.

TABLE 1. PRE-HISTORY AND HISTORY OF MANKIND

Year	Prime Movers	Major Events
~100,000 BC	Early homo sapiens in Africa during prehistoric era	Earliest record of human activity found in East Africa from archaeological records. Hunters ruled the land. God creates diversity of skin colors; black, white, brown, yellow and red. Humans get darker in hot climates.

50,000 20,000 BC	Migration of Humans from Africa	Human migration from Africa to Middle East, Asia, Europe, and America. Blood types variation around the world. Skin color changes depending on geographical area. Lighter-skin humans in cold areas.
~ 20,000 10,000 BC	Humans in Stone Age	First recorded stone tools found in Africa around 20,000 BC
15,000 – 4000 BC	Communities in India and Eurasia	Agrarian societies formed all around in Middle East Asia and Indo-Europe.
~3,000 BC	Hinduism religion	The beginning of the world's oldest religion in India.
~ 3000 BC	Mesopotamia and Egypt	Mesopotamia and Egypt develop early writing forms called cuneiform and hieroglyphics, respectively
~ 3000 BC	Mesopotamia and Persian astrology	Human begin to study the movements of the sun, moon and planets and develop astrology
3000 – 1300 BC	Bronze Age	Humans produce bronze from copper and tin to make metallic tools
~2,500 BC	Judaism religion	Beginning of the Jewish religion.
1300 BC – 700 AD	Iron Age	Age of Discovery
~500 BC	Buddhism religion	Buddha is the founder of Buddhism
~350 BC	Taoism religion	Lao Tzu is the founder. Sacred book is Tao Te Ching.
800 – 200 BC	Axial age	Age of revolutionary thought in India, China, Persian and Greco-Roman Empire
100 BC – 700 AD	Vedas philosophy	Sanskrit literature developed and made available in India and surrounding areas
~50 AD	Christianity Religion	The world's largest religion was initiated based on teachings of Jesus Christ and it quickly spread around the world. Old testament prepared around 300 BC. New testament prepared around 150 AD.
~ 650 AD	Islam	Muhammad founded Islam, the second largest religion in the world. Koran is the sacred book.
500 – 1400 AD	Middle Ages	Dark Ages in ~700 AD marked the end of the Roman empire and decline of living standards in Europe

1400 – 1700 AD	Renaissance and Age of Discovery	Cultural renaissance led to revolutions in science, philosophy and education.
1890 AD – present	Psychology	Freud founded psychoanalysis and the discipline of psychology has emerged as one the prime movers in study of human mind and human nature

(Source: Wikipedia)

Knowledge of Human Nature

Jesus knew who he was and he also knew human nature. He asked his disciples several times whether they knew who he was. The Bible says in John 2:24-25; *"But Jesus did not trust himself to them, because he knew all. And he did not need anyone to bear witness concerning man, for he himself knew what was in human nature."*

Everyone wants to understand human nature for their survival, protection, personal growth, and spiritual healing. As Steven Pinker said, *"Everyone has a theory of human nature. Everyone has to anticipate the behavior of others."* Even the ordinary man in the street feels he knows a theory or two about human behavior and can contribute to an understanding of human mind and nature based on his awareness of his own human nature and personality, observations of the nature of other humans, friendships and conflicts between groups of humans, and experience of the high and lows of daily life.

We are born into this world with a purpose, with parents who will nurture us, with talents, with personality, and lessons for our soul to learn for wholeness. In Taoism, Lao Tzu writes in the Tao Te Ching (verse 37):

> *"If you understood others you are astute.*
>
> *If you understand yourself you are insightful.*
>
> *If you master others, you are uncommonly forceful.*
>
> *If you master yourself, you have uncommon inner strength.*

If you know when you have enough, you are weak.

If you carry your intentions to completion, you are resolute."

Everyone has their viewpoints on human nature, including practitioners of psychology, religion, spirituality, sciences, philosophy, metaphysics, astrology, sociology, and biology. We want to find out from the experts and from religious revelations about the known, knowable, and unknowable nature of man. Our immediate help comes from our priest, pastors, and spiritual teachers who focus on the soul and spirit in relation to the mind. Scientists in various disciplines are also finding more about the science of human mind and human nature.

Humans Have a Three-fold Nature

Most religions believe that we humans are tripartite or three parts in one. Human beings have a spirit, soul, and body or some will say spirit, mind, and body. The true essence of a person is the spirit and soul. The body and mind are vehicles for the human soul to express itself. The spirit is our divine nature and where we receive inspirations and direction from God. The soul is who we are and our personality and purpose. The body is the vehicle for us to interact with our environment leading to experiences of pleasure or pain, service or selfishness, detachment, or lust. We are of divine nature, but we think we are our ego because we associate who we are with our personality, actions, successes or failures.

In essence, we are a complex, three-part being with body-mind intelligence, soul personality and spiritual consciousness. Every individual has to deal with problems of the body, soul, and spirit. Nobody is perfect. As a result, we love to celebrate our achievements when we beat the odds and learn to align our body and soul with our spirit for wholeness.

Our mind, soul, and spirit are made viable by our emotions, energy, and spiritedness. The Bible tells us that *"a happy heart makes the face cheerful."* (Prov. 15:13) and *"There is the beauty of a gentle and quiet spirit."* (1 Pe 3:4) The spirit guides us at all times. Psalm 23 says, *"He refreshes my soul, he guides me."* We pay attention to the spirit of God within us when we are in good or bad spirits. We pay attention to our soul to see whether we are troubled in relationships or not troubled. We are taught that our ego is our false self, not our true self. And so, we pay attention to our mind to watch our thoughts and ignore the chattering of the ego-mind or false self.

Your soul is at the center of who you are on Earth. If your soul is moving away from wholeness, your spirit becomes disconnected from your body and mind. Your soul is the lamp of your body and mind, or like the eye of your body. *'The eye is the window to your soul,"* The Bible says in Luke 11:34-36,

> *"The lamp of the body is the eye. Therefore, when your eye is good, your whole body also is full of light. But when your eye is bad, your body also is full of darkness. Therefore, take heed that the light which is in you is not darkness. If then your whole body is full of light, no part dark, the whole body will be full of light, as when the bright shining of a lamp gives you light."*

Evolution of the Body and Soul from the Spirit

John Garrison has written on the body-mind-soul-spirit connection and the narcissism of the human nature from the Christian and psychological point of view in his book entitled *"Psychology of the Spirit"*. He wrote:

> *"All life began with the Spirit of God. The Spirit of God then created out of himself the human spirit as a secondary life principle. As secondary life principle, the human spirit created and now maintains the soul. The soul then brought the spirit life it carried and made the body live. It is important to keep in mind that the life of the spirit itself receives its constant union with a renewed spirit or through the omnipresence God who is above all and through all and in all."* Beck said *"spirit*

is the principle and the power by which life persists, soul is the seat, guide or holder of it, while body is its vessel and organ. The three are specifically different, but they exist in connection with one another."

Garrison adds: *"The personification of the flesh comes about as a result of the personal way in which its corrupt and irrational impulses express themselves through the intelligence and personal soul. In other words, when these impulses from the flesh take possession of the soul's lower level, the impact is converted by the intelligence and personality of the soul into personal expressions through behavior."*

Different types of Leaders in Human Nature

It is human nature for an organization or community to select a leader who will lead them to meet their needs and goals. Psychology, religion and astrology describe different types of leaders based on different expectations and needs. Usually who a religious organization will select as a leader will be different from that of a private company which serves the interest of its shareholders and not the employees. Leadership style may also depend on the personality of the leader and the needs of the organization. In some of the leadership courses that I have taken over the years, I found that there are at least eight types of leaders who are chosen for leadership of companies, departments and institutions:

- Democratic Leadership
- Autocratic Leadership
- Technical or Directive Leadership
- Situational Leadership
- Coaching Leadership
- Strategic Leadership

- Transformational Leadership

- Visionary Leadership

On the spiritual type of leadership, the Tao Te Ching says in verse 17, *"There are four types of leaders. The best leader is indistinguishable from the will of those who selected the leader. The next best leader enjoys the love and praise of the people. The poor leader rules through coercion and fear. And the worst leader is a tyrant despised by the multitudes who are the victims of his power. What a world of difference among these leaders. In the last two types, what is done is withhold sincerity or trust – only coercion. In the second type, there is a harmony between the leader and the people. In the first type, what is done happens so naturally that no one presumes to take the credit."*

Human Nature From Religious Points of View

What do the various major religions say about human nature? Christianity teaches that man is made in the image of God. God created man and breathed into him the breath of life and man became a living soul.

In Hinduism, one's inner spirit or essential self is Atman, the part of the Spirit of God that dwells in all beings. Your individual soul is jiva. Man's true nature is divine.

Most religions talk about the need for humans to obey a moral code of conduct to lead a life of righteousness. Christians have to obey the Ten Commandments and avoid a life of sin or face damnation after death. Hindus have to move away from self-centeredness and move towards selflessness and unity with Atman.

Nature of the Human Relationship with God

Karen Armstrong has written a remarkable book, *"The History of God"*, in which she traces 4,000 years of the nature of relationship between man and God in Judaism, Christianity, and Islam. She has also written about the Bible, Buddha, and Muhammad. She found out that various ancient cultures set up a system of religion where they had a relationship with the creator of their world. We need a relationship with the Creator of the universe to be assured that someone is in charge of sustaining the world and keeping peace on Earth. The Bible says, *"Man shall not live by bread alone, but by every word of God."* (Luke 4:4)

We need God and God incarnate, Jesus Christ, to guide us through life on Earth to show us what our nature is and what we need to do to become perfect, as the Creator is perfect. We also learn about the laws of the universe, mind, soul, and spirit to discover new ideas that help us make progress in this life towards wholeness of the body, soul, and spirit.

Nature of Human Personality

We count on the expertise of psychologists, pastors, and astrologers to help us understand human nature, how we ought to behave, and how others will respond if we behave in a dysfunctional manner. To become whole, you have to work on your personality and overcome your weaknesses in your body, mind, and spiritual dimensions.

Personality psychologists have been able to categorize the nature of human personalities into thinkers, sensationalists, emotion-types, intuitive types, doers, perceptive-types, and judicious types. In addition, astrologers have also noticed the correlation between personalities of the planets and the personalities of human beings.

Based on the Sun sign and the ascendant of an individual, one can determine if the person is a competitive type, the possessive one, the deep thinker, the homebody, the affable performer, the critic, the lover of relationships, the transformer, the philosopher, the ambitious worker, the humanitarian and the sentimentalist.

Nature of Human Love

Love is the greatest thing that is inborn into human nature. Human beings could not survive without love because God created humans and the universe out of love. God is love. Love is the one quality that makes you understand what a spirit is. Love is not material, just as spirit is not material. Pure love, as opposed to sexual love, is spiritual and so it moves one into acts of goodness.

The parent's love for the child allows the child to trust the parent and not tremble with fear of abandonment. Love is what draws a child to its mother and father. Love sustains the unity and bonds of the family. As a child, love for your friends protects you and makes you feel good about yourself. As an adult, love for your boyfriend or wife lifts your soul and gives you that feeling of joy for life.

Innocent and Fearful Nature of Humans

Life begins innocently and takes us where we need to be to learn our lessons as adults and achieve wholeness. When you are a child, you play, have fun, learn about your body, and find out what you can say, laugh at, do to explore the world, and feel free. Growing up as a teenager, you learn at school, go to church with your parents, and learn to live a life of good morals, learn about the opposite sex, and enjoy outdoor activities with friends and family.

As one approaches adulthood, one may receive feedback about one's personality, strengths and weaknesses from friends, parents, family and teachers. You may begin to develop fears of making contact with people, of the opposite sex, fear of being disliked, and fear of other ethnic groups, tribes, and races. Conflicts and wars may arise that shed innocent blood.

In adolescence and adulthood, you have the option of beginning to search for your purpose in life and develop personal awareness. You have the option to find out who you truly are, come to know God, accept who you are, and overcome your personality defects and fears.

Good and Evil in Human Nature

Since God is Goodness and perfection, does it mean human nature is essentially good? According to Christianity, human goodness is the foundation of man's character and personality and our problems come from choosing evil over goodness and faith in God. *"All have sinned and come short of the Glory of God"* (Romans 3:23), as the Apostle Paul reflected in the Bible about behavior, righteousness, and sin. The Bible also adds, *"Why do you call me good? No one is good, but the Father."* (Luke 18:19)

The vast majority of human beings struggle to stay on the path of Goodness. Usually, we all have excuses where we treat our friends or people of our own race well but act evilly towards someone who is not our friend or is of a different race. In Matt 5:39-42, Jesus said we have to return evil with goodness:

> *"But I tell you not to resist an evil person. But whoever slaps you on your right cheek, turn the other for him also. If anyone wants to use you and take away your tunic, let him have your cloak also. And whoever compels you to go one mile, go with him two. Give to him who asks you and from him who wants to borrow from you, do not turn away."*

How do we get out of the cycle of good and evil? We need to look at ourselves, not as our body or ego, but as a spirit and soul. In this vein, Christians want to be born again of the spirit to move towards wholeness and perfection. Hindus aspire to be selfless and treat everyone well, if they want to move towards wholeness and unity with God. Buddhism and Hinduism talk about the law of karma. Good results come to those who perform good deeds. Everyone is encouraged by karma to change our bad habits and become a whole person.

Is it in Human Nature to Struggle or to be Blessed?

They say life can be good and fun and it all depends on you. You are the master of your own fate. Sometimes, things go so smoothly, with a few bumps here and there, that we may begin to take things for granted. However, no life is easy. For some of us, life can be a messy trip as we deal with human nature. You want to know yourself well in order to navigate the complex nature of life. Sometimes, we wonder what is wrong with us when things don't go the way we want. We ask ourselves why God created us this way to struggle without making any progress financially, increasing our will-power or mind power, and living a spiritual life.

In those situations of doubt, we need the patience to keep doing what is right on the course to wholeness of personality. When life is tough, we have to strengthen our faith and trust in God to carry us through the crisis. There is no time to wonder why one is made this way. We have to understand and make good choices in life. The Bible says in the book of Job 9:21-29:

> *"Though I am blameless, I regard not myself, I despise my life."*

Again Job 10: 1 says, *"I am weary of my life and loathe it. I will give free expression to my complaint. I will speak in the bitterness of my soul."*

Like all of us, Jesus did not have an easy time on Earth. He said, in John 8:19, to his fellow humans, *"You do not know me or know my Father."* He was watched closely by his family. He cultivated friendships in the village. His village neighbors did not think highly of him, so he had to demonstrate his leadership skills. He encountered great challenges, from his arrest to the crucifixion. Like all of us, Jesus had to grow strong physically, mentally, emotionally, and spiritually, while on earth.

Nature of Human Poverty and Wealth

To some worldly people, the value of human life or your human nature can be measured by how much money and how many possessions you have. Around the globe, everyone is busy trying to work or study and make money so they can pay their rent, buy food to eat, and have fun after work.

Do not think you have a hard life and other people have an easy life. Do not assume the poor have it worse than you. You do not know what lessons they have to learn in this life.

Likewise, do not envy the wealthy man in your town. You do not know what a wealthy life has done to his children and wife.

It is the nature of human life to be born into one of three types of families; a poor family, middle class family, or wealthy family. It is a great achievement when someone in a poor family has a breakthrough and ends up in the middle class or wealthy class. The impact of poverty is devastating because there are no easy routes out of poverty. Some of the poor choose to rob, steal, and beat people for money. Others just give up on a life of ambition. Individuals in a third group just do the best they can with what they have. The Bible says in Luke 12: 29-34,

> *"And do not seek what you should eat or what you should drink, nor have an anxious mind. For all these things the nations of the world seek and your Father knows that you need these things. But seek first the kingdom of God and all these things shall be added unto you. Do not fear, little flock, for it is your Father's good pleasure to give you the kingdom. Sell what you have and give alms; provide yourselves money bags which do not grow old, a treasure in the heavens that does not fail, where no thief approaches or moth destroy. For where your treasure is, there your heart will be also."*

The problems facing the poor are exacerbated by corrupt politicians and their cronies who divert any funding for development programs for the poor into their pockets. They become part of the unwholesome wealthy class where there is a lot of deceit, anxiety, lobbying, stealing, greediness, boasting, self-indulgence and materialism. As Socrates said, it is better to live a life of wholeness than to seek wealth and live an unwholesome life.

A life of wholeness, free from addictions and bad habits, for both the poor and wealthy is a life worth living. It brings the fruits of the spirit which are joy, love, self-control, and peace of mind. A life of wholeness is a life where you are not attached to your possessions and are prepared to give them away if you are wealthy or live with integrity. You do not crave what someone has if you are poor. We have to support each other and grow to become whole. If you are rich, you may help a poor person to get back on their feet by through acts of charity or the sharing your knowledge and experience. If you are poor, you may offer to care for the kids of the rich person who needs a caretaker.

Human Nature and Harmonious Life

According to Lao Tzu, the spiritual leader of Taoism, every individual has to *"take a specific path to live in accordance to the unity of the universe. It is the nature of everything in nature to issue from an inextricable relation of every path of the whole, to live life in accord with the Tao (path) is to be in harmony with all others, with the environment, and with one self, and to be authentic, sincere, natural and innocent."*

Human Nature of Suffering and Happiness

Buddha paid more attention to human suffering and spirituality than to the cult of his personality or the personality of other spiritual leaders. He found that the cause of human suffering or unhappiness is ignorance. Suffering was caused by desire, greed, or an attachment to possessions. One ends suffering by stopping the cravings for material things and overcoming ignorance through the process of enlightenment. The path to liberation from suffering or the path to happiness is the path of eight noble steps, which is right way of speaking, right aspiration, right understanding, right action, right type of livelihood, right thinking, right mindfulness, and right meditation.

Human Nature and Wholeness

If you have struggled with who you are as a personality, what God has in mind for your destiny, and what kind of progress you can make to over-come your weaknesses, you have to undertake a spiritual journey. Spiritual experience is a journey in the life of an individual who has the spirit of God to help the soul solve problems. The good news is that science, religious scriptures, astrology, and spiritual teachings have provided us with knowledge and understanding about human nature, personalities, and spirituality to move us from being a broken spirit to an unbroken spir-it, from division to unity, and from a splintered life to a life of wholeness.

CHAPTER FOUR

Obstacles to Knowing Yourself and Becoming a Whole Person

What is a Whole Person?

As a seeker of spiritual knowledge, I have always been attracted to knowledge about the human self, mind, soul, and spirit. The soul is described as your driving force. Everything we think about and our reactions to changes in life tell a lot about who we are. We also learn from our soul who we are and why we do what we do. I understand that some people don't want to go deep within themselves and find out who they truly are, perhaps out of fear. For the uninterested ones, it probably takes the fun out of life. They may prefer to focus on what they want to become rather than on what they are now or what they were in the past.

The essence of knowing ourselves is for improving ourselves towards wholeness of mind and soul. Would you like to be successful financially and career-wise in this life without making any progress towards the wholeness of your personality and soul? The process of knowing yourself is not to assign blame for who you are or point out your faults, but to empower you to use your God-given strengths and talents to transform yourself from imperfect soul to wholeness of your soul.

As Rabbi David Aaron says in *"The Secret Life of God" "We are not angels but rather low Imperfect Beings. We struggle with evil urges all the time. We live in a materialistic society. Thus God should give us his mission."*

Rabbi David goes on to say that, *"God created humanity to be his vehicle for the expression of dynamic perfection and to participate in the struggle to be perfect or whole. We have an evil inclination that challenges us every day but only humans can fight and overcome evil by choosing goodness."*

Personality is just one aspect of our true self. Our soul's personality includes deficiencies and weaknesses that provide challenges for us in life, in relationships, and at work. Your goal in the personal arena is to overcome your imperfections, improve your personality, and to become a whole or well-balanced person.

The definition of wholeness is completeness, with an absence of division. A life of wholeness is not a life of seeking pleasures and being happy all the time. It is about being well-balanced and cultivating a life of good virtues. It is not a life of renunciation, perfection, extreme behavior, or isolation. In the path to wholeness, you control your desires of the flesh, bad habits, self-centeredness, fear, greed, pride, anger, and hatred. Eventually you replace these with temperance, good habits, selflessness, courage, humility, kindness, and love. Since we are imperfect souls, a whole person will make mistakes and sin, but they will recover and stay on the path of wholeness.

A whole person is therefore one who is at ease, wise, approachable, well-balanced and without disabling weaknesses in his personality. He has high self-awareness, no addictive personality, understands, loves, and inspires others, he has great self-control, integrity, and faith in himself and God. A whole person is also knowledgeable, personable, content, not controlling of others, confident, friendly and adaptable in relationships, humble, truthful, non-judgmental, and fruitful in life.

Lao Tzu, the great spiritual teacher said, *"Knowing others is wisdom, knowing yourself is enlightenment. Mastering others takes force. Mastering yourself needs strength."*

The Bible also talks about the actions of a whole and prudent person in Prov. 14: 2-25 (I have left out actions of an imprudent person):

"He who walks in uprightness reverently and worships fears the Lord. The wise man preserves them. Knowledge is easy to him who understands; the wisdom of the prudent is to understand his way. Among the upright, there is the favor of God. The tent of the upright shall flourish. A good man shall be satisfied with his ways. The prudent man looks and considers well where he is going. A wise man suspects danger and cautiously avoids evil. The prudent are crowned with knowledge. The poor is hated even by his own neighbor, but the rich has many friends. He who despises his neighbor sins, but happy is he who is kind and merciful to the poor. Loving kindness and mercy, loyalty and faithfulness shall be to those who do well. The crown of the wise is their wealth of wisdom."

There are **10 obstacles** that prevent us from becoming a whole person and living with joy, self-knowledge, and a sense of purpose. The more we become like God or Christ, the more we come closer to the Spirit of God or Jesus.

Not Knowing Your Creator

We are all created by the God of this Universe to enjoy His glory and creations of beauty, pleasures, power and intelligence. We are sustained by His laws, grace, provisions, blessings, protection, revelations and relationships with His creatures. We do not see God because He is everywhere and infinite, but we feel His Spirit within us and working through us. Life's problems distract us from paying attention to the Spirit of God within us and staying in constant contact with God. The Bible says, *"God is spirit and those who worship Him must worship Him in spirit and in truth."*

The purpose of religion is to unmask our divine nature which is hidden by the distractions of our mind and body. We know God through our experiences, when our needs are met, when we are filled with love and joy, when we observe the wonder of nature and the planets, and when we are inspired by reading the scriptures. The spirit of God is in all human beings.

Not Knowing Yourself and Your Personality

Who are you and do you understand why you behave and do the things you do? What kind of personality do you have? Our personality is based on our thoughts, attitudes, and behavior. You have to find yourself to know yourself and turn your weaknesses into strengths.

Every person is born with personal characteristics of body, thoughts, behavior, and attitudes. Psychology is the study of the human mind. Although, psychologists have helped us to know who we are and how we act, you want to know yourself on a deeper level. You want to go beyond your body and mind to understand your soul and spirit. We also want to know what type of personal destiny or personality we have and whether they are changeable.

We all yearn to understand ourselves so that we can stop making the same, dumb mistakes that make our lives miserable at times. To know yourself at this time of your life, you need to understand human nature. I have heard some people say that human beings don't really care to know themselves or human beings cannot change who they are for the better, even if they know themselves. I agree that changing our bad habits of behavior requires great effort. We have the Bible, and other scriptures to show us how to transform our souls in order to enjoy the fruits of the spirit, such as *joy, peace, love, patience, goodness, gentleness, kindness, faithfulness, and self-control* (Gal. 5:22-23).

Poverty of Money and Spirit

The Bible says, *"Blessed are the poor in spirit."* The conundrum in life is whether we will seek money or seek the spirit of God if we are poor or rich. We know that poverty of money is not the only pressure that makes us struggle in life on the road to wholeness, but poverty is devastating to our body, mind, and soul. We also have to deal with loneliness, racism, loss of a parent or parents, joblessness, and illness, which can cause us to lose self-confidence.

We are taught in the Bible to seek first the spirit of God and His kingdom and all other good things will be added unto us, including money. If we seek only money, we deprive ourselves of the spirit, leading to poverty of spirit within us. The fruits of living in the spirit is a life of peace, joy and love.

We live our lives from the body and mind, and when we are poor or we do not have sufficient money to meet our needs, we lose focus on the importance of wholeness, vision, and a purposeful life. We will rely on others or break moral laws to acquire money rather than having faith in ourselves to go through the process of education, job training, building our character and spiritual development for wholeness.

I want to espouse and advocate the importance of knowing oneself in life, especially in Africa where people are struggling financially, economically, and psychologically because of the influence of poverty, self-centeredness, corruption, greed, and tribalism. There is a lot of hope in the world, despite these hardships from poverty. In Ghana, people are turning to religion and prosperity-preaching churches to save them from poverty and harm. It is therefore essential that people choose their church carefully as there are some unscrupulous pastors who could take advantage of their despair and take what people have saved from years of hard labor and sacrifice.

The benefits of being whole far outweigh the financial gain. The Bible asks what does a person profit if he gains the whole world and loses his soul. There is power in the alignment of your body and mind with your soul. If we do not think right, we will fail to make the right decision for success. When we consider how our lives are going, we need to examine all three aspects to ensure wholeness of body, mind, and soul. The result is the gaining the power of the spirit of God to have one's needs met.

Lack of Faith in Ourselves

Having faith in yourself is believing strongly in your abilities, capabilities, value, responsibility and reliability. The problem arises when we confuse the expectations of having faith in ourselves with having faith in God because of fear, ignorance and lack of trust.

Each of us has to develop the strength to believe in ourselves and develop self-esteem because of the spirit of God within us. It is common for people with low self-esteem to turn to their relatives to support them financially and emotionally. Humans are not aware of the power of their spirit to fulfill their purpose in life. Our full potential is realized when we bring our divine spirit into our actions in the physical world.

Fear and Negative Emotions

Life is a school for learning our lessons to improve our personality and character and to develop good relationships with others. When we fear to do what is needed for wholeness, it is usually from fear that we will lose love from others or from our circle of friends. We sometimes indulge in negative behavior to achieve pleasure or fun and avoid the narrow path of wholesome behavior. A life of wholeness may not be fun, but it brings joy, love, and peace of mind. Living in fear inhibits our ability to think right, act right, and seek God. We fear to give up our bad habits, bad relationships, and addictions. Having courage, knowledge of ourselves, and strong will-power helps to steer us away from fear to hope, faith in God, and wholeness.

Weakness in Our Personality

We falter in life because of the weaknesses in our personality. Be aware that there is a cause for every weakness that we have. The challenges that we experience in life tend to be in the areas where we are weak. The Bible says, *"Weakness is sown, strength rises"* (1 Cor. 15:39-40). Our weaknesses cause us to behave in a dysfunctional manner, such as drug addiction, alcohol abuse, obesity, conflicts with family members, and idleness. We also lose our focus through bad company and distractions from our weaknesses. Paul says in the Bible, *"I do not do what I want to do, but what I hate."* (Rom 7: 15-16).

Your weakness is the source for your growth in life. You cannot be a whole person without struggling in life. If we are not strong enough, we keep making the same mistakes and lose our opportunities in life. We are born to overcome the challenges we face in life from our weaknesses through our own efforts. We have to work hard to turn our weaknesses into strengths through knowledge of the self, increasing our awareness, developing will-power, and seeking spiritual power to solve our problems.

Rabbi David Aaron wrote, in his book, *"The Secret Life of God"*, that *"we are the imperfect vessels. God created imperfect beings who struggle to become better and gradually work their way into becoming more and more perfect. We are the broken vessels, and it is through us that God fulfills His desire to express and participate in a process of becoming perfect."*

Rabbi Aaron asked the question in his book, *"If God is perfect, why did He create such as imperfect world with imperfect people?"* Rabbi Aaron answers as follows, *"God's absolute perfection includes the possibility for dynamic perfection – becoming perfect. This type of perfection is expressed through imperfect you and me, struggling in this imperfect world to improve ourselves and this world, striving and working hard towards becoming perfect."*

Identification with Our Body and Mind

Your consciousness should not be limited to just your body and mind. Our body has desires that can distract us from our purpose. Our mind can be obsessed with different thoughts and keep us conflicted at times. A life of conflicts and negative emotions causes a lack of clarity of mind. Your awareness should cover the body, mind, soul, and spirit. The human being thinks his essential nature is his body and mind. He does not know that he is a spirit with a soul.

If you know yourself as a spirit with a soul, you stay in tune with who you really are and the Kingdom of God within you. A major step in our lives is for us to realize that our true self or real self is separate from our mind or ego self, which is preoccupied with thoughts and desires. This separation gives you the space needed for your true self to witness or observe your thoughts in a detached manner. Meditation relaxes your body and mind and allows your spirit to be more aware of your thoughts and alert to the truth in you.

Bad Habits and Relationships

Bad habits are destructive to our progress in life and health. Drug, alcohol and food addictions can hinder our path to wholeness. Toxic relationships are detrimental to our sanity and health. The goal of life is to discover yourself, meet your purpose, and interact with others to become whole. This guarantees a better route for a healthy, creative, and enriching life, as God is perfect and expects us to meet his high standards. The spirit within us is perfect but the body, soul, and mind are imperfect.

We need to overcome our bad habits and compulsions that keep us addicted and in bondage. Bad habits are bad choices for survival. A life of perfection means you become a whole person. In our journey of life, we have come to learn about God's incarnation on Earth as Christ Jesus. Jesus is described as the perfect personality, and the Bible says in 2 Cor. 5:21, he *"knew no sin."* Most of us are imperfect and we commit sins that set us back on the road to wholeness or perfection. Sin means missing the mark that God set for you on the road to wholeness.

Ignorance of Your True Self

When we do not have the knowledge to be educated, to become well-trained and successful in life, we go through a process of trial and error. We also do not pursue support systems and mentors that are available to us. J. D. Ouspensky, a spiritual teacher, taught that we do not really know ourselves well and that the ordinary man is ignorant of his true nature. He wrote in the book, titled, *"The Fourth Way"*, that *"We know how little we know about ourselves, we know how we make mistakes about everything, we know how we cannot foresee things, how we cannot understand things and we realized that it is the result of insufficient knowledge."*

Not Knowing Your Purpose and Destiny

How do we find out our purpose and destiny? The purpose of life is to make progress, improving our personalities and evolving from low to high consciousness. Each one of us was made in a unique way to play a role in meeting God's purpose for this universe. Each one has a destiny to do His will. Your destiny is created by the personality of your soul. Good actions lead you to a good destiny. Your destiny is in your hands to fulfill. You are a master of your own fate in life. Because destiny is created by your habits, thoughts, and character, you correct your destiny by improving your personality and turning away from evil.

We have to trust our Creator and have faith in Him to provide us opportunities to keep us on the track of the destiny He has for us. The Bible says that *"we are assured and know that all things work together and are for good to and for those who love God and are called according to His design and purpose. For those he foreknew and loved he also destined from the beginning to be molded into the image of his Son"* (Romans 8:28-29).

CHAPTER FIVE

Know Your Story and
Purpose In Life

What is Your Purpose?

Thomas Merton said, *"If you want to identify me, ask me not where I live, what I like to eat or how I comb my hair, but ask me what I am living for. In detail, ask me what I think is keeping me from living fully for the thing I want to live for."*

When God created you in the beginning, you were equipped with temperament, personality, and purpose. *"Before you were born, I knew you."* (Isaiah 1:5) If you know yourself, you will know the following:

- Which part of your personality lights up when you meet others?

- Who you are compatible or incompatible with?

- Which behavior gets you in trouble?

- What makes life thrilling for you?

- What you need for your personal and spiritual growth and development?

If you know your purpose, you have a great chance of living up to your potential and fulfilling your destiny. What is your mission in life? Your purpose is what drives you in the direction you need to go in life. Is your purpose in life primarily to use your God-given skills or uniqueness for contribution to the world? Some people know their purpose, while others do not know where to begin and have problems identifying their purpose and goals in life. If you understand who you are, you will know where your motivation, passion, and your source of strength lie in life.

It is important to follow your purpose in life to grow and evolve, rather than follow some other person's purpose in life. The Bhavagad Gita II, (Juan Mascaro, *Bhavagad Gita*) 35 says that *"Because one can perform it, one's own dharma (purpose), though lesser in merit, is better than the dharma (purpose) of another. Better is death in one's own dharma; the dharma of another brings danger."*

The purpose of a person who is a CEO will not be appropriate for a person who is a carpenter. In a similar vein, the purpose for God's creation of a particular tribe, race, gender, or nation will be different for another race, gender, tribe, or nation. The two genders or two races may follow a different path or they may be at different stages of evolution, learning different lessons and working under different standards of achievement.

How Do You Find Your Purpose?

Eckhart Tolle expounds on how we can find the purpose of our life. He writes in the book *"A New Earth"* that *"There is no substitute for finding one's true purpose. But the true or primary purpose of your life cannot be found on the outer level. It does not concern what you do but who you are – that is to say your state of consciousness."* He goes on to say that *"the most important thing to realize is this: your life has an inner purpose and an outer purpose. Inner purpose concerns Being and is primary. Outer purpose concerns doing and is secondary."*

Pastor Rick Warren has written an inspiring book called *"The Purpose-Driven Life"*. He shows us how we can find our purpose and lead a purpose-driven life. The book provides insight into tapping into the divine within us as a driving force to meet our purpose in life. Pastor Warren says that the *"purpose of your life is far greater than your own personal fulfillment, your peace of mind or even your happiness."* Pastor Warren goes on to say that *"it is only in God that we discover our origin, our identity, our meaning, our purpose, our significance and our destiny."*

In the book entitled *"The Seat of the Soul"*, Gary Zukav writes that *"in order to be whole, the personality must experience the effects it causes in order to heal."*

He explains that the law of karma is an important law in the search for our purpose and destiny. If the purpose you pursue is not putting you on the path to healing or wholeness, then you have to dig deep and find your true purpose. In the Eastern religions, each soul is unique because it comes into the world with unique karmic lessons to learn. Eastern spiritual philosophy informs us that the karma of your soul is created by the actions of your soul's personalities. Therefore, your individual personalities may give you some indication of your purpose, which will lead you to the lessons your soul has to learn in this life in order to achieve wholeness.

Jesus knew himself very well while on Earth. He knew that he was a human being whose spirit is one with the Spirit of God and his mind was one with the Mind of God (Philip 2:2). He kept telling his disciples that they did not know him. Although Jesus also had three beings in one, the body, the soul, and the spirit, he was highly aware of his spiritual consciousness and his unity of self with the Spirit of God. He was also highly aware of the consciousness of his physical body and the suffering he went through in his crucifixion.

Jesus had a perfect personality as a human being, to the extent that he went beyond wholeness into the transcended sphere. There, his spirit was in union with the spirit of the Creator, not temporarily, but permanently. Jesus did not worship God as an image of man, but rather he worshipped God as Spirit and truth. He knew that you can kill the body but you cannot kill the soul and spirit (Matt 28). He also understood how the forces of darkness wage war against the soul (1 Peter 2:11).

Fulfilling Your Purpose and Destiny for Wholeness

Once we are convinced about our purpose in life, we choose a spiritual path to meet our purpose. Your vision and spiritual path are now set for you to find out whether you have the strengths and ability to overcome the problems you may face in your journey to wholeness. Christ Jesus said that we have to be born again to achieve the Kingdom of God, which comes after you have achieved wholeness.

The Bible tells us again that Jesus came to Earth with a specific purpose. Jesus was born with a mission to save those who are lost and to redeem us from our sins. Jesus was raised in a village and yet possessed the power of the Spirit of God. Jesus was predestined to succeed in his purpose on Earth.

The destiny of Jesus was foretold many years before his birth and yet he had to make great efforts, like everyone else, to fulfill that destiny. In addition, he worked effortlessly to maintain a perfect personality and the highest level of spiritual consciousness.

John A. Sandford described in his book, "The Kingdom Within", that Jesus had the perfect personality while on Earth in terms of being without sin, balanced, and well integrated with the four areas of personality: thinking, feeling, sensation, and intuition. Jesus had a great ability to think, showed deep emotions and compassion for fellow man, had excellent intuition and an ability to grasp reality. He had a clear perception of value and made use of the spiritual and human laws to make a judgment about people.

Discovery of My Soul's Personality and Purpose

How did I become interested in the subjects that I discuss in this book? I am a liberal Catholic who found his purpose in the search for self-knowledge and joined others on the path to wholeness. I found my purpose because I had shown the inclination early on in my youth to broaden my experience of spirituality through the body-mind-soul-spirit alignment for wholeness.

Having been born, baptized, and raised as a Catholic, I naturally went to a Catholic elementary school and later attended a Catholic high school. After I received confirmation during my elementary school years, I began to receive communion. I recognize that my childhood upbringing in the church gave me a strong foundation for my faith and trust in God. I was religious in my youth and I think that this foundation helped me stay religious in my adulthood. I love being a Catholic because it fits with who I am and what my goals are in life.

The Roman Catholic Church in Ghana was well organized and well-funded in the 1960s and 1970s. There was a Catholic church in almost every town, city, and community. During my childhood, I sat through several catechism classes and had to pass my tests before confirmation. I was fortunate to receive a good education from the age of 12 to 19 at Opoku Ware School, a Catholic boarding school. The all-boys school consistently showed academic excellence, commitment to high moral code and preparing young men for a life of wholeness. We had a full time Catholic chaplain, Father Habits, who taught a lot of us to avoid the bad behaviors of youth and lead a life of holiness, peace, love and unity. He would not accept excuses for not attending mass every week. We all respected him as a devoted priest. He really cared a lot for the spiritual welfare and education of the students.

One of my biggest personality problems in life came early in my childhood. I was an introvert; too quiet and too serious during childhood, elementary school, and high school. I sought to understand where this seriousness came from since I have always been quiet, calm, and serious since childhood.

When I read *"Linda Goodman's Sun Signs"* and Sydney Omarr's *"Capricorn"* in my college years, they provided me the answer to the question of why I was made this way. Astrology is a tool to understand your personality and soul type. Why was I born to be so quiet and serious? When I found out from these two Astrology books that I am a typical Capricorn Sun sign, my introversion and seriousness in childhood, adolescence, and adulthood made sense. Fortunately, my spirit had guided me down the right path to understand my burden of seriousness. My love of music and outdoor sports activities, such as soccer, running, lawn tennis, table tennis and badminton, took the edge off of my seriousness and allowed me to enjoy adolescent life with my friends, school mates, and family members.

Throughout my life, I embraced the opportunity to seek important knowledge for my well-being and to expand my consciousness. I did not want to be limited to just my religious beliefs. Meeting a life coach and mentor changed my life and allowed me to pursue my purpose in life. When I was in high school, I had a mentor who was interested in spiritual truths and had studied the major religions, especially Christianity, and including Judaism, Hinduism, Islam, and Buddhism. He was a Yoga instructor and a Yoga practitioner. He taught me that yoga is another path to an integrated life and harmonious living, in addition to my religious faith. I started performing yoga exercises to achieve balance in my body movements and mind.

My mentor was also interested in Metaphysics and Astrology. He was a Sagittarius. Through my mentor, I found out that I was a seeker of spiritual knowledge earlier on in my life. Knowing that I was a Catholic, my mentor encouraged me to read the Bible regularly, as some Catholics tend to read the Bible only during mass on every Sunday. My mentor advised me to interpret the texts in the Bible with the following in mind; literal versus symbolic meaning, historical or cultural background, moral lessons or meaningful messages for my soul and spiritual renewal.

By the time I completed high school, my mentor had given me a lot of knowledge on the Bhavagad Gita, meditation, and astrology. He went back and forth to compare Bible scripture with the Gita to show that both scriptures are equally powerful if one understands the spiritual message. I read the Bible to understand the message of the Gospels and Paul's letters on the meaning of Jesus' message. The Gita was not as voluminous as the Bible and so it was easier to read over and over. In particular, I read the Gita to understand the mind, soul, spirit, consciousness, meditation and the various spiritual paths of Yoga.

My mentor showed me how I could learn about my soul's personality from my Astrology Sun Signs to understand what my strengths and weaknesses were. I think Astrology has a long way to go to convince psychology and religious organizations that they have similar objectives to help individuals behave in a wholesome way, based on the mental and spiritual laws that God has created in the universe. However, I find that astrology requires faith and experience, as does science and religion. If one's experience of astrology, religion, or science is not fruitful, then you have to try something else. For me, it was relatively easy to validate my experiences in science, religion, spirituality and astrology for the pursuit of happiness and wholeness.

As I got more mature in my academic career and in life, I pursued my interest in spiritual knowledge, yoga asana, meditation, psychological personality types, and astrology personality types vigorously. I was able to find challenges and weaknesses of my soul. As I continued to learn my life lessons to overcome my weaknesses, I found that the career that fit my personality was scientific research and that I was more of a thinker and doer than a person with strong emotions.

In addition to my Capricorn Sun sign, I found out in the business world that I had a Guardian personality after taking the Myers-Briggs personality test. Now I had a good sense of what my soul was like based on my personality. My psychology personality type is a Guardian, my Western Astrology sign is a Capricorn and my Chinese Astrology sign is the horse. This type of self-knowledge made a significant impact on my life and allowed me to accept my true self and understand my relationships with bosses, work mates, and close friends.

I found out which types of individuals I will tend to have fun with and those individuals that I will not be compatible with. The information on personality traits was shared openly in our management training courses and management meetings so I got to know those that gave me a hard time because of their nature and those that were easier to partner with at work. I knew whom to seek out for advice and who would protect me from people that did not like me. I also learned to serve others by accommodating their temperaments.

My Search for Purpose in Life

My Capricorn nature predisposed me to be a bookworm in my childhood. However, being very active in sports activities and games allowed me to have so much fun in my youth. Playing soccer in elementary school, high school and university also enhanced my leadership skills as in capacities where I was either captain of a team or coached others on the art of playing soccer. I did not even think once about being a scientist. Neither did anyone encourage me to be a professional soccer player.

My discovery of my life's career was God sent. One evening in my second year in college, about six of my friends and I were enjoying ourselves after dinner, just talking about girls and life. We took turns making jokes about each person. Then, my friend David said to me, "Andrew, you are so serious that I think you should be a scientist." I was surprised and so jolted in my being that I stood still for a moment and then told my friends, "Yeah, I want to be a scientist". Being a scientist was consistent with my disposition and my passion for seeking a knowledge of God at that time. If I did not know who I was in the moment, I might never have gone to graduate school and built a career in scientific research.

Struggling in Life

Recently, I attended my friend Peter's birthday party at the Mission Inn Riverside, and I saw a statue with the following words written on it, *It is not your position in life that makes you successful, and it is what you overcame that makes you a success.*

My early struggles during childhood came from my personality as a Capricorn and the absence of my father in my life. Another time of indecision and confusion came from trying to figure out what I wanted to study in college upon completing my high school education. I knew I was more interested in science than in liberal arts. The question was what should I study; should it be Chemical Engineering, Chemistry, Physics, or Pharmacy? I went with knowledge of my capabilities and selected Chemistry.

I put so much of my soul into academic studies at the expense of my social skills. I remember a friend of mine thought that I was going to be a hermit. I eventually earned a BSc degree in Chemistry from Ghana University of Science and Technology in 1978. I worked for a year as a teaching assistant before I left Ghana to pursue higher education at the University of British Columbia, where I obtained my Master's degree in 1982 and PhD in 1985, under the direction of Dr. Frank Abbot, a brilliant Professor and now Professor Emeritus at UBC.

Education and the drive for knowledge meant a lot to me with my Capricorn ambition for success. However, it was not easy dealing with the weaknesses of my personality and pressures of academic achievement. I had to overcome my fears of failure and of letting my parents down by getting my act together and overcoming the challenges of being sociable, in spite of my Capricorn personality, and developing the discipline and good habits needed in my young adult life.

I had my share of major crises in life. There were times after graduation when I did not have enough money to pay rent for an apartment and had to look hard for a good job. When I found a job as a research scientist, I found my real passion was in scientific research so I threw all my energy, body, mind, soul, and spirit into the job as scientist and rose to become scientific director. There were many days where I slept for only a few hours because I wanted to resolve issues and problems before I went to bed.

The leap of faith was when I felt the internal power and strength to apply for a position to lead a group of scientists. I found out during my scientific career that I was very good at being a deep thinker, a department manager, and director. With the grace of God in making me who I am, what made me succeed was taking advantage of my strengths, skills, and talents, and learning to get along well with people. As a Capricorn, I had a good sense of duty, enjoyed working and demonstrated prowess in management. My temperament as a Myers-Briggs Guardian was consistent with who I am and I found out that I loved the integration of knowledge, systems, procedures, and processes to achieve desired goals and objectives.

The saddest time for me was when my mother passed away at the age of 77. My mother was the one who had the vision to help me strengthen my knowledge and spiritual experience. She did not oppose my desire to meditate every day. She knew that education would be the catalyst for self-knowledge and worldly success. She was highly proactive, enrolled me in boarding school at the age of 5, and provided the financial, emotional, and advisory support for me to complete my preparatory, high school, and college education.

Our relationships with others can help us to know ourselves and know others. If several people or psychologists point out a negative personality trait in you, are you willing to acknowledge the fact and work on improving yourself? Relationships with others can help us discover ourselves or bring some balance to our lives. Some people may bring excitement, fun, seriousness, and laughter into your life. You and your best friend may perhaps help each other to grow in your personal and spiritual lives. This is why I lost my seriousness as time went by. I had so many friends who helped energize me and showed me how to be light-hearted and have fun.

I love what God has done for me. I was lost and now I am found. I know myself better now than I did several years ago. I was fortunate that as I matured in my life, I was able to find out that my purpose in life was to seek knowledge, increase my awareness of my behavior, make good choices, awake my spirit through meditation, and serve others from my knowledge as a scientist and the blessings that come from the good Lord.

PART THREE

Know Your Psychological Personality

CHAPTER SIX

Where does Personality Come From

Your Personality is The Karma of Your Soul

Each human being is a spirit, with a soul and a body. We are therefore complex beings with a lot of lessons to learn and distractions to deal with before we reach the right path to realize our dreams and purpose. What makes it difficult for us to know ourselves and find out who we are as individuals? People may not know how to discover who they are. One of the spiritual laws that you want to pay attention to is the law of karma. Your personality is considered to be the karma of your soul. As you sow, so shall you reap. What you do today affects your soul and what affects your soul affects your personality. Expressed in another way, your personality shines when you are a whole soul and it dims when you are a fragmented soul. One of the quotes from Buddha in Karen Armstrong's book called *"Buddha"* is:

> *"If you want to know what you did in your past life, observe your present conditions. If you want to know what your future conditions will be, observe your present actions."*

Psychological View of the Personality

How do you find out who you are? What will help you to know who you are is to profile your personality. Everyone has positive and negative qualities based on how they live, and the choices they make with their free will. You are equipped to fix your personality deficiencies and live a better life. Psychology has made significant progress in helping us understand who we are and how we behave.

Psychologists tell us that personality is based on our emotions, attitudes, and behavior. The personality is therefore developed through social interactions and influences, which leads to habits that are difficult to change. Where does personality come from and what is the relationship between our soul and personality? There is also debate about whether our personality is inborn or acquired during one's lifetime.

There are some spiritual teachers, astrologers, and psychologists who are convinced that personality traits or temperaments are God-given traits. They are convinced that the Creator of the Universe provides our personality traits for our lives on Earth. In his book, titled *"People Patterns"*, Stephen Montgomery writes that *"Temperament is a personal style, a predisposition that forms the basis of all our natural inclinations, what we think and feel, what we want and need, what we say and do. In other words, temperament is the inborn, ingrained, factory-installed, God-given, hard-wired base of our personality."*

What is the proof that personality is God-given? Stephen Montgomery indicates that:

> *"In Kiersey views the signs of the underlying makeup can be observed from an early stage long before families, peer groups or social forces have made their imprint on our character. This means that all of us, in the course of growing up – and unless seriously interfered with – will develop a consistent pattern of attitudes and actions that express our temperament."*

View of Spiritual Teachers on the Soul and Personality

In his book titled *"The Fourth Way"*, P. D. Ouspensky, a disciple of Gurdjieff, writes that our personality is acquired through knowledge, the influences of other people and culture on our life, and that personality is not who you really are. He used the word essence to describe a "person's own true nature or the truth of a person's being." This is consistent with what other teachers have written about our essence being our true nature. Our essence is described, by both scripture and spiritual teachers, as our soul, in that our soul is who we truly are. It makes it apparent then that knowing your essence or soul will allow you to do the work that is necessary to become a whole person.

Gary Zukav writes in his book, "*The Seat of The Soul*", that the personality is the karma of the soul. *"The soul is not physical and yet it is the force field of your being. The personality is never separate from its soul and the soul and its personalities are continuously assisted and guided by the spirit and wisdom of the soul. When a personality is in full balance, you cannot see where it ends and the soul begins. This is a whole human being."*

John Garrison also clarified the soul's personality. He wrote:

"The soul is that part of us that thinks and feels, and decides and acts for the whole person – body, soul and spirit – in the world. In this manner, the unity of the whole person in and before the world is centered on the soul. Because of this, the earthly responsibility of the whole person falls totally on the soul. This is its jurisdiction."

Garrison adds:

"The soul has personhood because it is self-conscious and self-determining. Yet, because the nature and qualities of the soul are determined by the creator spirit, personhood in an individual is fundamentally of the spirit. In this capacity of fundamental person or self, the spirit represents the entire human being – body, soul and spirit – before God."

It is interesting to note that an individual karma connotes a tendency to act in a certain or predictable way. The question is, what did you do in childhood or what did you do in your past that led to you behave in a predictable way? Gary Zukav writes that *"the karma of the soul determines the physical, emotional, physiological and spiritual circumstances into which the personality is born."* He also writes that *"Your personality is that part of you that was born into, lives within, and will die with time. To be human and to have a personality are the same thing. Your personality, like your body, is the vehicle of your evolution."*

The ego is the principle of separation from God in its will to indicate its uniqueness. John Sandford who authored the book *"The Kingdom Within"*, says that our personality can be compared to the ego. *"Although the ego is the center of your consciousness, human beings have a vast unconsciousness called the inner world. In the inner world, the center of the personality includes the whole self, where the ego is only the center of consciousness life. The whole self is in each of as a potentiality and seeks to be realized in the life process. In order for the realization to take place, the ego must come into creative relationship with the inner world."*

Swami Sivananda says in the *"Mind, its Mysteries and Control"* that a strong personality is a very valuable asset for the individual. He says:

> *"That which distinguishes one man from another is his personality. In reality, personality is something more than this. It includes a man's character, intelligence, noble qualities, moral conduct, intellectual attainments, certain striking faculties, special traits or characteristics, sweet powerful voice and so on. All these things put together contribute to the personality of Mr. So and So. The sum total of these things make up the personality of a man. Mere physical characteristics cannot make up the personality."*

Someone may have a magnetic personality, a great personality, or dynamic personality. Sivananda adds:

"Money has its own share of making up for the personality of a man. His charitable riches may cover licentious behavior. Personality can be developed. A cheerful man is more influential than a gloomy man. A man of humility is a powerful magnet to draw people. The temperament of a man can be greatly modified by environment, education and experience. It can hardly be changed in toto."

View of the Great Philosophers on the Soul and Personality

What do the great philosophers say about the soul and personality? T. Z. Lavine has written about the great philosophers from Socrates to Sartre. Plato used logic, knowledge, and metaphysics to shed light on the mind, soul, spirit, desire, intelligence, and human goodness. Plato talks about the conflicting elements of personalities and their potential for causing disagreements and productivity problems. Plato said the soul is the essence of a person and immortal. He came up with three types of soul or personality. There is the rational soul, who is dominated by reason. There is the soul who lives for success and status, and then there is the soul who lives only for money and material gain.

Plato also clarifies the tripartite nature of the soul, with each part having a role to play to serve the soul. Thus, the human soul is like a chariot pulled by a controllable white horse ('spirit' or emotions) and an uncontrollable dark horse ('appetite' or desire), and driven by a charioteer ('reason' or intellect). He described the nature of man as characterized by his intellect, will, desires, and emotions. The rational part has a desire for truth and goodness. The bodily appetite part is irrational. The high-spirited part of the self includes anger, ambition, courage, pride, and aggression.

Freud believed that the human self is shaped in early childhood and the behaviors of the essential personality remains consistent from childhood into adulthood. The human child does not have a blank mind when he is born. The child has an inborn personality. Freud thought that the driving force in each individual comes from the individual's past and that our thoughts and behavior come from hidden causes in our mind. In contrast, Immanuel Kant believed that we cannot know what we are or what our soul is. He defined the soul as the 'I' whose existence can neither be proven or disproven. The scriptures, however, say the soul is real.

Can We Change Our Personality or Who We Are?

There is significant knowledge that each person is unique. The soul's karma makes the journey to wholeness all important, as we have to purify ourselves to be whole or perfect. Bhagavad Gita 3:33-34, says, *"Even a wise man acts under the impulse of his nature. All beings follow nature. Of what is the use of restraint? Hate and lust for things of nature have their roots in man's lower nature. Let him not fall under their prey. They are the 2 enemies in his path".*

You are who you are for reasons that only God knows. God created you and your personality. Where do personality, thoughts, or talents come from? Some people are happy as talkers. Some are happy as doers to keep them busy. Some are happy with where they are in life. Others are not happy with where they are or in their jobs and are determined to change their circumstances. Some people do not want to change their jobs and are happy with the same job they have had for 30 years.

Are our personalities created for us because of our actions so that we can learn our lessons in life to meet our purpose? Did God create personalities to bring growth of character to us and allow relationships to build between individuals? The idea of human personality goes way back to ancient Greeks and Romans when people were divided into four temperaments, or the four humors. You were either sanguine, choleric, phlegmatic or melancholic. A sanguine person is cheerful, optimistic and extraverted. A choleric person is aggressive, temper-ridden, and extraverted. A phlegmatic person is worrisome, methodical, and introverted, and a melancholic person is pessimistic, a thinker, and introverted. Since then, psychology continues to help us in categorizing human behavior through the use of personality tests to determine our personality type or temperament.

Modern psychology is able to determine our personality based on five dimensions of personality; extrovert or introvert, neurotic or stable, open to new things or lacking curiosity, agreeable or antagonistic, and conscientious or lacking direction. Psychological tests, like the Myers-Briggs test or Kiersey test, also show that people of the same temperament type tend to behave in a certain way.

Carl Jung, an eminent psychologist, described four types of minds; thinkers, feelers, intuition, and sensation types. Keirsey came up with four temperaments; Artisans, Guardians, Idealists and Rationals. Artisans are spontaneous, playful and do what works, Guardians are sensible, judicious and do what is right. Idealists are intuitive, fervent and do what is right, and Rationals are ingenious, thinkers and do what works.

The personal behaviors you are trying to change may come from your genes. In his book, *"The Dimensions of Personality"*, Hans Eysenck believed that outgoing personalities or extraverts and those with inward-focused personalities or introverts are determined by our genes and that our genes led to specific brain functions and nervous systems which influenced our behavior. Others have suggested that our religious behavior or faith in God could come from our genes. Modern psychology has now come up with several methods of determining an individual personality type, including personality type that is based on five factors; extraversion, openness, neuroticism, agreeableness, and conscientiousness.

Views of Astrology on the Soul and Personality

When people want to know what type of personality you have, they may ask you, what your Astrological Sign is. You have probably had people tell you to be yourself. What invisible forces drive us to behave the way we do in a predictable way? The general response is that our behavior comes from our genes, environment, and interactions with people over the years. On the other hand, Astrology tells us that your fundamental personality traits are based on our planetary forces in the Universe created by God at the time, date, and location of your birth.

Astrology is one of the mystical philosophies and pseudo-sciences that began with ancient cultures and it continues to be fine-tuned by the observation of individuals with different signs. Some people do not want to believe that God created astrology to help us discover the foundation of our true personality.

As astrologers pursue their craft, they want to find out if there are basic laws governing the origin of our personalities. By coming up with the astrological signs based on birth date, astrologers determine order and compatibility in personalities and relationships. They also understand that each person is unique because of the uniqueness of his or her birthdate, location of birth, and purpose in life.

Astrology reveals our tendencies to act in a certain way. The 12 Sun signs describe specific personalities for each sign; Aries, Taurus, Gemini, Cancer, Leo, Virgo, Libra, Scorpio, Sagittarius, Capricorn, Aquarius and Pisces. Aries types are warriors, enthusiasts, and competitive. Taurus types are realists, sensual, and practical. Gemini types are communicators and educators. Cancer types are home-loving, care-givers, and intuitive. Leos are leaders, performers, and sociable. Virgos are perfectionists, analytical, and critical of others. Libras are diplomats, negotiators, and sociable. Scorpios are controllers, transformers, and detectives. Sagittarians are philosophers, optimists, and travelers. Capricorns are conservative, hard-working, and authoritative. Aquarians are humanitarians, friendly, and eccentric. Pisces are spiritual, easy to talk to, and emotional healers.

Carl Jung also believed in astrology. He thought that astrology represented the summation of psychological knowledge of antiquity and coined the term "collective unconscious". According to Jung, the collective unconscious is the collection of the totality of the evolution of man's experiences to the present time in the unconscious mind. The one astrology book that taught me a lot about the history, principles, and deeper meaning of astrology was Dane Rudhyar's book, *"The Personality of Astrology"*. According to Dane Rudhyar, *"Astrology deals with the creative process where there is a creator who develops an order of nature from the laws of nature. Psychology deals with the development of the personality of mind."* He wrote that every individual possesses both individual and group behaviors. Dane Rudhyar wrote that:

> *"Personality is the exteriorization of the ever-changing pattern produced by the interplay of the collective and individual in the whole human entity. It represents the balance to the process of living. The personality is therefore what the human being shows as it appears from day to day with its behavior, thoughts and feelings. It is the front that the total man presents to the world ... The personality, near the end of the true process of individuation, is fully integrated by and centered on the self ... At the very dawn of the process, the personality is normally divided by instinct and inherited impulses and the psychological and mental part ... The process of development of the personality deals with the interaction between the individual and collective forces towards integration or disintegration."*

Dane Rudhyar also wrote:

> *"Planets are the focal points for collective energy. What we call personality is a synthesis of patterns of behavior. It is the sum total of the outer motions and the inner motions (emotions) of the human being, from the way he walks, to how he speaks, to his behavior in public. It is a complex of activities. Personality behavior is a blend of inherited and environmental influence operating with a structure of selfhood. Like all planets are characterized as to their nature by the zodiac position and they operate in cortical ways according to their position in the structure of the houses. The sum total of the planetary pattern represents the personality as a whole."*

How is astrology related to religion and sciences? Religion, science, and astrology seem to be opposing forces. All three use different approaches, methods, and instruments to find out how and why people behave the way they do, especially when they act in a dysfunctional manner, how they should behave to be whole and how they inherit personality traits. In this aspect, Dane Rudhyar wrote that:

> *"Like religion, astrology approach deals with the beginning of all things and of all cycles. Like science, the psychological approach refers to the study of the life process or middle of the cycle in the world of change. Like philosophy, the aesthetics approach deals with the ultimate significance and ultimate synthesis of all that is in Religion in so far as it is a practical approach to life built on unity and identification with God. Focus on the beginning and principle of all things. Science is of course attempting to analyze and discover the laws of the world process of change of universal life and its myriads of transformation. This does not mean astrology is a religion but both astrology and religion are similar methods of creativity and order."*

As a scientist, all this knowledge is eye-opening and fascinating. It helps to support the theory of the intelligent design of our solar system and human beings by God and that all beings and systems did not originate purely out of chaos or random events. There is a source of the Universe, but the process of creation is not definite. So I have mentioned three theories for the creation of the world; the Genesis story in Christianity, Vedanta in Hinduism, and the theory of creation from Evolutionary Scientists.

Creation of physical forms in the universe comes from the laws created by God. God is in charge of directing and maintaining the universe and our solar system. Science, religion and astrology are making progress to understand our human nature, personalities and the power of order and creativity of the universe.

Astrology tells us that your personality traits and temperament are symbolic of the effect of planetary movements and vibration on Earth at the date and time of your birth. Astrology is one facet of our lives that we cannot ignore. When I found out as a young man that my Astrology sign is Capricorn it changed my life. I realized that it was acceptable for me to be myself. As a Capricorn of the Earth type, I have always been conscientious, serious, and ambitious, have a strong faith in spirituality, work all the time, and focus on achievement to enjoy life. I had to be aware of a tendency to be careful, materialistic, rigid, and pessimistic if the challenges were overwhelming.

To transform your life, you need to know who you are in terms of your strengths, weaknesses, purpose and the spiritual path in life that is right for you. Armed with self-knowledge and faith in God, you are in a better position to put in a great effort to face the challenges and learn the lessons that are needed to take you to a life of wholeness or a higher level of consciousness.

Does Astrology Put People's Personality in a Box?

I know some people who do not want to hear about their astrological sign because they feel that astrology is trying to box them in a particular group of human behavior. They may not want to know what their core personality is or they may not want people to categorize them or pigeon-hole them in a sun sign. They feel they can be who they want to be and transform themselves into whatever they choose to, but astrology seems to tell them that they accept who they truly are. It is not easy to change your basic nature or essence, but you can transform yourself to wholeness by correcting your flaws, negative behavior, and weaknesses.

The Islamic poet Rumi said in one of his famous poems,

"Define and narrow me, you starve yourself of yourself. Nail me down in a box of cold words. That box is your coffin. I do not know who I am. I am in astounded lucid confusion. I am not a Christian. I am not a Jew. I am not a Zoroastrian,

and I am not even a Muslim. I do not belong to the land or to any known or unknown sea. Nature cannot own or claim me, nor can heaven. Nor can India, China, and Bulgaria. My birthplace is placeless. My sign to have and give no sign. You say you see my mouth, ears, eyes, nose – they are not mine. I am the life of life. "

Every human being is a unique person and this is supported by the individual's astrological chart. Human beings are more than labels, such as nationalities, race, gender, and their earthly habitat. Likewise, your astrology sign does not put the individual in a box where he or she is limited in personal behavior and possibilities in life, as some believe. It helps you to understand what you usually feel you need and don't need in order to be whole, what careers may fit your personality and what your addictions or vulnerabilities might be in this competitive world. It also helps you to understand why you are compatible with some and not others in relationships, why some relationships may be easier for you but not transformative, and how to live or work with others with the same or a different sign.

We have free will to choose which path we want our lives to take or which decisions to make. However, we have challenges in the exercise of our free will when other forces impact our ability to survive and pursue peace and happiness.

The question that we have for the seekers of knowledge, wisdom, and scriptures, is this: Did God create astrology or provide the laws of the universe that led ancients to figure things out and come up with astrology? Is astrology associated with one or more of the universal laws? We can say that religion, astrology, chemistry, biology, medicine, and the other related sciences likely arose from God's creation and that all man had to do was to discover these systems of knowledge and their associated laws.

Astrology was discovered from the observation of planetary locations in association or correspondence with time and place of birth and behavior of different personalities. It is fascinating that ancient astrologers associated the personalities of individuals with their ruling planets and then came up with four elements of air, fire, water and earth for the four basic human temperaments; sanguine, choleric, phlegmatic, and melancholy (see Table 2).

I am humbled by the mysteries of relationships between humans and God. How do we come to know God and engage in a spiritual relationship with God? How do we find our romantic or marriage partners? How did the ancient people discover the principle of astrology in relation to personalities of individuals? The answer may be in the Tao Te Ching v.15, which says, *"In ancient times the people knew the Great Integrity with subtlety and profundity. Because they were so unfathomable to us, we can only describe the ancients with great effort.'*

Somehow, the ancient astrologers were able to predict the personality of an individual by knowing the birthday and the movement and positions of the planets at the time of birth. Even the Bible tells us that the astrologers were able to locate the birthplace of Christ by following the position of a particular group of stars.

CHAPTER SEVEN

Know Your Psychological Personality Type

Take a Psychological Personality Assessment Test

Psychology is the study of the human mind and human relationships. Personality is an important determinant of our behavior in a social environment. Personality psychologists have described the personality as patterns of thoughts, feelings, adaptations, and behavior that affects one's attitudes, values, and self-concepts.

Do you know how you behave? Self-observation, our relationships with others and with psychologists help us how we behave. External influences from the social environment interact with our personality to shape our adaptations, such as habits, attitudes, skills, jobs, and relationships. Personality develops from childhood and matures in adulthood and thereafter becomes consistent or stable. It is then hard to change our patterns of thought, feelings, and behavior, unless hard soul work is done on the individual soul for transformation of our inner self.

What do you know when you know a person? You try to figure out what you think is their pattern of behavior. Psychologists evaluate our personality through our personality traits. According to articles of scientists in the book titled *"Personality Puzzle"*, a personality trait is dynamic and involves more than a habit. Personality traits range from narrow and specific to broad and generalized characteristics.

Table 2 shows an account of the progress that philosophers and psychologists have made over the past 2,500 years in decoding the personality types of human beings. How personable you are can be assessed from your friendliness, cheerfulness, self-esteem, assertiveness, openness, moodiness, and social anxiety.

TABLE 2. HISTORY OF PSYCHOLOGICAL PERSONALITY TYPES

Year	Prime movers	Psychological Personality traits and types
~400 BC	Hippocrates	Four humors; cheerful (blood), somber (black bile), enthusiastic (yellow bile) and calm (phlegm)
~350 BC	Plato	Four types: artistic, sensible, intuitive, reasoning
~190 AD	Galen	Four types, sanguine, choleric, phlegmatic and melancholy. Elements of air, fire, water and earth associated with four types of humans.
1890s	Freud	Founder of Psychoanalysis. Introduced individual unconsciousness. Human psyche: comprise of unconscious id (instinctive), conscious ego (regulating) and super-ego (moral conscience)
1909	Carl Jung	Introduced extroverts and introverts and four mental types; sensational, thinker, emotional and intuitive
1912	Alfred Adler	Individual psychological identity or personality characterized by social skills and motivation
1920s	Carl Jung	He introduced concept of collective unconsciousness, and concept of individuation for integration of the conscious and unconscious parts for a person to become a whole person.
1946	Hans Eysenck	Noted for his contribution to personality based on neu-roticism (N) and extraversion (E). Introduced four types of personality: low N/high E (sanguine), high N/ high E (choleric), Low N/low E (phlegmatic) and high N/low E (melancholy)
1970	Myers-Briggs Type Indicator	Introduced MBTI to identify 16 types of personality based on sensing-thinking type (ST), sensing-feeling type (SF), intuitive-thinking type (NT) and intuitive-feeling (NF) with addition of extraversion or introversion and judging (J) or perceiving (P)

1988	Kiersey Temperament sorter	Introduced four temperaments; Artisan (SF), Guardian (SJ), Rational (NT) and Idealist (NF).
1990	T. M. Digman, R. R. McCrae and P. T. Costa	Five-factor model of personality types based on extraversion, introversion, agreeableness, conscientiousness, neuroticism and openness

Carl Jung, a renowned psychologist, was one of the first modern psychologists to classify characteristics of human tendencies. He concluded that humans have four characteristics of the mind that reveal something about their personalites. People are thinking types, emotional types, intuitive types, or sensation types. Modern psychologists tend to describe the basic tendencies of a person as extroversion, openness, agreeableness, conscientiousness, and neuroticism. The extrovert is outward looking, sociable, and outgoing. Introverts are inward-looking, quiet, and reserved. Openness to experience leads to a lack of inhibition and the development of interests. Agreeableness is the ability to have a forgiving attitude in cooperation and willingness to defer to others in conflicts. Neuroticism can lead to low self-esteem or pessimism.

Myers-Briggs Personality Test

Myers and Briggs expanded Carl Jung's psychological personality types and came up with a questionnaire that revealed 16 personality types. The Myers-Briggs Type Indicator (MBTI) is a test that is used extensively by employers to determine our personality type. The tests consider personality types as innate or inborn characteristics and theorized that if we focus on our strengths, we can accomplish more. Thus a person will do better to choose a job that matches his or her personality and skills. If we are aware of someone's personality type then we can solve problems through collaborative work by understanding that person better and avoiding a conflict of personalities.

This MBTI test is based on whether you are extrovert (E) or introvert, sensation (S) or intuition (N) person, thinker

(T) or feeling (F) person, and judgmental (J) or perceptive (P) person. One test looks at how we assess reality or information through sensation or intuition. Sensation types look at what is real through their senses. Intuition types look for internal validity of what is real through their unconscious mind. One test analyzes how we deal with people through thinking or feeling. Thinkers use logic for understanding, but feelers understand how important something is to them. One type makes conclusions about situations through being judicious and another type concludes through perception.

People tend to be consistent in their personality types. Analysis of MBTI personality tests by researchers have shown that about 70% of women are more feeling types than thinking types. Also, as expected, about 60% of men are more thinking types than feeling types.

The MBTI tests determine four basic behaviors that reveal our traits, habits, needs, and values. (1) Sensation and Thinking people (ST); (2) Sensation and Feeling people (SF); (3) Intuition and Thinking people (NT); and (4) Intuition and Feeling people. David Kiersey expanded on the Myer-Briggs personality pattern and came up with four basic human temperaments; Artisans, Guardians, Idealists and Rationals. In all, there are 16 personality types; ESTJ, ISTJ, ESFJ, ISFJ, ESTP, ISTP, ESFP, ISFP, ENTJ, INTJ, ENTP, INTP, ENFJ, INFJ, ENFP, and INFP. For example, the ESFJ person is an extrovert, sensing, feeling, and judgmental type. The INTP person is an introverted, intuitive, thinking and perceiving type.

Four Basic Temperaments

Stephen Montgomery has described the 16 personality types in his book, titled *"People Patterns"*. Guardians (SJ) are sensation and judicious types who need to see and judge facts before coming to conclusions. They are logistical, managerial, fond of schedules, cautious, and stoical. The negative qualities of guardians include being over-cautious, too serious, and nagging.

Artisans (SP) are sensation and perception people who need to see and perceive facts before coming to conclusions. They are spontaneous, easygoing, optimistic, playful, and tactical. Their negative tendencies include bad temper, impulsiveness, and unorthodox behavior.

Rationals (NT) are intuitive and thinkers who are strategic, ingenious, logical, self-reliant, analytical, and pragmatic. Their negative qualities include being passive, oblivious to schedules, too theoretical, unconventional, and uncaring.

Idealists (NF) are intuition and feelings types that are passionate, diplomatic, empathic, humanitarian, trusting, and people-oriented. Their negatives include being unconventional, irreverent, and escapists.

When I found that I am a Guardian, it made sense to me that the most stimulating and enjoyable jobs that suited me very well were jobs where I used my sensational and thinking abilities for scientific investigations, designing processes for workflow, and establishing structures and standard procedures. Some have tried to match the Myers-Briggs personality types with Astrological signs. For example, an ISTJ is supposed to be either Capricorn or Taurus.

As a Guardian inspector (ISTJ), with introversion (I), sensation (S), thinking and judgmental profile, I have areas of strengths and weaknesses. According to Kiersey temperaments, Guardian Inspectors are the guardians of institutions. The Guardian inspector is dependable, detail-oriented, determined and dutiful. He is a realist, who makes decisions based on facts and likes to provide service to others. He is one who likes to build systems and processes to provide structure and stability in his organization. They are quiet and love procedures. They inspect work to ensure that procedures are standardized, rules are followed, and standards are maintained.

My psychological personality profile at a leadership workshop showed that, as a Guardian Inspector, I need to improve in the following areas:

- **Empathy.** Even though, I am inner focused, I have to be aware of the feelings of others and influence their behavior in a positive way, as a director of the department. This weakness is also consistent with my Capricorn tendencies to be a bit bossy and sometimes unemotional

  To correct this weakness, I was trained to express confidence in people's abilities, observe the facial expressions and body language of others and inquire about their thoughts and feelings so that I can interpret their emotional reactions.

- **Optimism.** While I am confident about my abilities and I plan well for the future needs, I have to minimize negative or pessimistic thoughts when trivial or temporary problems surface or when providing a vision for the department. This weakness of pessimism is also consistent with my weakness of being a bit pessimistic and gloomy as a Capricorn.

  To correct this weakness, I was coached to adjust career goals so that they are more achievable. I have to make a strong effort to be solution-driven, rather than being problem driven. Instead of being pessimistic about goals being met and judgmental about the work of others, I was shown how to empower individuals, show enthusiasm in what they do, support their decisions and provide constructive feedback.

- **Social responsibility.** Though I get along well with people who are open-minded and believe in collaborative efforts, I have to increase my efforts and opportunities to connect with others within the company to cultivate a culture of co-worker community and cross-functional cooperation. I have to use my talents and develop strong social skills in underdeveloped areas of myself. This weakness is also consistent with my weakness, as a Capricorn, of being focused on my ambition to climb to the top and becoming insensitive about the interests, activities, and goals of others.

To make amends, I was taught to encourage group interactions between different groups and to increase my involvement and understanding in the goals and activities of others and charities in my neighborhood and church.

Perfect Personality of Jesus

Personality is not easy to change, but one can grow and expand in consciousness. In essence, coming to know thyself, as the philosophers say, through the word and grace of God, through your experience, and through psychological and astrological characteristics, helps you to do the soul work needed to transform your soul. You then make the right choices and understand your soul's journey into wholeness. In his book, *"The Kingdom Within"*, John Sandford applied Carl Jung's personality test and concluded that Jesus had a perfect personality. He presented evidence from Biblical texts to indicate that Jesus was well balanced in terms of his intuition, sensation, feeling, and thinking. In addition, he ascertained that Jesus personified the personality of a whole and unique person in his human life, since he was self-harmonized and operated at the highest level in all four functions of experience, which includes thinking, sensation, intuition and feeling.

CHAPTER EIGHT

Diverse Approaches to
Self-knowledge and Wholeness

Self-knowledge from Psychological Personality Traits

One approach to self-knowledge is through the ability to figure out personality traits from the nature of the mind of the individual. If you want to know how you think, reason, feel, judge and plan, you can take an online personality assessment test, such as the Myers-Briggs Test Indicator, to inform you about your personality type. Another approach is to see a psychologist and have your personality evaluated based on the measurement of key traits of extraversion, openness, agreeableness, neuroticism, and conscientiousness.

Once individuals are aware of their personalities and have a better understanding of who they are, with self-knowledge, they may work on themselves to correct their bad habits and dysfunctional behaviors so that they can become a better person or move towards wholeness. A healthy self-knowledge boosts self-esteem and confidence in life, as compared to being ignorant of who you are and what your talents and skills are.

Self-knowledge from the Cognitive-Affective
Personality Approach

The quality of a person's relationship with others is influenced by his or her cognitive, affective, and behavioral patterns. Your cognitive self is the conscious intellectual part of you that thinks, reasons, and remembers. It tells you whether you are rational or irrational, attentive or not observant, impulsive or deliberate. It involves planning, problem-solving, initiation, and monitoring of one's actions.

Your affective self is the part of you that expresses emotions or feelings. It includes your level of emotional expression (cold or warm), empathy, and body language. Your behavioral self is the executive part of you, which is involved in taking action, making decisions and choices, and self-control. Certain behavioral actions could be taken by you because of your motives, goals, creativity, or need for achievement. Different individuals have different cognitive strengths and weaknesses as well as different levels of emotional expression, communication skills, and moods.

In the book entitled, *"The Personality Puzzle"* (edited by David C. Funder and Daniel J. Ozer,) W. R. Norton, Walter Mischel discusses the cognitive-affective approach to personality, as opposed to the approach based on the five factors of extraversion, openness, agreeableness, neuroticism, and conscientiousness. Walter explained that the cognitive-affective approach evaluates a person's personality from the underlying situation or process of their patterns of behavior. It therefore assesses a personality based on cognitive learning, emotion, and behavior. In this situation, cognitive learning is a change in behavior after the acquisition of information in the person's environment. Walter favors an integrated approach of self-knowledge that involves personality traits, cognitive-affective determinants, motivations, genetic disposition, and cultural influences.

The Religious and Spiritual Approach to Self-Knowledge

At the spiritual level, self-knowledge is the knowledge of your true self, which seeks union with God to attain peace, joy, and harmony within yourself. Some individuals prefer the religious and spiritual approach to self-knowledge because they believe that psychology cannot help them discover how their souls can become whole, less fearful, and content. They may work with their pastor to help them to become a better person, one whom God will approve.

There appears to be great interest in the relationship between personality and the soul. Individuals who take the religious or spiritual approach for self-knowledge want to know who they truly are from the spiritual approach. They may want to know what they can do to align the soul with the spirit for the purification of their soul.

The spiritual approach to self-knowledge focuses on the influence of the spirit on the soul. The Bible describes the soul as the living soul and immortal essence of a person. The Bible says in James 2:26 that death is the separation of the soul from the body, meaning that the soul survives after death. Regarding spiritual psychology, John Garrison has written an excellent book, called the *"Psychology of the Spirit"*. He describes our conscious self as our soul. The soul is the decision-maker, the life of your body, and the self that is responsible for your thoughts, words, and deeds. Your inner self is your spirit. Your spirit is the self representing you in the presence of the Spirit of God. According to Pastor Rick Warren in *"The Purpose-Driven Life"*, our purpose and meaning in life comes from the Spirit of God which communicates with our spirit.

In Hinduism, the soul is the true self, the decider or witness who is aware of what is going on with the body and mind. Dharma is the principle of law, order, and harmony. Each person has to act according to their dharma. The Bhavagad Gita 6:12 says one practices *"Yoga for purification of the soul with the life of his body and mind at peace, his soul in silence before the One."* Hinduism espouses that there are four levels of the soul or consciousness; being, feeling, thinking, and doing based on the major scriptures of Hinduism. The Bhavagad Gita says in 7:16 that *"there are four kinds of man who are good and the four love me (Brahman); the man of sorrows, the seeker of knowledge, the seeker of something they treasure and the man of vision."*

Apostle Paul says in the Bible that our true self is different from our sinful nature. Our sinful nature comes from our inclination to gratify our desires of the flesh. Thus, your soul has a true self and a sinful self or false self (ego) that commits sin. The soul is connected to the body for survival on Earth and thus it tends to satisfy the desires of the body. When the body takes over the soul, and the soul overindulges the body, it leads to pain and suffering in the body and soul.

Buddha preached that the cause of suffering is desire or attachment to pleasures and possessions. Suffering comes to the unenlightened or unwholesome person who exhibits unhealthy habits and behavior. If you are spiritually-inclined and you perform your spiritual practices to increase your level of consciousness, you ought to follow the eight noble paths of Buddha, which require living with right thoughts or perspectives, right speech, right actions, right livelihood, right effort, right mindfulness, and right meditation to purify your soul. A spiritual person is a soul who is awakened to the spirit within and observes the spiritual laws and practices for purification or wholeness of the soul.

The Astrological Approach to Self-Knowledge

There are individuals who prefer the astrologic approach to self-knowledge. It provides information on your likes, dislikes, areas of your body at risk for health issues, strengths, weaknesses, motivations, and the types of people you are more agreeable or compatible with. Astrology appears to focus on the soul in its relationship with the body and spirit. Love of neighbor and love of God will help each sun sign overcome weaknesses and become whole. This is the greatest commandment that the ordinary man needs, on the road to wholeness. Unconditional love is the starting point for purification of the soul to wholeness, as our sinful nature is very powerful and hard to overcome.

The Bible says God breathed into man and he became a living soul. The living part of the soul comes from man's origin from the dust of the ground. According to astrology, Earth's crust is made up of elements of fire, air, water, and earth. In astrology, your personality is either a Fire, Air, Water, or Earth type. Fire Signs are the transformers or performers, Air Signs are the thinkers, Water Signs are the feelers and Earth Signs are the doers. Within each element, one is either generative or initiator of action (Aries, Cancer, Libra, and Capricorn), mutable and distributor of action (Sagittarius, Gemini, Pisces and Virgo) or fixed and concentrator of action (Leo, Aquarius, Scorpio, Taurus).

The Scientific Approach to Wholeness

According to David Hawkins in *"Power vs. Force"*, there appears to be a relatively small number of scientists who are investigating the science of wholeness. The advantage of a scientific investigation is that it will provide a systematic and objective analysis of the paths to wholeness for each personality type. However, science is limited when it comes to spiritual truths. So I turn to religion, spirituality, and astrology to complement what science can provide us when it comes to the search for truth about the nature of man, and our true self, which is our human soul.

Meaning of Wholeness from the Psychological Approach

I am not a psychologist, but I appreciate what psychologists do in professional practice to help others heal and move towards wholeness. I am a pharmaceutical scientist who wants to learn about psychological personalities because I believe it will help me in my journey to wholeness.

The psychological approach will be to attain wholeness of body and mind through addressing the negative behaviors of Artisans, Guardians, Idealists and Rationals and taking advantage of their strengths in life. Everyone has different lessons to learn when it comes to ability to deal with openness, agreeableness, neuroticism, and conscientiousness. Wholeness is therefore not about being rich or poor, but rather how you can change your life to become a whole person who is well-balanced, in harmony with oneself and others, and able to live a full life.

A 2012 UN research report on happiness found that the happiest people live in Denmark, Finland, and Norway. The report found that political freedom, strong social networks, and absence of corruption are important to people's sense of well-being. On the individual level, good mental and physical health as well as job security and stable families are important for happiness.

Those imbued with wholeness tend to be highly evolved individuals who have overcome selfishness, communicate with compassion and love and demonstrate high spiritual consciousness. These highly evolved souls have a great personality and personal power to function better socially, mentally, religiously, and spiritually than do others. They have fewer negative personality traits, cope better with stress, and exude positive emotions towards everyone whom they meet.

Astrology of Wholeness and Relationships

Astrology is a tool that has been used for more than 4,000 years to understand personalities. My interest in astrology is for the knowledge of the soul's evolution to wholeness and not for fortune telling or psychic reading. A lot of people know that their Sun sign or Ascendant reveals information about who they are but they cannot believe that God can design a system that requires Astrology to decode the journey of our soul toward wholeness. It requires faith to pursue research in science, religion, and astrology.

Are you frustrated with the ups and downs of relationships and your struggles in life? It is important to know how you react to stress, crisis, and addictions, to find out what relationships are rewarding for you, and to figure out what type of marriage partner or job will be suitable for you. I am sharing my experience in finding out who I am, what my strengths and weaknesses are, who I am compatible with in relationships, and how to build a relationship with God and get rid of my bad habits and addictions. Correcting dysfunctional behaviors of my personality allows me to move towards wholeness of mind, soul, and spirit, in alignment with the spirit of God within me.

Meaning of Wholeness from a Religious Approach

The Bible says Mary Magdalene had 7 demons. Where did the demons come from? Do we all have demons? Our ego and weakness tell each of us that we have demons. We seek God to heal our broken or demonic souls and save us from our destructive habits, such as drunkenness, drug addiction, hostility towards others, racism, prejudice, and gossiping. Religion looks at wholeness from the viewpoint of unity with the spirit within oneself, unity with others, and unity with God. An unwholesome person is vulnerable to temptation, suffers, and gets into a lot of pain.

Christianity describes wholeness through unity with Christ. It looks at the journey to wholeness as following the Way, Truth, and Life of Christ. Wholeness means using one's mind, heart, strength, and soul to attain holiness and avoid committing sins or letting one's sinful nature take over one's soul. Our sinful nature is born from our bodily desires and self-centeredness. Upon achieving wholeness, the individual continues to obey the spiritual laws and is rewarded with the fruits of the spirit, which include love, joy, peace, kindness, goodness, gentleness, faithfulness, and self-control.

We are all imperfect beings. We have personal concerns about our flaws, limitations, and incompleteness. These concerns about our personality may manifest in anti-social behavior, poor communications with others, lack of friends, inability to find a marriage partner, and low motivation to find a job. Our faith in God becomes important when we seek spiritual solutions for our brokenness and personal problems. Christianity warns us about the works of the flesh and wages of sin, which will lead to unwholesome life. Life is a battle waged in the mind for the soul of man between the forces of goodness and evil.

The whole person is described in the Bhagavad Gita 2:56, as *"His mind is undisturbed in adversity, he is happy and content in prosperity and he is a stranger to anxiety, fear and anger. Such a man is called a wise man."*

Wholeness is being at ease, feeling complete with no disabling weaknesses, and living in harmony with the universe in a state of equanimity or self-control. Wholeness is not the same as Nirvana in Buddhism.

The Tao Te Ching says in v.45, *"Completeness can seem incomplete, yet the completeness that we achieve can be remarkable. Fullness can seem empty yet the fullness that we achieve can be useful."* Nirvana is the transcendent state where the individual is perfection, free from suffering, and able to see the true nature of enlightenment in life.

Hinduism looks at wholeness as a union between the individual and God as well as a unity of one's soul with the collective soul, Atman. In Buddhism, suffering and a broken soul result from cravings. If we can avoid these cravings of the flesh and attachment to possession, we can overcome our suffering and brokenness. Achieving goodness and wholeness requires considerable effort to overcome the weaknesses of the human soul and its tendencies for self-centeredness and evil. In verse 8, the Tao Te Ching (translated by Ralph Alan Dale) says,

> *"The highest good is like water running life effortlessly, flowing without prejudice to the lowest places. It springs from all who nourish the community with a benevolent heart as deep as an abyss who are incapable of lies and injustice, who are rooted in the earth and whose natural rhythm of action play midwife to the highest good of each joyful moment."*

Meaning of Wholeness from a Spiritual Approach

Wholeness is about a higher state of being, thinking, feeling and doing. At the spiritual level, wholeness of a person requires the body, soul, and spirit to function with unity of purpose, love, harmony, balance, to be well-integrated, and in alignment with the Spirit of God within us. Wholeness is not the same as the happiness that arises from sensual pleasures, material gains, and the accumulation of wealth. Wholeness of the body and soul is needed for higher spiritual development. In wholeness, there is no division or conflict between the body and soul and the soul is in control of the body's desires. When there is a brokenness of the soul such that the spirit is estranged or alienated from the soul, one has to seek or awaken the spirit in order to restore the soul to its true self of peace and unity with the Spirit of God within us.

The Bible says, *"Blessed are the poor (who are) in spirit."* God forbid, but if one is poor, one has to have faith in oneself and in God to do whatever is required to move towards a wholeness of mind and soul, including observing the spiritual laws, increasing one's awareness of one's behavior, and gaining knowledge about human nature.

Being poor is not the end of the world, but the poor cannot afford to be idle or behave in dysfunctional activities. The poor and the rich both need to be rooted in the spirit within them in order to achieve wholeness. Buddha taught that humans ought to empty themselves of desires to be whole and so the poor certainly have an edge in having nothing and being in the spirit or aligning their soul with the spirit. The Tao Te Ching says in v.16, *"Allow the heart to empty itself of all turmoil, retrieve the utter tranquility of mind from which you issued."* The Bible says we can trust God to help us overcome more than we can bear (I Cor. 10:13). God forbid, but if you are poor, as you move towards wholeness opportunities for success will show up, such as education, mentoring, job training, healthy living, and strategies for financial gains.

Meaning of Wholeness from the Astrological Approach

Wholeness is unity and completeness. Astrology focuses on achieving wholeness of the soul, the true self, which requires unity with the body and spirit. Astrology looks at the flaws, weaknesses and strengths of individuals based on their date of birth and resulting astrological personality. The individuals need knowledge of who they are to understand their motivations and vulnerabilities, and make the necessary effort to overcome their weaknesses and failures. Because it is difficult to change our essence or personality, we need to seek the love and wisdom of God who provides support and opportunities for us to become whole. We also need to be aware of people that come into our lives to help us to mature into wholeness.

PART FOUR

Know Your as Trological Personality

CHAPTER NINE

Know Yourself from Your Sun Sign Astrology and Ascendant

Astrology is Not a Religion

Some people in science and religion are skeptical of the principles, concepts, and astrological charts in Astrology. Astrology is a mystical philosophy, like numerology. We are all living in a mysterious world. Some religious people are cynical about science's concept of evolution, and some scientists are suspicious of religious beliefs. We all have to be open-minded and allow our experiences and faith to guide us in whatever mystery of nature we get attached to in this life. After all, the scientist, religious person, and the astrologist are all trying to decode the mystery of life and human beings.

Astrology is not a religion as some of the religious think of it, but rather an artistic science. It does not have a moral code of conduct. It advises individuals on their personal characteristics, challenges, and the influences of the planetary motions on their lives. Table 3 shows a brief summary of the history of Astrology. There are references of astrology in the Bible, as astrology was well known in the Middle East and Asia during the time of the people in the Old and New Testament.

TABLE 3. ACCOUNTS OF THE HISTORY OF ASTROLOGY

Year	Prime Movers	State of Astrology
5000 BC	Priests of Chaldean people (current Iraq, Syria, Turkey)	Studies of maps of movements of Sun, Moon and stars form the initial basis for astrology, where the heavens influence the earth
3000 BC	Chinese	Chinese astrology started with heaven, earth, and water as the basic elements and yin-yang principles
2000 BC	Indian Hindu	Hindu astrology incorporated the 5 elements of space, air, fire, water, and earth later in its astrological development
1700 BC	Babylonians in Ancient Meso-potamia	Oldest known texts of Babylonian astrology. Astrology uses symbolism, analogy, and correspondence of changes in life phenomena with planetary changes and changes in seasons.
550 BC	Egyptians	Babylonian and Egyptian astrology integrated to form the Egyptian zodiac. Four elements of fire, air, water, and earth incorporated into astrology
500 BC	Judaism	Old Testament mentions astrology in Job 38:32-34, with references cluster of stars called Pleiades, constellation of Orion, and signs of the zodiac
500 BC	Ancient Greeks, Plato, Pythago-ras	Alexander the Great conquers Babylonians. Greeks intro-duced system of planetary gods, including Mars, Saturn. Philosopher, Plato writes about astrology. Mathematician and philosopher, Pythagoras visits Chaldeans and Egypt and learns about astrology.
50 AD	Christianity	Gospel of Matthew describes journey of three astrologers to the birth place of Jesus Christ in Bethlehem
100 AD	Astrologer and astronomer, Claudius Ptolemy	Ptolemy wrote a treatise on principles of astrology in Alexandria, Egypt. Introduced Western-type astrological tradition.
270 AD	India	One of the oldest astrological treatises in Sanskrit discovered. Indian, Egyptian, and Greek astrology intermixed.
600 AD	Islamic scholars	Introduced horoscope astrology to European astrologers
1100 AD	Plato of Trivoli	Ptolemy treatise on horoscope astrology is translated from Arabic into Latin
1500 -1600 AD	Copernicus, Galileo, Kepler	Astrology discipline revolutionized during renaissance with discovery of the sun at the center of the universe

1700 AD	Isaac Newton	Practices Astrology
1900 AD	Freud	Founding of Psychoanalysis reignites interest in astrology
1920-1960 AD	Carl Jung, disciple of Freud	Describes astrology as a symbolic system that operates by a-causal synchronicity or meaningful coincidences. He also introduced concept of col-lective unconsciousness, and concept of individuation for integration of the conscious and unconscious parts for a person to become a whole person.
Present	Modern astrologers	Astrologers divide the zodiac into 12 sections; Aries, Taurus, Gemini, Cancer, Leo, Virgo, Libra, Scorpio, Sagittarius, Capricorn, Aquarius and Pisces

(Source: Wikipedia)

The Bible says in Job 38:32-34, *"Can you bind the chains of the cluster of stars called Pleiades or lose the cords of the constellation of Orion. Can you lead forth the signs of the zodiac in their seasons? Or can you guide the starts of the Bear with their young. Do you know the ordinances of the heavens? Can you establish their rule on the earth?"*

Matt 2:1 says, *"Where is He who has been born King of the Jews? For we have seen his star in the east at its rising and have come to worship Him."*

Find Your Astrological Sun Sign

Western astrology is one of several paths to help us find out who we are and how we can overcome our weaknesses and take advantage of our strengths. Another advantage of astrology is that it helps us interact well with people. We are all aware that astrological sun signs are used in relationships and partnerships to assess whether individuals complement each other.

The first two astrology books that I bought and loved in the early 1980s were *"Linda Goodman's Sun Signs"* and Sydney Omarr's books released annually for each sun sign. Linda provided personality characteristics for the man, woman, husband, wife, lover, children, boss, and employees of all sun signs, while Sydney provided personality characteristics of each sun sign and changes for each year.

For those who want to learn about the soul lessons of their personality, I will recommend Linda Joyce's book, *"The Day You Were Born"*. If you want to find the astrological profile for your birthday and those of friends and bosses, review Saffi Crawford and Geraldine Sullivan's book entitled *"Power of Birthdays, Stars and Numbers"*. Lastly, those whose birthdays are on the cusp may want to read Sally Cragin's book, *"Astrology of The Cusp"*.

Some personalities we meet in life are hostile or negative to us. Others are friendly and positive to us. We do not fully understand the reasons why interactions with other souls can be positive or negative. The reasons of natural antagonism appear to be hidden from us. However, astrology, psychology, and other disciplines are making progress in understanding the relationships between different personality types.

Astrology is a formula or symbolic system used to decode our personality and behavioral tendencies by analogy with positions and influences of planets, the sun, moon, and stars in the cosmos at the moment of one's birth and in our daily lives. Astrology helps individuals understand patterns of their soul's personalities and relationships with others. Each soul is unique because it comes into the world with a unique purpose in life, unique personality, unique karma, and soul lessons. Western astrologers use Sun signs, Ascendants, and other astrological points to describe the personality of individuals and the challenges involved in the individual soul's journey to wholeness.

The astrological chart is largely built from two movements of the Earth. One is the Earth's rotation around the Sun, which produces the seasons over 12 months. The other is the rotation of Earth around its own axis over 24 hours.

Your sun sign is based on the day and month just as seasons are related to the day and month. Seasons affect body development and physiology. The sun sign is the sign in front of which the sun is positioned at the time of one's birth, as Earth orbits around the sun.

The 12 sun signs are Aries (21 Mar – 20 Apr), Taurus (21 Apr – 20 May), Gemini (21 May – 21 Jun), Cancer (22 Jun – 21

Jul), Leo (22 Jul – 21 Aug), Virgo (Aug 22 – Sep 22), Libra (Sep 23 – Oct 21), Scorpio Oct 22 – Nov 21), Sagittarius (Nov 22 – Dec 21), Capricorn (22 Dec – 20 Jan), Aquarius (Jan 21 – Feb 20), and Pisces (Feb 21 – Mar 20). Sun signs provide general descriptions of the personality profiles based on the birth date. Your sun sign is one of the most important signs. It is the part of yourself that shines brightest.

The Zodiac sign personality profile is not an end by itself. You still have the free will to make your choices in life, relationships, career, and spiritual paths. Astrology does not cause us to behave certain ways. The Bible tells us that the three astrologers found the location where Jesus was born using the position of the stars. This indicates that astrology has been with us for thousands of years and astrologers continue to learn more about ways to develop their system and predict our behavioral tendencies.

Some people fear astrology. Astrology does not judge the personality profile of one type as better than the other. Like the Myers-Briggs personality types, the sun signs provide general descriptions of personality types and each personality's strengths and weaknesses. The universe of your life consists of layers of other realities that have an impact on you, such as gender, race, tribe, genes, culture, environment, parents, family, and so on.

People Born on the Cusp Between Two Sun Signs

People born at the edge between two signs or the cusp have difficulty in determining their Sun sign. If you were born on days between the 18th and 24th of each month, you are classified as born on the cusp, at the boundary between two signs. For example, if you were born between March 18 and March 24, you could have Aries traits, Aries with Taurus traits, Taurus with Aries traits or Taurus traits.

Another example is someone born on the cusp, between December 18 and December 21. This person will be a Sagittarius with some Capricorn traits. In this case, the person may not be as outgoing, funny and adventurous as a typical Sagittarius born between November 25 and December 17. You may be more serious, ambitious, hardworking and go-getter than other Sagittarius because of your Capricorn traits. That is why people on the cusp tend to have a dynamic personality because they tend to be multidimensional, incorporating traits of the two signs that meet at the cusp.

Elements of Astrology

The Western Astrological Sun Signs (Zodiac) are classified in three ways: *Element, Quality, and Polarity*. Women may be slightly different from men of the same sign. Fire signs and Air signs are masculine (yang). Water and Earth signs are feminine (yin).

Astrology has four basic elements; earth, fire, air and water:

Earth forms the ground structure or platform of life.

Water is the dissolver or universal solvent.

Fire is the transformer that changes one form or nature into another in life. Air is the harmonizer that brings harmony into all aspects in life.

Fire Signs are Aries, Leo, and Sagittarius. Fire signs are energetic, lively, passionate, courageous, quick tempered, and aggressive.

Air Signs are Gemini, Libra, and Aquarius. Air signs are intellectual, lively in mind, social, thoughtful, and fluent in expression.

Water Signs are Cancer, Scorpio, and Pisces. Water signs are emotional, sensitive, intuitive, kind and sympathetic.

Earth Signs are Taurus, Virgo, and Capricorn. Earth signs are down to earth, sensible, capable, practical and skillful. Tend to be shy in social situations.

The Qualities represent modes of operation. Quality of each sign is either Cardinal, Fixed, or Mutable.

Cardinal Signs (Aries, Cancer, Libra and Capricorn) are

initiators, go-getters, are independent, and represent activity at the beginning of a season or project.

Fixed Signs (Leo, Scorpio, Aquarius and Taurus) demonstrate steadfastness, stubbornness, persistence, consistency, reliability, and ability to see things through and represent the middle of a season.

Mutable Signs (Sagittarius, Pisces, Gemini, and Virgo) exhibit adaptability, changeability, flexibility, and represent the transitional ending of a season, leading to increased flux at the end.

Astrology does not have a one-size-fits-all for each sun sign member. There are different layers that impact the individual astrology based on an individual's gender, ascendant sign, proximity to the cusp, and the locations of other planets at the time of birth.

Each astrological Sun sign is tasked with making improvements in that personality to become a whole person who is personable, well-balanced, self-controlled, without disabling weak points, and purposeful in actions.

General Personality Characteristics of Your Astrological Sun Signs

The positive and negative personal characteristics of each sign are described below. You have to be aware that people are evolving at different levels, and so people in the same sign may have different types of strengths or weaknesses. Also, you may see the same type of weakness in your sign and other sun signs and maybe conclude that everyone behaves the same. When you look at the list of each sign, look at the big picture of common strengths or common weaknesses.

The birthdays of celebrities can now be found in Wikipedia. Wikipedia shows the day, month, and year of birth. Individuals, like myself, can see whom I share a birthday with.

Along with a list of celebrities and their sun signs, here are the general characteristics of strengths and weaknesses of each sun signs:

Aries (I am a Competitor and Leader)

Aries Strengths: leader, fearless, strategist, direct, assertive, optimistic, active, enthusiastic, aggressive, passionate, competitive, energetic, pioneer

Aries Weaknesses: impatient, cold, selfish, reckless, impulsive, quick tempered, compulsive, inconsiderate, tactless, domineering

Decanates of Aries: Aries-Aries (Mar 23-31), Aries-Leo (Apr 1-10) and Aries-Sagittarius (Apr 11-19)

Aries Celebrities: Al Gore, Maya Angelou, Celine Dion, Eddie Murphy, Hugh Hefner, Marlon Brando, Marvin Gaye, Lady Gaga, Diana Ross, Colin Powell, Aretha Franklin, M. C. Hammer, Richard Dawkins, Jackie Chan, Robert Downey Jr.

Celebrities on Aries-Taurus Cusp (Apr 18-24): Adolf Hitler, Queen Elizabeth II, Jack Nicholson, Michael Moore, Barbra Streisand, and Kelly Clarkson

Taurus (I am Practical and Strong-willed)

Taurus Strengths: Calm, endurance, loyal, generous, pragmatic, creative, sensible, determined, patient, deliberate, sensual, fashionable, enjoy luxury, strong will

Taurus Weaknesses: stubborn, greedy, uncompromising, rigid, possessive, materialistic, rebellious, jealousy and suspicious

Decanates of Taurus: Taurus-Taurus (Apr 21-30), Taurus-Virgo (May 1-10), and Taurus-Capricorn (May 11-20)

Taurus Celebrities: Wayne Dyer, Andre Agassi, David Beckham, Chris Brown, Tim Duncan, Janet Jackson, Jay Leno, Adele, Dennis Rodman, Andy Murray, Emmitt

Smith, Barbra Streisand, Shirley Maclaine, George Lucas, Madame Albright, Kelly Clarkson, Tim McGraw

Celebrities on Taurus-Gemini Cusp (May 19-24): Jamie Fox, Grace Jones, Naomi Campbell, Al Franklin, Novak Djokovic, and Patti Labelle

Gemini (I am a Communicator and Deep Thinker)

Gemini Strengths: good communicators, optimism, affectionate, intelligent, wit, curiosity, adaptable, lively, enthusiasm, expressive, imaginative, changeability

Gemini Weaknesses: indecision, restless, feisty, harsh, nervousness, gossip, undependable, moody, argumentative, procrastination.

Decanates of Gemini: Gemini-Gemini (May 21-31), Gemini-Libra (Jun 1-10) and Gemini-Aquarius (Jun 11-20).

Gemini Celebrities: T. D Jakes, Joyce Meyer, Joan Rivers, Venus Williams, Kanye West, Donald Trump, Prince, Angelina Jolie, Johnny Depp, Mitt Romney, George H Bush, Mehmet Oz, Tupac Shakur, Raphael Nadal, Ce Lo Green, Pam Grier, Suze Orman, Heidi Klum, Kendrick Lamar, Paul McCartney, Lauryn Hill

Celebrities on Gemini-Cancer Cusp (Jun 18-24): Paul McCartney, Paula Abdul, Solanges Knowles, Prince William, and Lionel Richie

Cancer (I am Homebody and Intuitive)

Cancer Strengths: Emotional, courageous, sensitive, tenacity, resilient, good sense of humor, sympathetic, protective, shrewd, nurturer, compassion, strong intuition

Cancer Weaknesses: demanding, oversensitive, eccentric, rebellious, judgmental, moody, calculating, unforgiving, secretive

Decanates of Cancer: Cancer-Cancer (June 21-30). Cancer-Scorpio (Jul 1-11) and Cancer-Pisces (Jul 12-21)

Cancer Celebrities: Bill Cosby, George W. Bush, Richard Branson, Mandela, Tom Cruise, Tom Hanks, O. J. Simpson, Lindsay Lohan, Meryl Steep, Angelina Markel, 50 cents, Ross Perot, Mike Tyson, Michael Vick, Lil Kim, Khloe Kardashian

Celebrities on Cancer-Leo Cusp (Jul 19-24): Danny Glover, Jennifer Lopez, Barry Bonds, Selena Gomez, Carlos Santana, Robin William and Ray Allen

Leo *(I am Boss and High Performer)*

Leo Strengths: leader, dynamic, charismatic, cheerful, creative, bold, outgoing, confident, generous, personable, responsible, compassionate, performer, fun, flamboyant

Leo Weaknesses: arrogant, attention seeker, snobbish, domineering, bossy, materialistic, extravagant, egocentric, vain, narcissistic

Decanates of Leo: Leo-Leo (July 22-31), Leo-Sagittarius (Aug 1-12), Leo-Aries (Aug 13-21)

Leo Celebrities : Magic Johnson, Barack Obama, Bill Clinton, Michael Kors, Mario Balottelli, Sandra Bullock, Madonna, Halle Berry, Ben Affleck, George Clooney, Arnold Schwarzenegger, Vivica A. Fox, Meagan Good, Martha Stewart, Sean Penn

Celebrities on Leo-Virgo Cusp (Aug 18-24): Wilt Chamberlain, Don King

Virgo (I am Articulate and a Critic)

Virgo Strengths: Analytical, perfectionist, intelligent, articulate, brilliant, reflective, health conscious, orderliness, detail-oriented, flexible, meticulous, charming, critical, responsible, excellent memory, dutiful, career-focus

Virgo Weaknesses: worrier, overcritical, pessimism, procrastination, faultfinder, overbearing, emotionless, miserly, grouchy, workaholic.

Decanates of Virgo: Virgo-Virgo (Aug 22-31), Virgo-Capricorn (Sep 1-10), Virgo-Taurus (Sep 11-21)

Virgo Celebrities: Michael Jackson, Beyoncé, Pink, Chris Christie, Tyler Perry, Barry White, Jennifer Hudson, Lyndon Johnson, Charlie Sheen, Prince Harry, B. B. King, Anthony Weiner, Raquel Welch, Shania Twain, Florence Welch, Phil McGraw, Cameron Diaz, Iyanla Vanzant

Celebrities on Virgo-Libra Cusp (Sept 18-24): Stephen King, Nichole Richie, Jimmy Fallon, Sophia Loren, Faith Hill, Ray Charles, David Chappelle, Kobe Bryant

Libra (I am Relationships-Focused and Mediator)

Libra Strengths: Sociable, charming, friendly, communicative, gracious, good judgment, love of beauty, fair, relationships, creative, idealistic, analytical, balanced, diplomatic.

Libra Weaknesses: insincere, escapists, passive, indecisive, materialistic, jealous, dependency, flirtatious, resentful, undisciplined

Decanate of Libra: Libra-Libra (Sep 23-Oct 2), Libra-Aquarius (Oct 3-12), Libra-Gemini (Oct 13-20)

Libra Celebrities: Serena William, Vladimir Putin, Usher, John Lennon, Roger Moore, Simon Cowell, Will Smith, Jesse Jackson, Barbara Walters, Eminem, Desmond Tutu, Jimmy Carter, Lil Wayne, Kevin Durant, Bruno Mars

Celebrities on Libra-Scorpio Cusp (Oct 18-24): Deepak Chopra, Kim Kardashian

Scorpio (I am a Passionate and Intuitive)

Scorpio Strengths: Loyal, strong-willed, determined, endurance, ambitious, deep emotions, forceful, passionate, hardworking, clever, competitive, methodical, highly intuitive, transformation

Scorpio Weaknesses: too serious, secretive, jealous, eccentric, obstinate, selfish, stubborn, arrogant, moody, dominating, revengeful, possessive.

Decanates of Scorpio: Scorpio-Scorpio (Oct 23-Nov 1), Scorpio-Pisces (Nov 2-11), Scorpio-Cancer (Nov 12-20)

Scorpio Celebrities : Billy Graham, Bill Gates, Karen Armstrong, Hillary Clinton, Sean Combs, Julia Roberts, Gabrielle Union, Demi Moore, Whoopi Goldberg, Ciara, Sinbad, Keith Urban, Larry Flynt, Lamar Odom, Condoleezza Rice, Susan Rice, Russell Westbrook, Roseanne Barr

Celebrities on Scorpio-Sagittarius Cusp (Nov 18-24): Ted Turner, Larry King, Bo Derek, Robert Kennedy, Meg Ryan, Miley Cyrus, and Goldie Hawn

Sagittarius (I am Adventurous and a Philosopher)

Sagittarius Strengths: optimistic, jovial, friendly, philosopher, independent, self-expression, resilient, freedom, honest, intellect, witty, spiritual, expansive, fair, adventure

Sagittarius Weaknesses: restless, unreliable, too outspoken, overoptimistic, fickle, tactless, undisciplined, exaggerate, vain, stubborn

Decanates of Sagittarius: Sagittarius-Sagittarius (Nov 22-30), Sagittarius-Aries (Dec 1-10), Sagittarius-Leo (Dec 11-20)

Sagittarius Celebrities: John McEnroe, Jane Fonda, Pope Francis, Nicki Minaj, Nene Leakes, Sammy Davis, Winston Churchill, Christina Aguilera, Rahm Emmanuelle, Mariah Carey. Richard Pryor, Jimi Hendrix, Tina Turner, John Kuffuor, Janelle Monae, Britney Spears, Tyra Banks, Taylor Swift

Celebrities on Sagittarius-Capricorn Cusp (Dec 19-25): Jane Fonda, Samuel Jackson, Brad Pitt, Diane Sawyer, Christina Aguilera, and Ryan Seacrest

Capricorn (I am Hardworking and Ambitious)

Capricorn Strengths: ambitious, resolute, achiever, responsible, take charge, determined, disciplined, practical, endurance, hardworking, stylish, generous, happy working, trustworthy, reliable

Capricorn Weaknesses: too serious, too cautious, bossy, authoritative, pessimism, controlling, rigid, opportunistic, materialistic, cold, unimaginative.

Decanates of Capricorn: Capricorn-Capricorn (Dec 22-30), Capricorn-Taurus (Jan 1-10), Capricorn-Virgo (Jan 11-20)

Capricorn Celebrities: Michelle Obama, Muhammad Ali, Stephen Hawking, Mel Gibson, Kevin Costner, Christina Amanpour, Martin Luther King, Frederick K. C. Price, LeBron James, Tiger Woods, John Legend, Howard Stern, Richard Nixon, Elvis Presley, Denzel Washington,

Eli Manning, John Legend, Rush Limbaugh, Katie Couric, Donna Summer, Nicolas Cage

Celebrities on Capricorn-Aquarius Cusp (Jan 18-23): Janis Joplin, Brad Pitt, Bill Maher, Dolly Parton, and Antonio Villaraigosa

Aquarius (I am Friendly and Humanitarian)

Aquarius Strengths: humanitarian, friendly, intellectual, visionary, inventive, outgoing, forward thinking, imaginative, strong will, good communicator, creative, tolerant, intuition, activist, spiritual

Aquarius Weaknesses: too detached, private, overcautious, calculating, stubborn, unrealistic, eccentric, critical, rebellious, cold, unpredictable, demanding

Decanates of Aquarius: Aquarius-Aquarius (Jan 21-29), Aquarius-Gemini (Jan 30-Feb 10), Aquarius-Libra (Feb 11-20)

Aquarius Celebrities: Oprah Winfrey, Michael Jordan, Ronald Regan, Rick Ross, Jennifer Anniston, Ellen DeGeneres, Paris Hilton, Alicia Keys, Justin Timberlake, Kerry Washington, Ken Wilber, Thomas Merton, Phil Collins, Natalie Cole, Arsenio Hall, Wayne Gretzky, Martin Lawrence, Kelly Rowland

Celebrities on Aquarius-Pisces Cusp (Feb 18-24): Neal Diamond, Rihanna, Charles Barkley, Julian Michaels, Seal, Floyd Mayweather, Steve Jobs

Pisces (I am Sentimental and Mystic)

Pisces Strengths: emotional strength, strong will, playful, compassionate, psychic, sensitivity, spirituality, sentimental, kind, inspirational, talker, spontaneous, generous, mystic

Pisces Weaknesses: oversensitive, selfish, withdrawn, escapist, melancholy, secretive, lying, enigmatic, private, procrastinate

Decanates of Pisces: Pisces-Pisces (Feb 19-29), Pisces-Cancer (Mar 1-10) and Pisces-Scorpio (Mar 11-20)

Pisces Celebrities: Henry Belafonte, Carrie Underwood, Joel Osteen, Didier Drogba, Rupert Murdoch, Nat King Cole, Justin Bieber, Albert Einstein, Spike Lee, Julius Erving, Sharon Stone, Billy Crystal, Flavor Flav, Anita Baker, Shaquille O'Neal, Queen Latifah

Celebrities on Pisces-Aries Cusp (Mar 18-24): Gloria Steinem, Adam Levine, Queen Latifah, Bruce Willis, Spike Lee, Pat Riley, and Chris Bosh

Ascendants and Descendants

Your sun sign is probably the most important sign. In addition to your sun sign, your rising sun or ascendant is also important. Your ascendant in a particular sign can change you into a different type of sun sign. The time of the day you were born determines your ascendant. Your ascendant is the Zodiac sign that was on the horizon at the time you were born, as the Earth rotates on its axis every 24 hours. The ascendant is the seed point of the lower hemisphere and the ascendant colors the outlook and orientation of your Sun sign personality. It is the hidden or inner person and takes on the meaning of self-awareness. For example, a Capricorn sun sign with a Libra ascendant in the first house will be a different type of Capricorn. If you know someone's sun signs and ascendants you get a good idea how they basically act.

Your Descendants, Bottom of Sky sign (IC) and Middle of Sky sign (MC) are considered to be important factors in your life. Your Sun sign describes your personality. The time of the day you were born determines your ascendant. Your Descendant is the seed point of the upper hemisphere and takes the symbol of awareness of others. Your MC sign describes your ego or true calling and vocation in life and it is revealed from your 10th house. Your IC sign describes your deeper sense of self or root of your being which supports and nourishes your inner life. It is described by your 4th house.

Astrological Houses

Your sign in a particular house can change you into a different type of sun sign. For example, a Capricorn sun sign with a Leo in first house will be a different type of Capricorn. Here are the attributes of each house:

First House: Personal image, Ego, Creativity

Second House; Money, Personal value, Possessions

Third House: Communication, Intellect, Perception

Fourth House: Home life, Family, Friends

Fifth House: Children, Fun, Creativity, Love affairs

Sixth House: Health and Work

Seventh House: Partnerships, Marriage, Social Activity

Eight house: Transformation, Sexuality, Hidden Talents

Ninth House: Philosophy, Religion, Travel

Tenth house: Career, Status, Ambition

Eleventh House: Friends, Group activity, Ideas

Twelfth House: Spirituality, Karma, Psychic Talents

Planets and Their Rulers

Planet	Rule	Attributes of the Ruling Planet
Mars	Aries	Aggression, Individuality, Energy
Venus	Taurus, Libra	Love, Beauty, Possessions
Mercury	Gemini, Virgo	Communication, Intellect, Thinking
Moon	Cancer	Emotion, Intuition, Security
Sun	Leo	Creativity, Self-Expression, Ego
Pluto	Scorpio	Dark Side, Sex, Transformation
Jupiter	Sagittarius	Luck, Expansion, Spiritual Growth
Saturn.	Capricorn	Discipline, Responsibility, Structure
Uranus	Aquarius	Individuality, Originality, Eccentric
Mercury	Pisces	Visionary, Illusion, Psychic

Your moon sign is the sign the moon was passing through at your birth. For example, you may have Moon in Aries, Moon in Taurus and so your moon sign will reflect the type of your emotional nature. Your Venus sign is the sign Venus was passing at the time of your birth. Your Venus sign will show how you relate to others.

Mars provides the energy and aggression you need. Your Mars sign is the mover and shaker in your life. Jupiter is the source of abundance, fun and prosperity. Saturn slows you down and provides discipline in your life. It makes you become responsible and shows your karmic lessons.

If you were born on July 11, 1955, you have Venus in Cancer, Mars in Leo, Jupiter in Leo, and Saturn in Scorpio.

CHAPTER TEN

Know Your Compatibility
With Other Astrological Sun Signs

Astrology and Relationships

Thomas Merton said, *"Love is our true destiny. We do not find the meaning of life by ourselves alone we find it with another."* He also says in *"No Man is an Island"* that *"The beginning of love is the will to let those we love be perfectly themselves, the resolution not to twist them to fit our image. If in loving them, we do not love what they are, but their potential likeness to ourselves, then we do not love them; we only love the reflection of ourselves in them."*

Relationships are important in everyone's life for the development of wholeness. To have a relationship with another human being is an awesome task, whether the other person is a baby, child, teenager, adult, boyfriend, girlfriend, wife, or husband. You are dealing with a human spirit with a soul and purpose in life. You are either a part of the solution for wholeness or you are one of the problems on the individual's path to wholeness.

Compatibility between individuals in interpersonal relationships plays a significant role in enhancing the emotional and physical health of a person. When we love people, cry together, laugh aloud with them, and jump up for joy when we see them, it makes us feel good about who we are. Soul mates help you know yourself, address your weaknesses, and grow personally and spiritually. This is because they are compatible with you, accept who you are, love and trust you, are not argumentative and want to see you become successful and whole.

Choosing a partner in life requires one to be careful and wise in order to dig out information and references about the partner. The law of attraction suggests that people of similar mind tend to attract each other. But others say you choose your opposite who will complement you well. Astrology, on the other hand, points out that you could be attracted to someone you are compatible with or you may decide to be attracted to someone with whom you are not compatible. It depends on the types of energies, love, attitudes, characteristics, and dynamics of the union when the two people meet. Whatever you choose, choose wisely, and shoot for win-win relationships.

Whatever relationships you are in you want to be conscious of the impact it can have on your purpose and goals in life. If you can avoid negative people who want to grieve your soul and establish good relationships with positive people who will inspire and support you, you will be on the right road to the wholeness of your soul. Relationships between a female and male sign will have dynamics that bring slight changes to the compatibility assessment, compared to two males or two females, due to differences in male and female brains and attraction between the sexes.

Build Relationships and Trust with All Sun Signs

It is wise to have relationships with individuals with each of the 12 different signs so that you discover yourself, evolve from a fragmented life to wholeness and get a good perspective on compatibility between your sign and other signs. Expose yourself to people who are different from you and have different personal needs. Having relationships with people who have a diversity of signs will cause you to experience different ideas of life, different responses from disagreements, and different energies in the interactions. However, some say that the more balanced you are, the better it is to choose someone who is also well-balanced in terms of his or her personality.

Do some people trigger your negative tendencies? Do strangers show love to you when you least expect it and you wonder what that means? The soul's personality shows up in body language, emotions, thinking, and communications. Two individuals who are attracted or compatible to each other feel as if a power or force is pulling them together. Also, two individuals may not know each other but when they meet for the first time, they may feel love at first sight or they may dislike each other at first sight. What explains this instant dislike or attraction between two people? Does it arise from their body type, essence, soul's personality, intelligence, or spiritual consciousness?

The joy and problems in relationships stem from having two different souls involved. The two souls are complex beings and there may not be much time at a 'first meeting' to find out what the other person's personality is like and if the two personalities will be compatible. Astrology has come up with a formula or language that can be used to determine compatibility or incompatibility between two people based on their sun signs, ascendants, qualities, elements, gender and astrological chart.

Principles of Astrological Compatibility

You can build good relationships and find happiness with different types of individuals or Astrological signs. People who have common interests with us tend to be easier to build relationships with. However, people who are different from you can make life enjoyable because they complement you and challenge you to grow. However, we have to be aware that our differences can destroy our relationships, whether we are compatible or incompatible.

To be compatible with someone in terms of astrology, you need to have at least one constituent in common with that person. The constituent in common can be the same astrological element (e.g., both fire sign), same astrological quality (e.g., fixed sign) or same planet sign (e.g. moon in Venus). Two mutable signs are compatible. Two Cardinal signs are compatible. Two fixed signs are compatible. Incompatibility bring challenges in the relationship that must be overcome. When you dominate another person, you bring conflict into the relationship. Withdrawal of love and affection shows that there is a conflict that has not been addressed. Even if one is not compatible with someone, there is a reward for learning how to adapt to the person you are not compatible with.

Alternatively, to be compatible, there has to be a strong attraction from natural forces, such attraction between opposite Sun signs, polar opposites or yin and yang types and complementary signs. For example, one observes strong attraction between opposite Sun signs, such as Cancer-Capricorn, Libra-Aries, Scorpio-Taurus, Gemini-Sagittarius, Aquarius-Leo and Virgo-Pisces. Example of polar opposites are introvert-extrovert and low energy-high energy individuals.

Astrologers have investigated the relationship between two people with known sun signs or ascendants and have come up with patterns of best, good, moderate, modest, and low compatibility that are worth validating in the real world. The compatibility formula is based on the energies involved with an astrological aspect and tendencies of each astrological sign. An astrological aspect is the angle the planets make to each other in the horoscope and also to the ascendant. A sextile relationship has a 60 degree aspect. A square relationship has a 90 degree aspect. Since each sun sign has 30 degrees on the zodiac circle, signs that are 90 degree aspects are 3 sun signs apart. A trine relationship has 120 degrees of aspect and is 4 signs apart. An opposition relationship has 180 degrees aspect and are 6 signs apart. A conjunction has a 0 degree aspect and is the same sign.

Astrology reveals our inclinations, tendencies, and energy levels. The sun sign provides dominant general characteristics of each person's birth. The ascendant provides a colorful influence on the Sun Sign. Whether the union or relationship between two individuals is positive or negative depends on the angle between their sun signs on the zodiac circle or the angle between their sun sign and ascendant sign or between the sun signs of their ascendants.

There is a connection between these elements and our body and mind. The relationship between any two elements provides clues on the type of relationship that will ensue. A water sign may douse the flames of a fire sign with water or a fire sign may heat up the watery emotions of a water sign and transform them. An air sign may blow the structure of an earth sign into dust, while an earth sign may suffocate the brainstorming nature of the air sign.

Astrological compatibility patterns can be used with dating, business relationships, friendships, soul mates, and acquaintances. The types of compatibility are described below based on the sun sign or ascendant of the two individuals.

Best Compatibility (Four sun signs apart)

Some individuals are very well suited for each other. Two individuals with sun signs that are four signs apart have the highest compatibility. These sun signs are 120 degrees apart on the zodiac circle. Examples are Aries-Leo, Aries-Sagittarius, Taurus-Virgo, Taurus-Capricorn, Gemini-Libra, Gemini-Aquarius, Cancer-Scorpio and Cancer-Pisces.

They show great compatibility, mutual ease of expression, and harmony. The two personalities reinforce each other in such a way that the qualities they share are strengthened. The two individuals are of the same element (fire, earth, air or water) and so they mix perfectly. Effort should be expended to bring dynamism into the relationship, such as the inclusion of others who are of a different element. Otherwise, the fact that both partners are of the same element can occasionally lead to predictability in the relationship and boredom at times.

As a Capricorn, I found out that I was very compatible with Virgos, who are four signs away from my sign. I have good compatibility with a Taurus. The Virgos I know tend to protect me and help me with love to grow and mature mentally and spiritually. However, they also get tough with me and provide constructive criticism of my behavior, while supporting me at the same time.

I get along and chat easily with the Water signs, Pisces (2 signs away), Scorpio (2 signs away), and Cancer (6 signs away) as well as Capricorn (same sign). The Air signs; Aquarius, Libra, and Gemini are my spiritual partners because we bond well and understand each other spiritually. The air sign is fulfilled in the earth signs; Capricorn, Taurus, or Virgo.

When it comes to friends that I want to have fun with, they tend to be Fire signs; Sagittarius, Aries, and Leo. I have lots of fun when I am with a Sagittarius because they make me feel comfortable in a big group by taking the focus onto themselves. They are philosophers, so my interest in spiritual knowledge brings some good debates. My relationship with my Aries friend is one of fun and competition. We have to compromise, otherwise no one wants to give in on what to do or where to go.

High Compatibility (Two sun signs apart)

Two individuals with sun signs that are two signs apart have high compatibility and often become friends. These sun signs are 60 degrees apart on the zodiac circle. Examples are Aries-Gemini, Aries-Aquarius, Taurus-Pisces, and Scorpio Capricorn. Two individuals from these signs have high compatibility, energy of friendship, and good communication between them. The compatibility in the relationship shows that air and fire signs mix easily or earth and water signs mix easily.

Good Compatibility (Opposite signs, Six signs apart)

These two individuals have sun signs that are diametrically opposites in the zodiac circle or they have a 180 degree angle between them. Examples are Aries-Libra, Leo-Aquarius, Sagittarius-Gemini, Virgo-Pisces, Cancer-Capricorn, and Scorpio-Taurus. Even though they are opposites they relate well to each other as they complement each other as yin and yang. By complementing each other, the relationship is more dynamic than two individuals with signs of the same element.

The relationship is good for both souls as they balance each other in a wholesome way. They are compatible because fire sign mixes well with air sign or earth sign mixes well with water sign. However, the drawback in the relationship is that their opposite nature may causes conflict from an exaggerated contrast of ideas and misunderstanding of each other. This will require some effort in compromise to understand each other and avoid disharmony and discord.

Medium Compatibility (Same sign)

These two individuals have the same sun signs. They have 0 degree angle between them and the aspect is called conjunction. This is the most powerful aspect. Examples are Aries-Aries, Taurus-Taurus, Gemini-Gemini and Cancer-Cancer.

Two individuals that are of the same sun sign have a powerful relationship that can be intensified. They will make a good team if they have the same goals. It is wonderful because they accept each other for who they are, see the world similarly, and show similar interests in life. However, being too much alike can lead to predictability in the relationship and boredom. Two people of the same sign are so much alike that they act more like siblings than marriage partners. They also tend to be stuck in their similar ways. To have fun, you need someone who is a little different and outrageous, compared to yourself. That is why life is a conundrum. It is good for compatibility to be similar, but not fun to be similar.

The powerful energy between same sun signs results in exaggerated harmony when they are in sync or intensified disharmony when they are out of sync and disagree with each other. For the relationship to work, they both have to be open-minded, become more whole, less insecure, and build trust in each other.

Modest Compatibility (Five signs apart)

The individuals that are five Sun signs apart have a relationship that is attached-detached or on-off. The relationship is turned on at one moment and turned off or detached at another time. These two sun signs have a 150 angle between them on the zodiac circle. Examples are Aries-Virgo, Aries-Scorpio, Sagittarius-Taurus and Sagittarius-Cancer.

The relationship is highly dynamic when the spark of attraction is there. Because of the tendency to be detached-attached, they appear to handle changes better and learn their lessons well, so that they are able to compromise to continue to live in harmony. They are from sun signs that are not next to each other and are of elements that do not mix well, such a fire and earth, fire and water, air and earth or air and water. Being of two different elements, it takes effort to make the relationship work. When it works, it is an attractive and dynamic one.

Modest Compatibility (One sign apart)

These two individuals are one Sun sign apart. The Sun signs are 30 degrees apart on the zodiac circle and the semi-sextile relationship occurs between adjacent Sun signs. Examples are Aries-Taurus, Aries-Pisces, Sagittarius-Capricorn, Capricorn-Aquarius and Sagittarius-Scorpio. The two signs have a slight ease in getting along, as the semi-sextile aspect is a minor aspect. The slight attraction energy that unites them may come from the spiritual partnership of the two Sun signs that are adjacent to each other, as if one sign is evolving into the other. The spiritual partnership leads to growth of the individuals in the relationship through awareness of each soul and compromise through objectivity. The difficulty in the relationship may come from the slight to neutral attraction energy brought into the relationship to generate excitement and overcome discords.

Modest Compatibility (Three signs apart, same quality)

These two individuals are three Sun signs apart. The Sun signs are 90 degrees apart on the zodiac circle and thus the aspect is square and the energy of relationship is stressful. Examples are Aries-Cancer, Aries-Capricorn, Sagittarius-Pisces, and Sagittarius-Virgo. They are compatible from both being fixed signs, but the relationship may show energy of tension, stress or tug of war, as each wants to control the other or be in charge. The relationship can be a dynamic one when there is respect, compromise and understanding between the two, as both are from different elements.

One of my friends is married to a lovely woman who is three signs apart. They have been married for over 30 years because of the hard work and commitment that they have shown in the relationship. Both of them are fixed signs which make them get along very well and compromise. They are close and do almost everything almost together. In addition to other factors, their compatibility also comes from both being fixed signs. They have a beautiful home and have created a harmonious environment for friends and family.

I also have a family member who has been married to his elegant wife for more than 15 years. Both of them are fixed signs which make them easy to get along well. They are disciplined and work together as a strong team.

Best Choice for Compatibility and Personal Growth

They say love conquers all in a relationship. Some couples stay in love despite the drama that surrounds them. Others have rocky relationships; hot one day, and cold another day. Finding the right partner requires strong effort for building a strong bond, whether the person is compatible or not.

Life is not a piece of cake. Only people with good hearts, strong minds, and caring spirits get to experience loving and dynamic relationships. If you are willing to change your bad habits, adapt to changes, compromise with partners, and overcome challenges created by incompatibility, you may transform any failed or struggling relationship into a powerful union between two evolved souls who know how to love and serve one another selflessly.

Based on the compatibility of signs, remember the following:

- In a relationship, choose someone you are compatible with, but be willing to work hard and compromise if there are disagreements and conflicts.

- If the person you are interested in is not astrologically compatible with you, understand that if both of you are willing to work hard and compromise in the relationship, you will develop and grow faster because you will overcome challenges that will make both of you stronger than before.

- Choose someone who is consciously aware of who he or she is, aware of who you are, and how he or she treats others.

- Choose someone who will be able to support you, meet your needs and purpose, and someone who will permit you to contribute to meet his or her needs and purpose.

- Choose someone who will help you grow personally towards the goal of wholeness of the body, mind and soul.

- Choose someone who is willing to be your spiritual partner.

- Choose someone who is as evolved as you are or whom you are willing to help evolve to minimize their weaknesses and dysfunctions.

CHAPTER ELEVEN

Evolution of Each
Sun Sign to Wholeness

Evolutionary Astrology

Evolutionary astrology deals with the progress of individual souls towards wholeness. It is used to denote significant changes in the personality of human souls as they progress toward wholeness. Where you are on this journey depends on how evolved you are. We have several layers of identity that affect our progress to wholeness, including religion, spirituality, gender, culture, upbringing, and karma. If you are highly evolved, you have very few areas of weaknesses and are closer to wholeness.

Evolutionary astrology seems to have been practiced by Indian Vedic astrologers for hundreds of years. Several astrologers have written about the evolution of each sun sign on the path to wholeness of the soul, including Dane Rudhyar, a pioneer in modern transpersonal astrology, who wrote an excellent book entitled, *"Astrology of Personality"*. Raymond Merriman and Jeffrey Green are considered leaders who developed the concept of evolutionary astrology in the late 70s.

One interesting quote from Dane on the evolution of souls is that evolution *"starts from Aries, the generative fire, to the end of the zodiac, Pisces, which is the distributive water that baptizes the body, mind and soul to be born again."* This quote is interesting when juxtaposed with Jesus statement that, *"Verily, verily I say unto thee unless a man is born again he cannot enter the kingdom of heaven."* (John 3:3)

Evolutionary Astrology to Wholeness

The principles, elements, and evolution of human souls in Astrology should be of great interest to those who want to know God, those who want to know who they are, why they are here in their present personality type, what obstacles they are facing, and what lessons they have to learn. The aim of the soul's evolution in the transpersonal or spiritual experience of humans is to align the body, mind, and soul with the spirit so that it is awakened or possessed by the Spirit of God, may achieve wholeness, and eventually transcendence of the spirit. One can say that the story of Jesus Christ is the story of a human being achieving wholeness, becoming a perfect personality or transpersonal figure, and transcending the human spirit to become one with God.

Early in my job career, I felt that my personality was limiting my ability to advance to a higher position. Since the personality is the karma of the soul, my personality was limiting my soul in its ability to transform itself. Now I understand why I had to practice mindfulness, perform self-observation, and expand my spiritual consciousness to address the deficiencies in my personality, before I could climb up the ladder of high expectations. By first purifying the body and mind through mindfulness, the soul is better prepared for alignment with the spirit. This is because the human spirit is masked by the soul. Therefore, purification of the soul reveals the power and purity of the spirit.

According to Dane Rudhyar in the *"Astrology of Personality"* and Linda Joyce in *"The Day You Were Born"*, there are 4 phases of the transpersonal journey that human souls go through in their evolution to wholeness. The cardinal signs; Aries, Cancer, Libra, or Capricorn are the initiators or generators of activity in one of the four phases. The fixed signs; Taurus, Leo, Scorpio, or Aquarius are the concentrators or fixers of problems to see things through in the middle of each phase. The mutable signs; Gemini, Virgo, Sagittarius, or Pisces are the distributors or the changeable ones who handle change in the transition from the end of one phase to the beginning of a new phase

The first phase of the transpersonal journey starts with the incarnation of the spirit in the body for separate selfhood in Aries, the generator of the will and of the energy required to survive the objective life. The impulsiveness and ego of Aries is supported by the soul pursuing desires and seeking possessions in Taurus, the concentrator of the link between spirit and the body. From the materialistic Taurus, the soul seeks the distributive power of the intellect in Gemini to solve problems by linking the body to the mind.

As the individual's desires for separation from the spirit wane from Aries to Gemini, the personal soul has a home in Cancer, generator of nurturing, for objective maturity of the soul. The soul then leaves the emotional Cancer to experience love and enthusiasm in Leo, the concentrator of the power of creativity of the soul in alignment with the spirit. The soul then leaves the generous Leo to the sign of discrimination and service in Virgo, the distributive power of the mind for critical analysis of choices for the inner and outer life of the individual.

Once it reaches Libra, the inner life of the soul emerges from its objective focus. The soul then seeks love and connection with the spirit in Libra, the generator of power for relationships, followed by the concentrative power of transformation of the soul in Scorpio to move towards unity with the spirit. This is followed by the optimism and distributive power of ideas in Sagittarius who connects the mind to the spirit through religion and philosophy.

The soul then leaves the passions of Sagittarius to seek knowledge and spiritual fulfillment and reach subjective maturity in Capricorn, the generator of power of the subjective to reawaken the spirit in the body. The soul then moves from the pessimism of Capricorn to the detached and visionary Aquarius, the concentrator of the power of the mind for interconnection with the spirit of all human beings. The cycle for subjective focus ends with a spiritual transformation of the soul in Pisces, the distributor of power of mysticism. The cycle of evolution in one's life then continues with the re-awakened spirit incarnated in the body in Aries and moves on until the body, mind, and soul are aligned with the spirit to achieve wholeness.

Must a Person be Born Again in Spirit in a Lifespan?

Jesus taught in John 3:4 that *"unless a man is born of water and the spirit, he cannot enter the kingdom of God."* There is opportunity in life for everyone to be born again in the cycles of selfhood in the zodiac of life by making improvements in their personalities, body, soul, and mind to become whole. When we lose hope or give up on life, we get back on the road to wholeness through being born again by water and by spirit. We have the spirit of God within us for hope, faith, and charity. Hope makes us feel better. Faith renews our trust in ourselves and in God. Charity leads us to move from self-centeredness to selflessness.

According to the astrological chart, each person is affected by 10 planets and 12 houses and therefore all 12 signs of the zodiac can influence the individual in different proportions, with the birth sign and ascendant predominating. In their book titled *"Birthdays, Stars, and Numbers"*, Saffi Crawford and Geraldine Sullivan reveal that some astrologers look at important turning points in a person's life using *"sun progressions to indicate important years in an individual life where the person's progressive sun changes."* Again, this is interesting as if we evolve from one sun sign to the adjacent sun sign and then on to the next. It is like being born again into other sun signs along the zodiac circle. Crawford and Sullivan go on to point out the following:

> *"In astrology, all twelve signs are embedded in the psyche of an individual and humankind alike, and although a person is born in one particular sign, in order to integrate into the whole, he or she must relate to the other twelve signs."*

Dane Rudhyar says in *"Astrology of Personality"* that *"progressions and directions are based on an analysis of the actual motion of planets or cusps after the moment of birth. They are based on the idea that birth is not a final gesture and that the act of birthing prolongs itself in time, spreads over a period of hours (Primary direction) or days (secondary progression) and in so doing affords a means to foretell the actual occurrences that will become objectivized during the whole life span."*

Love Provides Power for Transformation to Wholeness

We want to know who we are and love who we are. A healthy self-love is said to provide self-esteem and confidence. Once we have accepted our loving self, we do the soul work of transforming ourselves and our lives to meet our purpose and goals in life.

Each individual in a Sun sign has to know his or her strengths and weaknesses and use love as the motivation to transform from imperfection to a state of wholeness. If human beings would love their neighbors as themselves, they would live in the Kingdom of God where there is peace and joy, rather than a hell of distrust, conflicts, wars, pain, and suffering in the current world. Most Sun signs are susceptible to self-centeredness and selfishness because of the need for self-preservation. If love is adopted as the model of behavior for each Sun sign, from Aries to Pisces, then there will be hope that all people may eventually overcome their weaknesses and transform their souls to wholeness. The Bible says love is needed for wholeness:

> *"Love is patient, love is kind. It does not envy, it does not boast. It is not proud, it is not rude. It is not self-seeking, it is not easily angered. It keeps no recording of wrong-doings. Love does not delight in evil, but rejoices with the truth. It always protects, always trusts, always hopes, and always perseveres"* (Cor. 13: 4-7).

In contrast, the Bible describes unwholesome habits, attitudes, and behaviors as coming from works of the flesh to satisfy the desires of the body and ego. The unwholesome activities includes: sexual immorality, debauchery, hatred, discord, jealousy, rage, selfishness, envy, and drunkenness (Gal. 5:19-20).

Making Prudent Choices on the Path to Wholeness

We struggle to choose love for transformation from unwholesome to wholeness. Love enables each one of us on the journey to wholeness to make prudent choices, such as the following:

1. Choose harmony over conflict, sharing over greed, selflessness over selfishness.

2. Choose trust over suspicion, calm over anger, and generosity over stinginess.

3. Choose humility over pride, moderation over greed, meekness over bossiness.

4. Choose cheerful over moody, optimism over pessimism, silence over gossip.

5. Choose openness over secretive, carefree over worry, easygoing over hostility.

6. Choose cooperation over separateness, caution over impulsiveness, truth over lies.

7. Choose non-attachment over possessiveness, encouragement over judgment.

8. Choose charity over materialism, forgiveness over revenge, and discipline over recklessness.

9. Choose a relaxed and confident demeanor over nervousness, goodness over self-righteousness.

10. Choose sociability over withdrawal, calmness over restlessness and impatience.

11. Choose self-control over compulsiveness, flexibility over control and inflexibility.

12. Choose compassion over hatred, goodwill over envy, contentment over lust.

13. Choose being candid over scheming, shrewd, calculating and manipulative behavior.

Transpersonal Astrology

I recommend that those interested in Astrology obtain a copy of Dane Rudhyar's book; *"Astrology of Personality"* and a copy of an outstanding book entitled, *"The Day You Were Born"*, by Linda Joyce. Both books describe the essence of each sun sign, what each sun sign seeks and charts the evolution of each sign to wholeness. For my own research, I observed individuals that I know personally in order to validate my understanding of their sun sign personalities and their astrological paths to wholeness, based on work done in the area of evolutionary and transpersonal astrology.

What are The Sun Signs of People You Know?

In my life, in high school, at the universities, and at work, I have come to know interesting individuals and their Sun signs. These relationships helped me to know myself and understand my family members, friends and work mates.

As shown in the table below, I have come to know at least 10 individuals in each sun sign. This gave me insight into other signs and my own sign, Capricorn. I also know the profession of each individual so I can classify them according to their profession without listing their names.

TABLE 4. ASTROLOGICAL SUN SIGNS AND PROFESSIONS OF KNOWN INDIVIDUALS

Sign	Scientist	IT	Engineer	Finance/ Sales	Service/ Admin
Aries	5	1	2	3	1
Taurus	2	1		2	2
Gemini	5	2	2		1
Cancer	4		2		
Leo	2			1	1
Virgo	4	1		1	3
Libra	3	1			1
Scorpio	1	2	1	1	
Sagittarius	9	1		4	4
Capricorn	7	2			3
Aquarius	3	1	2	1	1
Pisces	4				1

The Aries Astrological Path

I know about 17 individuals with the Aries sun sign. In general terms, Aries is the sign of selfhood, action, and the courage of a leader. They are highly individualistic and do not take orders from others easily. As their cardinal quality, they like to initiate activities. They have a brilliant mind, strong will power, and strong faith in themselves. I know a natural Aries who focuses a lot on the job. She has excellent leadership skills, but had conflicts with others unnecessarily. She was assertive, creative, and loved to wield power over others. But this Aries had the typical Aries weaknesses of being selfish, reckless, impulsive, impatient, and inconsiderate.

Nurse	Business Mgmt	Teachers/ Professors	Banking	Counsel/ Coach	Politician
Aries	2			1	1
Taurus				3	
Gemini	1		2		1
Cancer	3	2	2		
Leo	5	2	3	1	1
Virgo	2	3	3	1	1
Libra	2	1	1	2	
Scorpio	1	2	3		
Sagittarius	1	1	1	2	3
Capricorn	2			1	2
Aquarius	3	1	1		1
Pisces	3	1	1	3	1

Two of my buddies from childhood are Aries. Both are intelligent, highly competitive, have a wonderful memory, and show tremendous energy and enthusiasm when handling several projects at the same time. You will think that they hardly sleep, but come the following day, you will find that they have refilled their tank of energy and are ready to go full throttle.

In general, the Aries seek action, control, independence, pioneer projects, and admiration, but they have a strong ego and need to compromise and balance aggression and anger with caution, generosity, love, and humility on the journey to wholeness. A highly evolved Leo will be less belligerent, less conflict-prone, and choose love over selfishness.

The Taurus Astrological Path

I know at least 10 people with the Taurus sun sign. Taurus is the sign of practicality and possessions. I know several Taurus friends who are calm, pragmatic, strong-willed, and determined. They seem to be loyal and family-oriented. Some love to be fashionable, materialistic, and enjoy experimenting with different styles. I have observed Taurus natives who can be really jealous and possessive.

My Taurus friends are home bodies, like Cancer types. They can be the strong silent type. They are described as the bull because they have a fixed nature, are susceptible to stubbornness and not easily pushed around.

Taurus people generally seek security, opportunities, friendships, and creativity, but need to replace jealousy, holding grudges, and possessiveness with flexibility, unselfishness, and self-control. A highly evolved Taurus will be less jealous and revengeful and choose love over suspicion and jealousy of others.

The Gemini Astrological Path

I have come to know about 14 Gemini individuals, three of them for a long time. Geminis seem to have a dual nature. They can be easily excited about something and then get bored easily or turn quiet suddenly. They have good communication skills, a penchant for being inquisitive, and enjoy conversations and gossip with friends. They seem to be wary of being overemotional and can get into really deep thinking to solve problems. My Gemini friends show strengths of liveliness and intelligence, but they can be restless, changeable and unpredictable. It is not easy to get close to their inner lives.

In general, Gemini people seek novel ideas, brainstorming opportunity to exercise their intellect, and lively communication with friends to feel secure and enjoy themselves. They need to balance gossiping, unpredictability and being too imaginative with an increased self-awareness, consistency, and unity of purpose. Highly evolved Gemini's will be secure in themselves, aware of their dual nature, and will choose love over harshness and strictness.

The Cancer Astrological Path

I know about 13 Cancer persons. Cancer is the sign of domestic and psychic feelings. They see life through their emotions. They are emotionally sensitive, intuitive, and determined. Three good friends of mine from childhood and one of my mentors show the typical Cancer traits. You can recognize them by their loud laugh and changing emotions as you talk to them. They love to be at home with their family and like well-established relationships. It is not easy to get close to them and their secrets, but they are popular with their friends because they are compassionate, love to laugh out loud, and enjoy good company. They love to be the center of attention.

Generally, Cancer natives seek solid roots, harmonious family lives, emotional space, inner life security and self-awareness to protect themselves, but they need to balance moodiness, a withdrawn nature, and insecurity with openness, generosity, and forgiveness, especially with those individuals who hurt their feelings. A highly evolved Cancer will be more generous and trusting and choose love over selfishness.

The Leo Astrological Path

I know about 16 Leo natives. Leos are performers. They love to have fun with friends, be in charge, and express themselves. They are sociable, graceful, optimistic, and have strong personalities. They tend to be charismatic leaders, and are friendly and generous. One of my best friends from graduate school shows the typical Leo traits. He is a strong leader in his business and community. He is very confident of his skills, cheerful, outgoing, bold, and fun to be with. Leo natives may go to extremes and become bossy, egocentric, materialistic, and extravagant.

Leos generally seek attention, freedom, fun, creative projects, harmonious relationships, and opportunities to shine, but they need to balance their huge ego and domineering nature with humility and introspection. Highly evolved Leos find balance by being humble, empathic and less egoistic.

The Virgo Astrological Path

I know about 21 Virgos. Virgo is the sign of articulate communication, orderliness, and judgment of self and others in life. As a Capricorn, I am so compatible with Virgos that I tell people that Virgos protect me from harm. Virgo women tend to be charming, graceful, and have a distinctive style of beauty. I get along very well with Virgos. The Virgos that I know very well are intelligent, love to talk, and articulate their viewpoint well. They are well known for being health conscious, sharp dressers, and stylish.

I seem to be surrounded by Virgos at home and at work. I had a wonderful Virgo boss and a dependable and efficient Virgo partner for 15 years of my professional career. Three of my best friends are Virgos. My soul mate is a Virgo. There are six Virgos in my family and extended family. My oldest, caring sister is a Virgo.

Virgos are serious and can be worriers. Criticism is a Virgo's area of specialization. The overcritical Virgo will criticize you if are not orderly and productive. They may criticize not only big mistakes, but little mistakes as well. They have high performance standards.

In general, Virgo natives seeks perfection, friendships, material security, productivity, but they need to balance a tendency to be worriers, to be overcritical and judgmental with spontaneity, generosity, the right perspectives, and positive emotions.

Highly evolved Virgos will be aware of their tendency to criticize, have fun with friends, choose love over being judgmental of others, and compliment others when needed.

The Libra Astrological Path

I know about 13 Librans. Libra is the sign of social consciousness and relationships. Librans are sociable, charming, fair-minded, and diplomatic, but they love their privacy. I enjoy the company of Librans. They know how to entertain their guests. My Libran friends like relationships so much that they talk a lot about relationships. They love people. They love to talk, but they don't like large parties which overwhelms them and makes them restless.

Librans tend to seek sense of self, fun, love, intimate partnerships, and harmony, but need to balance materialism, indecisiveness, and dependency with increased self-awareness, discipline, and self-reliance.

Highly evolved Librans love people, are well-balanced, and good mediators of conflicts. They are not withdrawn and do not swing between two extremes. They enjoy having people visit them and are not overly sensitive about their feeling being hurt.

The Scorpio Astrological Path

I know about 12 Scorpio natives. Scorpio is the sign of transformation and longing to unite with others, especially in marriage. My Scorpio friends and I get along well. They tend to be honest, calm, and sociable. They have strong determination and it can be hard to convince them of something when they have made up their mind about it.

They are honest, independent and want to be in charge and they enjoy fine things in life. They are not easy to understand and are skeptical of others and their motives. They can be secretive and would rather be in control than be controlled. They demonstrate an air of coolness that is attractive. They work hard and cultivate a sense of independence.

Generally, Scorpios seek love, intimacy, transformation, the secrets of others and vision, but they need to balance manipulation and possessiveness with selflessness, generosity, and openness.

The Sagittarius Astrological Path

I know about 28 Sagittarian natives. Sagittarius is the sign of optimism, expansion of relationships, and passion for ideas and life. They are visionaries, outgoing, and love outdoor activities, travel, and philosophizing. I get along very well with Sagittarian natives. Three of my best friends are typical Sagittarians. They are outgoing, vocal, philosophers, and religious, extravagant, generous, and enjoy a battle of the mind and ideas. They love their freedom and independence and like to have fun, experience the good life and travel even with short notice. They are not as egotistical as other fire signs; Leo and Aries.

They enjoy making our circle of friends laugh, but they are well known for their fearlessness and bluntness, even with their friends. They tend to be restless and prefer activities that keep them busy or outdoors. In college, one friend would pick me up in his truck on the weekends and we would go out to play soccer, go to the clubs, and go hiking or party with friends at his place.

The typical Sagittarian seeks freedom, outdoor life, spiritual truth, higher knowledge, expression of their beliefs and purpose in life. They need to balance their passions, unconventional nature, and adventures with self-control, attention to detail, flexibility, and good organizational skills.

The Capricorn Astrological Path

I know about 17 Capricorns. This is the sign of individual stability, ambition, and a strong reliance on spiritual ideas. When I found out that I am a typical Capricorn, it made me understand why I am so serious and quiet. My purpose to seek knowledge for spiritual growth and development is consistent with the Capricorn quest for spiritual practices and ideas. Capricorns are gentle, ambitious, responsible, and hardworking. They want to take charge, find material and financial security and achieve goals for career and spirituality goals. They are devoted to their jobs, realistic, and seek facts before making decisions.

They have singular vision, like rules and routine, and struggle with their imagination. They are insensitive and need to learn to be empathic. They tend to have difficulties in their lives because they are too serious, thanks to the restrictive influence of their ruling planet, Saturn. They seek pleasure and the luxurious things in life to escape the restraints discipline imposed on them. I get along well with other Capricorns because we tend to be similar, with a serious outlook, and strong minded.

Some of the Capricorns that I know well tell me that one of their concerns is that they are too serious in life. My understanding is that this comes from the restrictive and disciplinary influence of the planet, Saturn. This may explain why Capricorns seek pleasure to escape from seriousness. Two of my extended family members are also Capricorns. They are so very like me, in terms of their sense of humor, introversion, generosity, and seriousness. Two notable differences are that they are less serious and affable underachievers. They could have a different Ascendant, but it seems they have the basic personality of a Capricorn. I noticed that these family members have improved their social skills and artistry and did not become as academically studious as I was in my upbringing.

In general, Capricorns seek higher self, security, friendships, spiritual ideas, love, intimate partnership in their work and activities, and spiritual growth, but need to balance their pessimism and authoritative natures with fun, being less controlling, going beyond limitations and being warmhearted and spontaneous. The highly evolved Capricorn knows how to balance ambition, work, and spiritual goals with fun, love, vision for the future, lively communications, and enriching relationships.

The Aquarius Astrological Path

I know about 18 Aquarius individuals. Aquarius is the sign of humanitarianism, intelligence, ideas, and idealism. They are

friendly, even-tempered, kind, expressive, and forward thinkers. They value their freedom and think outside the box. They
love people and reach out to help others to the extent that they
can be neglectful of themselves. They don't like rules, nor do
they conform to conventional attitudes, so they tend to be private, detached, and eccentric. They feel that they are right in
their thinking because they do their homework to ensure they
have the facts to back it up.

I was astounded at how often Aquarian women feel no
interest in marriage, though they are delightful, graceful, and
smart. They love their freedom and feel good about their single
lives, as they find friends easily. However, they feel hurt easily
and like to probe into your feelings if you are a friend, as they
have good concentration, psychic ability, and they don't trust
easily.

Generally, Aquarians seem to seek freedom, excitement,
harmony, purpose in life, equality, spiritual partners and
friendships, but they need to balance their detached and calculating side with more focus on the direction of their life, being
warmhearted and expressive, and demonstrative of emotional
feelings.

Highly evolved Aquarians have learned to trust people,
enjoy people, make friends through philanthropy and not sab-
otage relationships in order to avoid being hurt easily if they
don't get their way.

A Model of Aquarius Nature

My mother was a model Aquarius, like Oprah Winfrey. Both
Oprah and my mother have similar birthdays (day and month)
and the same Chinese astrological sign; the Snake. As an Aquarius, she was a humanitarian, intuitive, strong-willed, friendly,
intelligent, stubborn, critical, unpredictable and demanding.
As a snake, she was wise, a leader, assertive, confident, shrewd,
sophisticated, secretive, graceful, and psychic. She loved to talk
and give advice to people who sought help from her because of
her wisdom, spirituality, and friendliness.

My father married my mother in a Catholic church. They were in love and he swept her off her feet. His Chinese sign was a Rooster and hers was a Snake. The Snake and Rooster are very compatible. He was a gentleman, conservative, serious, hardworking, and a good provider as a departmental store manager, where he led a group of about 50 employees.

My father was a handsome man, poised, lively and adventurous. He was very popular and admired in the neighborhood because of his job, personality, and lifestyle. He had a keen eye for fashionable clothes, quality shoes, and other fine things of life. He loved to attend parties, flirt with women, and crack jokes. My mother felt hurt, later on in the marriage, by his decision to marry two women, in addition to her. He was the type of man who followed his own rules, but he lost a good woman when they separated.

My mother was a midwife who was popular in the community because she took good care of the health of pregnant women and their babies, and showed concern for other people. She had great social grace in the community. She was powerful, resilient, patient, bold, intelligent, a little detached, and a pillar in the community.

Her faith in herself and in God was the cornerstone of her life. She was one of a selected few women who built her own house in the neighborhood by budgeting her money well. She took great care of her children and ensured that we all had a good education. She was a devout Catholic and rose to the level of Grand Lady in the society of Ladies of Marshall.

Family was very important to my mother. However, like a lot of Aquarians, she felt comfortable living alone in her house. After my father passed away, re-marriage was not a priority. Because my father could not handle her devotion to her midwife career, she had been heart-broken with her first love and talked little about the relationship. The love of family, friends, neighbors, and church members meant a great deal to her and gave her the joy and peace that she cherished.

The Pisces Astrological Path

I know about 15 Pisces individuals. Pisces is the sign of idealism, judgment of relationships, and psychic mysticism. As a Capricorn, I get along well with Pisces friends. They love deep mysteries and like to figure people out. They surround themselves with luxurious things in life and set up their own rules of life. They tend to be self-conscious and moody. They are meditative, spontaneous, lively, and sympathetic.

A notable characteristic of my Pisces friends is that they are helpful, compassionate, and put on a cheerful face, but they can be secretive, manipulative, and may get their feeling hurt easily. They like to embellish the truth a little bit. Some of my Pisces friends change husbands or jobs more easily than I would expect. They can be attracted to destructive and mysterious people.

In general, Pisces individuals tend to seek faith, harmony between their emotion and heart, healing of their soul and spiritual connection, but they need to balance an oversensitive and judgmental nature with a sense of purpose, selflessness, and confidence for personal growth.

PART FIVE

Know Your Chinese Astrology and Birthday Number

CHAPTER TWELVE

Chinese Astrological Signs and Relationships

Background of Chinese Astrology

I was introduced to Chinese Astrology by a Chinese colleague who told me astrology is used for varied reasons in China, including verifying partner compatibility in relationships. I studied Chinese Astrology and selected three books for reference, because of the relative accuracy of the descriptions of the signs of my friends and family members. The books were *"Simple Chinese Astrology"* by Damian Sharp, *"Chinese Astrology"* by Suzanne White and *"Chinese Horoscopes"* by Debbie Burns.

Chinese astrology is based on the Chinese lunar calendar. Indian, Chinese, and Western Astrology are all based on the elements of fire, air, water, and earth. Chinese astrology is based on the year of your birth, whereas Western astrology is based on your day and month of birth. Thus, the two astrology types complement each other for a whole reading of your personality profile.

In Chinese Astrology, the characteristics of 12 animal signs represent 12 different personality types. Chinese astrology is based on a cycle of years and lunar months. You don't have to believe in Chinese astrology but I suggest you pay attention to how Chinese astrology works. Then, compare your own personality traits with the astrological predictions of the Chinese Astrological signs.

Principles of Chinese Astrology

The Chinese Astrological signs are classified in three ways: Animal sign, Element, and Polarity. Chinese astrology has five basic elements; wood, fire, earth, water or metal. These elements are important in the quality of our existence on Earth. Out of the 105 elements in the world, about 83 of them are metals, such as iron.

The connection of elements are: wood produces fire, fire collects as earth or dust, earth produces metal and molten metal collects as water or liquid, water leads to wood, like a tree. Wood is controlled by metal, as trees are cut by metals.

The controlling relationships are as follows: Metal is controlled by fire as fire melts metal. Fire is controlled by water, as water puts out fire. Water is controlled by earth, as earth directs flow of water in rivers. Earth is controlled by wood, as the roots of trees hold the soil together.

The conducive relationships are metal and water, water and wood, wood and fire, fire and earth, and earth and metal.

Within each Animal sign, there are five distinct sub-personality traits, depending on the element governing the sign in the particular year of birth. In terms of polarity, the element of each sign is either feminine (yin) or masculine (yang). Women may be slightly different from men of the same sign.

The Chinese Astrology Signs

What is your Chinese Astrology Animal sign? The Chinese calendar year starts from approximately beginning of February to end of January. The Chinese Zodiac signs are of the order: Rat (1948), Ox (1949), Tiger (1950), Rabbit (1951), Dragon (1952), Snake (1953), Horse (1954), Sheep (1955), Monkey (1956), Rooster (1957), Dog (1958), and Pig (1959). The cycle of signs occurs every 12 years. Each sign is repeated after 12 years.

The Innovator Signs are: Rat, Dragon, and Monkey. These are the thinkers, innovators, initiators, doers, performers and progressive individuals.

The Visionary Signs are: Ox, Snake, and Rooster. These are the intellectuals, purposeful, and determined individuals.

The Free Spirit signs are: Tiger, Horse, and Dog. These are the humanitarians, honest, idealistic, active and high-spirited ones.

The Artist Signs are: Rabbit, Sheep, and Pig. These are the expressive, intuitive, compassionate and sensible individuals.

The following are general characteristic of the 12 personality types:

Rat Sign

Rat Strengths: leader, hardworking, initiator, intuitive, resourceful, inquisitive, adaptable, shrewd, caring, outgoing, self-motivated

Rat Weaknesses: reserved, gossipy, thrifty, a busybody, selfish, nervous, anxious

Rat Celebrities: Richard Nixon, Mehmet Oz, Stevie Nicks, John McCain, Prince Charles, Sean Penn, Jimmy Carter, Marlon Brando, Ben Affleck, Shaquille O'Neal, Ralph Samson, Kate Perry, Eminem, Tom Flores, Donna Summer, Cameron Diaz

Ox Sign

Ox Strengths: Conservative, authoritative, determined, calm, reliable, dedicated, hardworking, honest, confident, patient, kind, dignified

Ox Weaknesses: rigid, stubborn, naïve, unapproachable, uncompassionate, narrow minded, has difficulty expressing feelings, and has difficulty expressing love

Ox Celebrities: George Clooney, Barack Obama, Bill Cosby, Colin Powell, Adolf Hitler, Margaret Thatcher, Eddie Murphy, Jack Nicholson, Tupac Shakur, Lionel

Richie, Meryl Streep, Madeline Albright, Forest Whitaker, Janelle Monae, Heidi Klum

Tiger Sign

Tiger Strengths: courageous, curious, passionate, energetic, charismatic, generous, optimistic, humanitarian, enthusiastic, loyal, honorable

Tiger Weaknesses: impulsive, egotistical, dictatorial, restless, selfish, rebellious, indecisive, and unreasonable

Tiger Celebrities: Hugh Hefner, Lady Gaga, M. C. Hammer, Queen Elizabeth II, Jay Leno, Ce Lo Green, Paula Abdul, Solanges Knowles, Tom Cruise, Richard Branson, Chris Christie, Steve Wonder, Demi Moore, Rush Limbaugh, Phil McGraw

Rabbit Sign

Rabbit strengths: peaceful, diplomatic, sensitive, elegant, intelligent, resilient, kind, intuitive, good judgment, graciousness, alert, and artistic

Rabbit weaknesses: over-sensitive, private, ruthless, secretive, moody, and fearful

Rabbit celebrities: David Beckham, Andy Murray, Joan Rivers, Albert Einstein, Ray Allen, Harry Belafonte, Mark Harmon, Angelina Jolie, Johnny Depp, Kendrick Lamar, Suze Orman, Lauryn Hill, Ralph Lauren, Nicolas Cage, Tina Turner

Dragon Sign

Dragon strengths: Dynamic, energetic, optimistic, courageous, intelligent, decisive, vitality, exciting, feisty, strong willed, dominating, commanding, well dressed, good instincts, warm-hearted, and adventurous

Dragon weaknesses: bad tempered, dogmatic, eccentric, egotistical, despotic, malicious, domineering, brusque, arrogant, overconfident, and restless

Dragon celebrities: Maya Angelou, Sarah Palin, Jimmy Connors, Wayne Dyer, John Lennon, Barry Bonds, Walter Mondale, Vivica Fox, Susan Rice, Anthony Weiner, Russell Westbrook, Wendy Williams, Sandra Bullock, Roseanne Barr, Richard Pryor

Snake Sign

Snake strengths: wise, leader, alert, sophisticated, confident, intuitive, shrewd, cautious, powerful, resilient, graceful, elegant, skeptical, psychic, and sensual

Snake weaknesses: power-hungry, ruthless, cold, calculating, laid back, vicious, highly secretive

Snake celebrities: Oprah Winfrey, Viola Davis, Chris Brown, Kanye West, Martha Stewart, Jackie Onassis, Charlie Sheen, Howard Hughes, Richard Dawkins, Martha Stewart, Shania Twain, Howard Stern

Horse Sign

Horse Strengths: energetic, athletic, action-oriented, strong, ambitious, bold, perceptive, passionate, hardworking, independent, optimistic, flexible, self-reliant, and confident

Horse Weaknesses: restless, unpredictable, opportunistic, capricious, fickle, petty, self-centered, bad tempered

Horse celebrities: Aretha Franklin, Paul McCartney, Angela Merkel, Ross Perot, Barbra Streisand, John Legend, Janet Jackson, Mike Tyson, Nelson Mandela, Mario Balotelli, Halle Berry, Sean Connery

Sheep Sign

Sheep Strengths: courageous, graceful, generous, gentle, compassionate, determined, sincere, easy going, refined, good-natured, friendly, honest, sympathetic, fashionable

Sheep Weaknesses: worrier, sensitive, pessimist, indecisive, shy, extravagant, live beyond their means, overspends, self-pitying, moody, risk-averse

Sheep celebrities: Joyce Meyer, Muhammad Ali, Don King, Desmond Tutu, Julia Roberts, Bill Gates, Jamie Foxx, Adam Levine, Nicole Kidman, Mick Jagger

Monkey Sign

Monkey strengths: intelligent, energetic, brilliant, curious, spontaneous, lively, sociable, clever, entertaining, alert, insightful, optimistic, competitive, charming

Monkey weaknesses: mischievous, selfish, critical, secretive, restless, egotistical, revengeful, unscrupulous, vain, and undisciplined

Monkey celebrities: Celine Dion, Patti Labelle, Christina Aguilera, Karen Armstrong, Venus William, Mick Jagger, Mel Gibson, Pope John Paul II, Tom Hanks, Selena Gomez, Lyndon Johnson, Elvis Presley, Martina Hingis, George Lucas, Kate Couric

Rooster Sign

Rooster strengths: Efficient, colorful, courageous, detail-oriented, ambitious, conservative, organized, knowledgeable, expressive, perfectionist, decisive, frank

Rooster weaknesses: critical, egoistic, vain, opinionated, obsessive, proud, provocative, uncooperative

Rooster celebrities: Beyoncé Knowles, Jennifer Lopez, Gloria Estefan, Meagan Good, Goldie Hawn, Emmitt Smith, Elton John, Jennifer Hudson, Dolly Parton, Nichole Richie, Larry King, Steve Martin, Bette Midler, Sean Combs, Kelly Rowland

Dog Sign

Dog strengths: Loyal, friendly, just, warm, honest, intelligent, amiable, dutiful, fearless, outspoken, generous, practical, trusting, faithful, noble, compassionate

Dog weaknesses: pessimist, erratic, critical, belligerent, argumentative, highly opinionated, cynical, caustic

Dog celebrities: Bill Clinton, Michael Jackson, Naomi Campbell, Donald Trump, Kelly Clarkson, Andre Agassi, Elvis Presley, Jane Fonda, George W. Bush, Danny Glover, Kelly Clarkson, Octavia Spencer, Nicky Minaj, Jimmy Buffett

Pig Sign

Pig strengths: affectionate, generous, honest, persevering, strong, hardworking, courageous, fun, lighthearted, sensual, considerate, generous, eager, peaceful, flexible, thick skinned

Pig weaknesses: bad-tempered, depravity, materialistic, debauchery, corruptible

Pig celebrities: Ronald Regan, Hillary Clinton, Henry Kissinger, David Bowie, O. J. Simpson, Magic Johnson, Michael Kors, Arnold Schwarzenegger, Elton John, David Letterman, Brian William, Carlos Santana

Best Compatibility Between Animal Signs

When looking at the wheel of the zodiac circle, the signs in each group or trine are evenly spaced at 4 years apart. People born under these signs in each group or trine will share similar mindsets, outlooks and personalities. This makes them very suitable for close relationships.

> Group 1. Rat, Dragon, and Monkey are very compatible with each other. These are the innovator signs.
>
> Group 2. Ox, Snake, and Rooster are very compatible with each other. These are the visionaries.
>
> Group 3. Tiger, Horse, and Dog are very compatible with each other. These are the free spirits.
>
> Group 4. Rabbit, Sheep and Pig are very compatible. These are the artists.

Incompatibility Between Opposite Animal Signs

It is easy to determine which relationships could be difficult for any people whose animals' signs are directly opposite one another on the zodiac wheel. Their personalities and views are just not going to mesh well. Therefore, the two incompatibles will have to put in extra effort to face and overcome ensuing challenges and learn from them to become more understanding of each other.

The incompatible pairings are: Rat and Horse, Ox and Sheep, Tiger and Monkey, Rabbit and Rooster, Dragon and Dog, and Snake and Pig.

Compatibility of Couples with Different Combination of Chinese/Sun Signs

If we have 12 Sun Signs and 12 Chinese Signs, then each person has the opportunity to meet 144 different individuals with a different combination of Chinese sign and sun sign. In other words, each sun sign/Chinese sign person will have 12 sun signs with one Chinese sign, and each of the 12 sign signs can have 12 different Chinese signs.

If one wants to go into detail, for each of the 144 different individuals that you can meet, there are 12 ascendants, 12 descendants and 3 decanates for each sun sign. If you also break down each Chinese sign, there are 5 different elements of wood, metal, water, earth and fire. Thus, each person has the opportunity to meet over 100,000 individuals with different combinations of sun sign and Chinese signs. This is what makes the world go around, when there are so many interesting possibilities for dynamic and interesting relationships between individuals. There is harmony and unity in the compatible relationships and dynamism and fun in diversity in the unevenly-yoked relationships.

If one wants to enhance the compatibility of a pair in friendships, business partnerships, and romantic relationships, you want to partner with someone whose sun sign is compatible with your sun sign and whose Chinese sign is also compatible with your Chinese sign. However, some relationships can be powerful when the two seemingly incompatible individuals develop a strong bond over time and grow up painfully through hard work and compromise to become less self-centered.

Every marriage has good times and bad times. It takes love, commitment, and some compatibility to sustain successful, long marriages. I found the following combination of sun signs and Chinese signs for the successful married couples that I know.

Leo/Snake Woman and Aquarius/Ox Man

My friend, Francis and his wife Rebecca have a strong partnership. They have been married for over 40 years. They have two adult sons and a grandchild. Linda dated four guys before she met Francis, and Francis had a short relationship with someone before he met Rebecca. Francis knew in the beginning when he met her that she was the woman for him. Their relationship blossomed so well that they have become a model of a good marriage in the extended family.

Astrology shows they are soul mates. Aquarius is compatible with Leo. The Ox is highly attracted to the charm of the Snake and is happy in marriage. Francis is patient and hardworking. He provides loving support to Rebecca.

Rebecca is a Leo/Snake woman who is charming, wise, serene, intelligent, lovely and graceful. As a Leo, she is a good performer and a strong leader in her professional work. As a lioness Leo, she wants to be treated like a queen. As a snake, she is charming, wise, a leader, shrewd, and confident. Francis is an Aquarius/Ox man. People who know Francis love him because he is handsome and possess a good personality. He knows he has a gem of a wife. His Aquarius nature comes through well. He is a humanitarian and a friendly person who will come to the aid of any extended family member, work mate, or friend who needs help. His Ox nature makes him serious, calm, patient and hardworking, the kind of man who takes care of his family.

Capricorn/Dragon Woman and Virgo/Rat Man

I have known Pedro and Paula for most of my life. They have been happily married for over 35 years because of the great compatibility between them. This is supported by their Chinese signs and sun signs. He is a Virgo/Rat and she is a Dragon/Capricorn. The Rat is very compatible with the Dragon, and Capricorn is a perfect match for Virgo. They have an adult daughter and an adult son who are doing well in the corporate world.

As a Virgo, Pedro is a handsome, flexible, intelligent, health conscious, orderly and honorable man. As a Rat sign, he is self-motivated, smart, hardworking, and determined. As a Dragon, Paula is dynamic, warm, powerful, domineering, and discreet and has strong leadership skills. As a Capricorn, she is generous, serious and one of the hardest working women you've ever met. She is a task master with strong leadership abilities. Paula is lively, vivacious and charismatic. Pedro offers her advice and supports her dreams.

Pedro admires her wife and her accomplishments in a corporate life dominated by men. She rose to become the CEO of a small company for about 10 years. He was a director and head of a department with 50 employees. Both of them can work for long hours and need to have fun to balance things out. Since Paula tends to dominate everyone in her vicinity through her strong personality, Pedro has found a way to be supportive and calm things down when she wants to release some tension. He is diplomatic and a gentleman, and she is a lady who can be charming as well as boisterous depending on the occasion. Paula has come to appreciate the support that Pedro has given her and the way he has handled the demanding and challenging side of her nature over the years.

Libra/Sheep Woman and Taurus-Gemini/Horse Man

Steve and Victoria are highly compatible and have been happily married for 23 years. They have two daughters. In Chinese astrology, the Sheep is a perfect match for the Horse. Their Sun signs and Chinese signs show a strong attraction between them. As a Taurus-Gemini cusp and Horse person, Steve is smart, materialistic, enjoys playing soccer, and loves a big house. As a Libra/Sheep woman, Victoria is well composed, charming, sociable, and a good communicator. She is a devoted mother who loves to talk and entertain her guests. They are a great team and coordinate well to handle the load at work and at home in order to raise the kids well in their beautiful house.

Virgo/Rooster and Capricorn/Horse Man

James and Elizabeth have been married for about 20 years and have one adult son who has exceeded expectations in his service to his community. James works long hours to run his own business, and Elizabeth works as a financial advisor. These two are soul mates. They are comfortable with each other, have mutual interests, and help each other to grow personally and spiritually. As Earth signs, they are both materialistic, pragmatic, rational, and hardworking.

As a Virgo/Rooster, Elizabeth is calm, hardworking, perfectionist, critical and health conscious. She works out a lot and enjoy dressing well. She is beautiful, loyal, analytical and a procrastinator. She is a Virgo and Rooster like Beyoncé Knowles and Jennifer Hudson. As a Capricorn/Horse, James is athletic, tall, demanding, serious, intense, independent, and spiritual minded. He is quiet, reserved and devoted to his job. Elizabeth is easy going and brings fun into his life. However, she is more critical and puts everyone and everything under a microscope. He is very confident and like to take charge and get things done.

Both Elizabeth and James have a strong union and a close-knit family. James is the romantic one. Elizabeth is protective of everyone in the family. After so many years together, James knows how to handle her Virgo/Rooster critical nature. She has learned to handle the controlling nature of the Capricorn James. They love going out for dinner, dancing, travelling, and spending time with family and friends.

Aries/Rooster and Virgo/Tiger Man

Lucy and Joseph have been happily married for about 27 years. They have two adult daughters and an adult son. They are a great team and love each other very much. Whenever you see Lucy, you will see Paul beside her. It is not easy to separate them, until they have go their separate ways to work. They love to shop and take long walks.

As an Aries/Rooster, she is elegant, charismatic, direct, a good leader, impulsive, and competitive. As a Virgo/Tiger, he is suave, courageous, religious, and an honorable man. It is surprising that he is a procrastinator, for he seems to manage his business very well. They both enjoy the finer things of life, love to talk, and enjoy a good conversation. She knows how to throw a party and keep the guests happy. He loves to tell good jokes and keep the guests laughing in their seats.

Aries/Rabbit Woman and Gemini/Monkey Man

Robert and Marie have been happily married for over 25 years. Robert is a Gemini/Monkey man who is lively, critical, cautious, and a deep thinker, with a good sense of humor to boot. Marie is an Aries/Rabbit wife who is feisty, sympathetic, courageous, witty, and sensitive. She cares very much for her family and makes sure the house is run well. Aries and Gemini have good compatibility and friendships. Monkey and Rabbit also have moderate comparability. They work as a good team and are very focused on their four kids, three of whom have just completed their first degrees at Ivy League schools. They have sacrificed a lot for their kids and they tell me it is their time now to shine.

Pisces/Monkey Woman and Scorpio/Monkey Man

John and Vera have been joyfully married for about 25 years and they have two adult sons. Pisces and Scorpio are very compatible together since both are water signs. In addition, both of them are monkey types. They get along well and understand each other. Vera is emotional, cheerful, charming, understanding and a good mother in running her household. John is forceful, loves music, and is an entrepreneur. Being with someone who is confident and boastful has given Vera a lot of strength and security.

They are a formidable and united team, and no one can cause a rift between them. They work well together and know what they need to do to have a strong marriage. They have raised and disciplined their kids well to be good students, be polite, and respect of others. He looks after and protects her, while she supports his plans for the family. They are soul mates and are devoted to each other.

Aquarius/Ox Woman and Sagittarius/Horse Man

Tom and Cecilia have been happily married for about 10 years. Both of them are on their second marriage, but they appear to have made the right choice this time. They both love and care for each other. Aquarius and Sagittarius have good compatibility and friendship. The Horse is also compatible with the Ox.

As an Aquarius, Cecilia is friendly and loves to talk. Tom is an athletics coach, funny, restless, and a big talker. Cecilia is a hardworking social worker and humanitarian. They are both friendly, honest, independent, motivated, religious, and love politics. At home, she runs the household well. The kids have to do their chores as Mommy is strict and does not tolerate any mess. Tom has been able to make her relax and laugh, as love and commitment to another person is a challenge for a lot of Aquarius females. Aquarians like to love everybody and so sometimes she takes off and visits her friends.

Virgo/Sheep Woman and Capricorn/Horse Man

Charles and Jennifer have been happily married for over 30 years and have two sons. Charles is an executive and Jennifer is a nurse. They are soul mates and both Chinese and Sun sign astrology back it up. In Chinese astrology, the horse is the best partner for the sheep. Virgo may be the best marriage partner for Capricorn. Both are down-to-earth, hardworking, and calm.

They have different personalities. Jennifer has a chic lifestyle and she is more outgoing and sociable than Charles, who is a little reserved and serious looking. She is elegant, charming, and counterbalances his quiet demeanor when they go out. She also has great taste for fashion and can be extravagant. He is generous and tries hard to provide her with the finer things in life. She is more imaginative, reflective, and seems to take her time before making a decision. They enjoy throwing a party and having lively company in the house. She does not like argumentative people, so he likes to encourage and support her in managing difficulties at work.

Charles and Jennifer are blessed to get along so well that you never see them having a big argument or conflict. He loves sports and works out in the gym regularly. She does not like working out because she says she walks a lot in the hospital.

Charles works long hours and takes good care of the family. They enjoy going to the clubs for dancing and travelling to visit friends and family.

Aquarius/Dog Woman and Taurus/Tiger Man

Anthony and Gail have been married for about 32 years with two adult daughters and one adult son. They make an excellent couple and have cooperated to raise their children who are now gainfully employed. As an Aquarius/Dog wife, Gail is intelligent, friendly, loyal, caring, and cautious. As a Taurus/Tiger husband, Anthony is calm, determined, friendly, and supportive. They are a great team and have overcome various challenges to enjoy a good life. They have shown that it takes commitment, understanding, good communications, partnership and love to make a marriage work.

Libra/Tiger Woman and Aries/Snake Man

I have known Simon and Joyce for a long time. They get along very well and dated for a while before they decided to get married. They have now been married for over 20 years and have two sons and a daughter. As an Aries/ Snake man, Simon is a good leader, intelligent, a family man, self-directed, and devoted to his job. As a Libra/Tiger, Joyce is graceful, sociable, and charming. As a devoted wife, she balances her career job and household work very well. The two demonstrate good compatibility as Simon is Aries and Joyce is Libra. Both of them have demanding jobs but they support each other to keep the relationship strong.

Sagittarius/Monkey Woman and Sagittarius/Rabbit Man

I also know Eddie and Lisa who have been married for about 35 years and have an adult daughter and two adult sons. They are both outgoing and sociable, love the outdoors, and possess a good sense of humor. When they go out, they look like a powerful pair. Eddie is a charmer and loves to socialize. Lisa is elegant and talkative. She is highly committed to him and supportive.

In all, there is great understanding between them. They know how to have fun with each other and with everyone in the family. He goes out often as he needs excitement and fun. He is interested in different exotic cultures around the world. He is able to communicate and collaborate well with job associates from different countries. Lisa provides a stabilizing influence in the family. Her personality is highly attractive. She has worked in the same company for about 35 years.

Cancer/Rat Woman and Cancer/Ox Man

I have known Sam and Christina for a long time. They have been happily married for over 45 years. He is a teacher and she is a nurse. With the same sun sign of Cancer, they are both homebodies and enjoy spending time with family and friends. There is a strong love between them. Their sun signs and Chinese signs support the strong attraction between them.

Sam is intelligent, sensitive, emotional, compassionate, hardworking, and reliable He has a wonderful sense of humor. Christina is hard working, compassionate, loving, emotional, patient, and caring. When Sam comes home from a long day at work, there is no fuss, only support. He will not miss dinner with his family, that is how committed he is to his family. They are both empathic and appear to pick up on the sensitivity and vulnerabilities of others. He likes to work hard and explore new ideas. She likes to shop and work in her garden. They have 6 grand kids and are very close to them. They love to travel for vacation, visiting family members and attending conferences.

Intimate Relationships of Soul Mates

Soul mates are individuals, male and female, who have a deep attraction for each other in terms of their love for each other, friendship, understanding of each other, and sexual connection. They accept and admire each other for who each one is.

Studies have shown that male and females differ in the brain structure, function, and hormones released into their bodies. To become whole, the male needs the interaction with the female in a relationship to overcome his weakness from a dominant left brain. Likewise the female needs a relationship with the male to conquer her weakness from a dominant right brain.

A man and woman who are soul mates embark on a journey of union of two souls to help each other to achieve wholeness. The journey will require both individuals to do the soul work needed to counteract their biological differences by learning to integrate the right and left brain functions of each individual in their interactions.

A soul mate is someone who connects to your soul's desires and aspirations and vice versa. The expectations for right behavior of soul mates are as follows:

- Soul mates get along well with each other, as they are compatible and authentic with each other. They are true friends who support each other. They should be open and honest with each other.

- They are comfortable with who each one is as a person and are not anxious to change the other person to fit his or her own image.

- Soul mates focus on love and right behavior, rather than faultfinding, to help each other grow and become a whole person. The Tao Te Ching v.81 says, *"Profound words are not clever. Clever words are not profound. Wise people are not quarrelsome, quarrelsome people are not wise."*

- They should score high in agreeableness and cooperation, as they have to be careful about being disagreeable, argumentative, overcritical, and defensive repeatedly, as anger, bad temper, and vengeance can sow seeds of hatred. They should be able to resolve conflicts quickly with forgiveness and kindness. The Bible says, *"Do not let yourself be overcome by evil, but overcome evil with good"* (Rom 12:21).

CHAPTER THIRTEEN

Numerology and
Generational Influences

Numerology

According to experts in numerology, names and birthdays have special meaning in your life. As a scientist, I am fascinated by numerology. I read that Pythagoras and other early mathematicians got really deep into numerology to find the meaning of numbers. Over the years, I have paid more attention to astrology than to numerology. I took some time and dug deep into numerology. So far, it appears that numerology and astrology are connected in the decoding of a person's personality and the evolution of the soul to wholeness.

Numerology is obviously based on numbers. There is power in numbers. It is said that Chinese culture considers the number 8 to denote prosperity. The numbers 4 and 13 are considered to be unlucky. Practitioners have found that each name or birthday number provides a certain energy that tells a lot about a person's tendencies, personality, purpose, and lessons in life. The numbers of the letters of your name are added up and reduced to a single number. According to numerology, Andrew becomes 2 and Andy becomes 8. The numbers of your birth day can also be added and reduced to a single number, which is used to describe your purpose in life, lessons in life, and motivation.

Since I have limited understanding of numerology, I will refer the reader to two books. The first one is titled, *"Hot Numbers"* by Jean Simpson and the second one is *"The Power of Birthdays, Stars and Numbers"* by Saffi Crawford and Geraldine Sullivan. According to Saffi and Geraldine, numerology, like astrology, is a symbolic system, one of the many systems that humans are developing to decode the mystery of life and understand ourselves and our lives in a better way.

Birthday Number (Soul Lessons for Wholeness)

Table 5 provides the meaning of birthday numbers. Your birthday number provides clues on your purpose, personality and the challenges you have to overcome in your life to achieve wholeness.

For your birthday number or lesson number, add the month, day and year you were born. January = 1, February = 2, March = 3, April = 4, May =5, June = 6, July =7, August = 8, September = 9, October = 10 = 1, November = 11 (1 + 1) = 2, December = 12 (1 + 2) = 3

Thus, birthday of October 1, 1963 = 1 + 1+ 1 + 9 + 6 + 3 = 21 = 2 + 1 = 3.

TABLE 5. MEANING OF BIRTHDAY NUMBERS

Source: from *"The Power of Birthdays, Stars and Numbers"* by Saffi Crawford and Geraldine Sullivan

Birthday Number	Dynamic Force	Strengths	Tendencies	Weakness	Needs for Wholeness	What to Avoid
#1	Individuality, Sense of Self	leadership, driven	strong will, inspiration	Insecure, demanding	responsibility, confidence	selfishness, arrogance
#2	Partnerships, Diplomacy	sociable, harmonizer	patience, cooperation	restless, insecurity	tact, self-esteem	discouraged, oversensitive
#3	Emotional expression	talker, socializing	creativity, imagination	worry, self-doubt	emotional growth, social skills	Indecision, intolerance
#4	Organization, Structure	detailed, builder	practical, patience	stubborn, immoderate	stability	laziness, extravagance

#5	Instinctive, Adventure	Sociable, exploring	travel, opportunistic	Impulsive, listening	open to change, ideas, freedom	Irresponsible, heartless
#6	Universal, Humanity	Caring, compassion	Perfectionist, adviser	snobbish	loving, harmony, responsible	injustice, dissatisfaction
#7	Analytical, Intuition	Detail-oriented, reflective	self-analysis, overcritical	self-absorbed	Independent, greater self-awareness	secretive, unfeeling
#8	Material Power	leadership, strength, hard worker	material success, management	Emotional imbalance, handling money	tolerance, patience, exercise	domineering, overworked
#9	Collective, Humanitarian	compassion, integrity, big picture	patience, psychic	escapism, moody	spirtual path, concern for others, generosity	stubborn, selfishness, prejudice

Table 6 shows birthday numbers of some celebrities in the US and other countries. The birthdays of the celebrities were obtained from Wikipedia.

TABLE 6. BIRTHDAY NUMBERS FOR CELEBRITIES THAT ARE OF INTEREST

Source: Birthday based on birthdays in *Wikipedia*

Birthday Number	Dynamic	Celebrities with Birthday Number
#1	Individuality	Maya Angelou, Chris Brown, George Clooney, Tom Cruise, Miley Cyrus, Steve Jobs, Magic Johnson, Sophia Loren, Robert Murdoch, Tiger Woods, Mark Zuckerberg, LeBron James
#2	Partnerships, Diplomacy	David Beckham, Bill Clinton, Michael Jordan, Jennifer Lopez, Madonna, Barack Obama, Michelle Obama, Tyler Perry, Colin Powell, Ronald Regan, Diana Ross, Alice Walker, Kanye West
#3	Emotional expression	Hillary Clinton, Robert Kennedy, Kate Perry, Rihanna, Joan Rivers, Xi Jinping, Rick Warren, Snoop Dog, Nia Long, Kendrick Lamar, Kelly Clarkson, Forest Whitaker
#4	Organization, Structure	Jennifer Hudson, Nicole Kidman, Kwame Nkrumah, Dolly Parton, Brad Pitt, Frederick Sanger, Desmond Tutu, Donald Trump, Oprah Winfrey, Nicky Minaj, Seal, Malcolm Gladwell
#5	Instinctive, Adventure	Anita Baker, Harry Belafonte, Simon Cowell, Selena Gomez, Beyoncé Knowles, Al Sharpton, Howard Stern, Ted Turner, Tina Turner, Keith Urban, Gayle King, Angelina Jolie, Donald Knuth

#6	Universal, Harmony	Kofi Annan, George W. Bush, Albert Einstein, Jesse Jackson, Michael Jackson, Angela Merkel, Eddie Murphy, Raphael Nadal, Meryl Streep, Florence Welch, Elizabeth Banks
#7	Analytical, Intuition	Muhammad Ali, Ben Bernanke, Winston Churchill, Queen Elizabeth II, Mel Gibson, Steven Hawkins, Vladimir Putin, Julia Roberts, Taylor Swift, Phil McGraw, Leonardo DiCaprio
#8	Material Power	Adele, Sandra Bullock, Naomi Campbell, Deepak Chopra, Richard Dawkins, Jane Fonda, Lyndon Johnson, Nelson Mandela, Martha Stewart, Barbra Streisand, Barbara Walters
#9	Collective, Humanitarian	

Effect of Generational Influences on Individuals

Another factor in Astrology that impacts our relationships and personalities is the generation into which one is born. It is like a cycle of years with unique characteristics. There have been several publications on the different generations over the years; traditionalists, baby boomers, generation X, generation Y. Astrology explains the generational influence from influence of Pluto and Uranus.

Traditionalists are the depression era generation born between 1920 and 1940. They are more practical, respecters of authority and traditions, and worked hard for the welfare of the family. They enjoyed the good life of owning a car, having a job to take care of the family, and they developed traditional values.

Baby boomers are described as those born between 1941 and 1960 in the time of economic expansion. The baby boomers are described as being optimistic about their future. Their life was their work so they worked hard to build their job careers and to generate enough income. They are characterized as being greedy, selfish, and independent.

Generation X folks were born between 1961 and 1980. Generation X are independent, travelers, and the spenders, who hardly save. They enjoy the moment, enjoy changes in their lives, have a more balanced work life, and will not kill themselves working long hours at work.

Generation Y people are those born between 1981 and 2000. They are described as Millennial. They now range from

12 years old to their early 30s. They are more confident of their future, are sociable, and inclusive, well educated, want to be promoted faster in order to move up the ladder, are financially cautious, tend to pay their bills as they come due, and prefer new cars to used cars. They are frugal and save some money and use credit card wisely.

PART SIX

Know Your Spiritual Path to Wholeness

CHAPTER FOURTEEN

Align Your Body, Mind and Soul with Your Spirit

The Outer and Inner Self

According to Maharishi Mahesh Yogi, in *"The Science of Being and Art of Living"*, the *"life of any individual in creation has three aspects: the outer, the inner and the transcendental. The outer aspect of life is the body; the inner is the subjective aspect of the personality which is concerned with the process of experience and action and the transcendental aspect of life is being."* He adds that the *"inner being is unmanifested absolute being which manifests as the ego, intellect, mind, senses and prana. All these subtle states of life make the inner man (soul) or the subject within, the subjective aspect of life".* Essentially, the life of the individual is made up of body, personality, and the soul.

In comparison, Thomas Merton described the interior self in the book, *"The Inner Experience"*. He says, *"The inner self is as secret as God and like Him, it evades every concept that tries to seize hold of it with full possession."* He goes on to say that *"At the same time, however, every deeply spiritual experience whether religious, moral, or even artistic tends to have in it something of the presence of the interior self. Only from the interior self does any spiritual experience gain depth, reality, and a certain incommunicability."*

Thomas Merton also adds, in *"Thoughts in Solitude"* that, *"when society is made up of men who know no interior solitude it can no longer be held together by love; and consequently it is held together by a violent and abusive authority. But when men are violently deprived of the solitude and freedom which are their due, then society in which they live becomes putrid, it festers with servility, resentment and hate."*

The Body, Mind and Soul

The spirit of a human being is masked by the consciousness of the soul and body. The aim of the journey to wholeness is to liberate the spirit to experience the power of God's consciousness. The path of wholeness enables us to purify the body, soul, and mind for alignment with a liberated spirit. Otherwise we become a self with several personas or identities, namely the body self, soul self, mental self, and spirit self, each with its own agenda. We need balance and harmony between the body, mind, soul, and spirit to achieve wholeness. What do you value more, wholeness of your soul and body, or your wealth and professional career?

The soul is the observer or decider, the mind is the process of observation or knowing, and the body is the observed or object of observation. The mind is where the ego resides. The mind is not the soul, but the soul includes the mind. The soul is what has to be born again if one wants to enter the Kingdom of Heaven. The vision of the soul is limited by the mind and body. The soul cannot control the mind because the mind is constantly changing, unless the ego is humbled and the mind purified. The body is said to be the vehicle of the soul. The eyes are said to be the window to the soul.

We are whole when we have integrated and aligned the body and ego with a wholeness of soul and spirit. When the desires of the ego mind and body dominate in our lives, the soul gets out of alignment with the spirit within us. Thus, we seek God who is holy, without sin or limitation, for salvation of our soul.

Relationship Between Body and Mind

We can see the body, but not the mind, soul, and spirit. John Garrison wrote in the *"Psychology of The Spirit"* that *"The body and the mind are like the attraction between a magnet and iron filings that are not joined together. However as the magnet moves, the filings will twist and turn in various directions, forming different patterns. In doing so, the filings were merely following what the invisible magnetic field was commanding. So it is with the body, its life functions and the mind."*

Our understanding of the differences between the body, brain, and mind come from scientific investigations. The brain is part of the physical body. The mind is not the brain, but the brain provides the hardware for the mind. The mind provides the software for us to think, feel, and do, and so the mind and body are connected. We cannot see the mind, just as we cannot see electricity. However, we feel and see the mind's effects, like we see the effects of electricity. The body and mind are always busy with activities. We exercise the body, acquire knowledge with the mind, have relationships and love others with the soul, and perform meditations for peace and joy of the spirit within us.

The Bhagavad Gita says in 3:32, *"They say the power of the senses is great, but greater than the senses is the mind. Greater than the mind is the Intelligence and greater than Intelligence is He-the Spirit in man and in all."*

Stress and Its Effects on the Body and Mind

We all deal with physical and mental stress in our lives. Too much stress can damage the brain's hippocampus leading to memory loss. Stress comes from various sources, such as the lack of finances to meet one's needs, losing a loved one, resisting change in the work place, overworking and driving ourselves to meet demanding timelines and goals, and dealing with personal crises. We also experience unnecessary stress from trying to stand our ground in dealing with unscrupulous bosses with big egos who use fear of job loss to make us cower in their presence.

Chronic stress is not healthy for the individual, unless the individual knows how to release tension in a harmless and healthy way. Chronic stress can cause heart disease or diabetes. If you have to choose between a high-paying stressful job and a lower-paying rewarding job, what would you do? It is important to choose a life of wholeness, rather than a life of fear and insecurity. Stressful jobs and fearful situations produce high levels of stress hormones, including cortisol and adrenaline, that may be harmful over a long period of time.

Stress takes a lot out of us. Some people cope with stress by going out and having a good time, having a couple of beers with the buddies, taking a stress pill, drinking a glass of wine to soothe the nerves, or by going to church. Of all the ways that we take to try to deal with stress, exercise and meditation are among the most effective practices. It is important. Having a good job, nice boss, good sexual life, adequate savings in the bank and compatible relationships in a marriage help to reduce our stress level.

To avoid a stressful way of life, health gurus advise us that we need proper rest, acupuncture, massages, healthy diets and regular exercise, such as daily walks, cardiovascular exercises, strength training, and yoga flexibility asanas.

All these healthy practices help to dissolve stress, elevate our mood and put us in a better physical shape, frame of mind, and spiritual attitude. The endorphins, serotonin, and other neurotransmitters we get from exercise put us in a better mood after a stressful time.

Meditation calms the mind of the meditator. The incessant thinking, distractions and restlessness of the mind settle down and the meditator's attention becomes focused and restfully alert. Scientific studies have shown that meditation results in reduction in levels of the stress hormone, cortisol, and harmonization and integration of the right and left brain hemispheres for improved physical, mental health and spiritual health. When the spirit of the meditator is stilled in silence, a certain peace of mind is restored on the person. The Bible tells us in Psalm 46:10, *"Be still and know that I am God."* Meditation takes us into the deep silence of God.

What is Your Body Type and Mental Type?

What is the connection between our body and mind? Even our body reveals how we are feeling inside and how confident we are in our emotional and soul life. According to P. D. Ouspensky in *"The Fourth Way"*, our body type correlates with our temperament since our physique depends on our gut reactions, instincts, feelings, thinking, habits, and environment. He learned about three basic body types. The endomorphic person, characterized by a big belly and wide waist and high fat storage, is more instinctive, intuitive, and sensual. The mesomorphic person, being more muscular, is more emotional and aggressive. The ectomorphic person, with bony features and low fat storage, is more wiry and intellectual.

These types of relationships between body types and temperament have not impressed personality psychologists, who like to see more rigorously-designed studies. However, these are the types of stereotypical correlations we all deal with in life. Whether you are white, black, brown, yellow-skinned, British, American, African, Chinese, Indian, Canadian, or French, there is always a stereotype for your group's behavior. The fascinating difference with body types could be that as you change your body-type through exercise or conscious efforts, your temperament and outlook in life could change.

The Bhavagad Gita says there are three types of gunas or mental energies; the sattvic mind is pure, the rajasic mind is passionate and the tamasic mind is dull and inert. It says in 14:5-8, *"Sattva, rajas, and tamas – light, fire and darkness – are the three constituents of nature. They appear to limit in finite bodies the liberty of their infinite Spirit. Of these, Sattva because it is pure and gives light and is the health of the life, binds to earthly happiness and to lower knowledge. Rajas is of the nature of passion, the source of thirst and attachment. It binds the soul of man to action. Tamas, which is born of ignorance, darkens the soul of all men. It binds them to sleepy dullness, and then they do not watch and then they do not work."*

In India, personality types have also been related to body types in Ayurveda teachings. The three basic body types are vata (ectomorphic), pitta (mesomorphic), and kapha (endomorphic). However one's personality could be a combination of body types such that there are a total of 12 body types, such as vata, pita, kapha, pitta-kapha, pitta-vata, vata-pita, vata-kapha, etc. Vata body types are thin, bony, quick to learn, lively and imaginative, walk quickly, tend to show anxiety under stress, and show variable appetite. They have cold and dry skin, with elements of space and air. Pitta body types are muscular, assertive, focused, efficient, and prone to anger under stress. They have a determined walk. They are warm and have moist skin, with elements of fire and water. Kapha people are calm, relaxed, slower to learn, affectionate, stubborn. They are slow walking, slow to anger. They have cold and moist skin, with elements of earth and water.

Some people are not aware of their body type and the areas of their body that are vulnerable. Astrology provides each sun sign information on the parts of their body where they are vulnerable and thus require protection. Examples include the head and face of Aries; neck and throat of Taurus; lungs, arms, shoulders and nervous system of Gemini; chest, breast and stomach of Cancer; back, spine and heart of Leo; intestine, liver, pancreas, gall bladder and bowels of Virgo; kidney, lower back and liver of Libra; bladder, urinary, sexual organs and reproductive system of Scorpio; thighs, hips, and muscular system of Sagittarius; knees, teeth, spine, skeleton and joints of Capricorn; leg, ankles and circulation of Aquarius; feet and immune and hormonal systems of Pisces.

The Relationship Between the Body and Soul

Meister Eckhart, a Catholic mystic, describes in the book, *"Meister Eckhart: The Man From Whom God Nothing Hid"*, that the "*body and soul are like twins. They are like one being, or man and woman born together. The body is from the earth and the soul is from God. Body and soul are opposed to each other.*

Body wars with the soul. The soul desires eternal things, but the body desires temporary things." He also says that the soul is the observer or witness inside us. Swami Sivananda says that the mind is mysterious. "*The mind is no other than Ego. It is only the mind that asserts itself as "I" in the body. The mind is constantly changing. Body and mind are two aspects. The body is the object and the mind the subject.*"

The Relationship Between the Mind and Soul

Ralph Emerson said that the soul is light, it is neither the intellect nor the will. He said the soul is the master of the intellect and the will. Some say that the soul is in the subconscious level of the mind. Others say the soul is where your psychological make-up or personality resides.

Swami Sivananda says that "*during waking state the mind occupies the brain. In dream state, senses are quiet and mind alone plays the dreams. The individual soul is the one that sees the dreams.*" He adds that the soul is the only source of intelligence in the mind and the soul is the subject when it comes to the mind, not the object. Gurdjieff, a spiritual teacher in the early 1900s, described the body-mind-soul-spirit relationship in terms of a carriage. The carriage itself is the body that houses the passengers. The horse is the mind with feelings and desires. The driver of the carriage who controls the direction of the horse is the soul and the master sitting in the carriage is the divine spirit. The soul driver calls on the master spirit when he needs the all-powerful and all-knowing master.

Meister Eckhart, a Catholic mystic, describes in the book, *Meister Eckhart: The Man From Whom God Nothing Hid*" that "*The soul has three powers; mind, will and rage. He also says that the soul is the observer or witness inside us. The highest power of the soul is his will followed by his intelligence.*" The Bible describes the soul as the inner man in the deeper part of your mind.

The mind is experienced as thoughts, will, intellect, memories, emotions, desires, and ego. The conscious level of the mind is what is actively experienced when we are awake. The controller of the physical actions of our conscious mind is the ego, the false self. The ego provides the sense of it as the doer of the action. The ego-mind is difficult to control. The conscious mind is where the ego calculates how to meet your desires. You need the ego for motivation and survival, so you cannot eliminate the ego. The whole soul lives with the ego, but does not identify with it.

The Relationship Between the Soul and Spirit

Our understanding of the differences between the soul and spirit come from the scriptures and spiritual teachers. The soul is described by many scriptures and spiritual teachers as the true self or real you. The self is not the spirit. The self is the soul. The self is the internal witness and it resides in the soul. Meister Eckhart and other Spiritual teachers say the soul is the witness within you. It is the soul that is observing your thoughts. According to Meister Eckhart, *"God's essence is in the soul as God's nature pours into the light of the soul. However, God is not the soul."*

Swami Sivananda, in the *"Mind, Its Mysteries and Control"*, says that the *"soul is from God. The spirit is the way God multiplies. It unites us with God. If you separate yourself from God, you unite with your Ego. You then identify yourself with the ego or body. The spirit is not connected to your senses, so it is free from desires. It never dies, It goes back to unite with God."* He espouses that in a deep sleep state or dreamless state, there is no play of the mind. *"There are no thoughts and no world. The self continues to exist, but it is united with the spirit. When the mind is free from passions, desires and thoughts, you are shut out from the external physical world. Then you experience bliss, joy and deep peace. These are the traits of the spirit."*

Bhagavad Gita says in Chap 6 vs. 5-6: *"Arise therefore. And with the help of thy Spirit lift up thy soul. Allow not thy soul to fail.*

For thy soul can be thy friend or thy enemy. The soul of man is his friend when by the Spirit he has conquered his soul; but when a man is not lord of his soul, then this becomes his own enemy."

Alignment of the Body-Mind-Soul-Spirit for Wholeness

How do you envisage your soul's journey to wholeness? Every soul has to transform itself from unrighteous behavior to righteousness and from ordinary consciousness to higher consciousness in its spiritual journey towards union with the Spirit of God. The soul's journey to wholeness depends therefore on the work needed to resolve the karmic debts. The individual soul is considered by some as the part of you which reveals your purpose in life, as some eastern spiritual teachers have taught that your personality comes from the karma of your soul. If that is the case, then God created you for a specific purpose --to learn your lessons in life using a specific set of behavioral traits, which is your personality. If your soul needs to heal from your karma to transform your life, then your personality will need to be aligned to your healed soul.

Your soul is connected with your spirit which is in the unconscious level of your mind. Your intuition lies in your spirit or the unconscious level of your mind. Your spirit is where you have no thoughts and thus it is your pure consciousness. Since your body and mind are also connected, your body, mind, soul, and spirit are connected. Thus, the higher your level of consciousness, the closer your soul is to your spirit. When your soul is in alignment with your spirit, you are your best self. You enjoy the fruits of the spirit which are love, joy, peace, patience, kindness, goodness, faithfulness, gentleness, and self-control (Gal. 5:22-23). When you identify with your personality instead of your spirit, you fail to know your essence in relation to God. So, when your soul is not in alignment with your spirit, your soul need transformation and healing.

Another way to look at the body-mind-soul-spirit connection is that your mind is the connection between your body and your soul. Your body operates with your DNA, senses, and mind. Your mind operates with your ego, soul, and spirit. Your soul operates with your karma and spirit and your spirit operates with God's consciousness or pure consciousness. Since your soul is connected to your body and mind, your soul is activated when you meditate or when your body is asleep. When you meditate or sleep, the senses of the body are quieted, your ego is pushed out as your thoughts are silenced, and your soul gets in touch with your spirit which is in the Spirit of God. Therefore, meditate on God in you and you in God.

Jesus Christ showed us the Way, the Truth, and the Life (John 14:6) in order to reach higher consciousness or pure consciousness, which is the spirit of God. He said no one comes to God or pure consciousness except through Him or his Way (John 14:6). Your essence is your soul and spirit. What happens when you pass away from the world and your soul and spirit leave your body? Jesus said, *"You are not of this world"* (John 15:19). But you live in the world. When your body dies, your soul and spirit go to where you came from.

The Soul's Journey to Wholeness

In yoga, the individual soul is the silent witness in your consciousness or awareness. The soul is the witness that observes your aura. As consciousness, it is aware of consciousness. The personality is designed so that the individual soul may learn his or her lessons on earth. Each of us is here on earth to know ourselves well, our personality, and our purpose in life, and thus to live the spiritual life that gives us victory over the limitations of our personality and ego-mind. As one enjoys the kingdom of heaven within, which includes peace, joy, freedom, blessings, and constant communion with God, one is closer to discovering one's spiritual self.

What are the struggles in the journey of the soul towards the higher self? In Romans 7: 4-25, Paul talks about the war or struggle between the body and the spirit to influence the soul and provide identity to it. The *'law of sin'* dwells in the body or flesh and is considered in the Bible to be the cause of unhealthy or dysfunctional human behavior. The personality, ego, and karma provide challenges in the journey of the soul towards the spirit self.

According to Swami Sivananda, *"The spirit and soul is eternal, but the mind is finite. The mind has will, action and knowledge. What separates you from God is your mind. One purifies the mind with acts of compassion, knowledge of the truth, acts of charity, study of the Bible, Gita and other scriptures, association with wise people and regular visits to church. He who has purified his mind becomes a center of force or power. Others are then drawn to this force for influence. Like the spirit, the mind also has aura which is both psychic aura and mental aura. The aura of those who have developed their mind greatly is effulgent. Spiritual aura is more powerful than psychic aura."*

CHAPTER FIFTEEN

Know which Spiritual
Paths Fit You

What is Your Spirituality?

Spirituality is the unveiling of the spirit within you and a connection with the Spirit of God. What is the connection between the spirit, soul, mind, consciousness, and personality? You are a spirit, but you have a mind and soul and you live in a body. Ephesians 4:23 says, *"Be renewed in the spirit of your mind."* The individual consciousness is finite, whereas God's consciousness is infinite. Spirituality is a living experience with the unfolding of the Spirit of God within you.

Eckhart Tolle points out in his book, titled *"A New Earth"* that *"many people are already aware of the difference between Spirituality and Religion. They realize that having a belief system – a set of thoughts that you regard as the absolute truth – does not make you spiritual, no matter what the nature of those beliefs is."*

Spirituality is having your attention and mind on God at all times. The experience of the spirit motivates one on the spiritual path. The Bible teaches that the fruit of the spirit includes love, joy, peace, kindness, patience, faithfulness, gentleness, and self-control. I know my spiritual path, which fits me as a practicing Catholic. My spiritual path is the path of self-knowledge, meditation, and identification with the spirit of God. My purpose is to share my knowledge with others and heal my soul in relationships so that I can be of service to others. My spiritual development entails development of a high state of awareness or consciousness in order to see and imitate the truth, the way, and the life of Christ Jesus.

How do you awaken to the Spirit of God and create the awareness of the Presence of God in each moment of your life? Humans can see each other because of the body, but humans cannot see God. How do we visualize God when we talk or pray to God? If we are spirits and God is a spirit, one expects that we communicate to God in spirit. The Bible says that we should *"worship God in spirit and in truth."*

The key for spiritual enlightenment is to go beyond personality, karma, and astrology as Jesus did in achieving unity with God the Father. Ignorance of who we are in God also leads to wrong understanding of ourselves and under-development of the soul.

Spiritual development starts with the ability to expand your conscious awareness through love of everyone, knowledge of the self, self-observation, social awareness, meditation, and the ability to separate one's beliefs from the beliefs of dogma and myth. Just as we have institutions of learning, we need institutions to teach us about spiritual development so that we can move people from lower levels of spirituality to higher levels of spirituality. According to Ken Wilber in *"The Integral Vision"*, we evolve from primitive spirituality to magical spirituality, mythic spirituality, rational spirituality, and from pluralistic spirituality to integrated spirituality or wholeness, and then to a transcendent level of spirituality.

Typically, the experience and progress made by the spiritual practitioner provide the evidence that the person is on the right spiritual path.

Knowing yourself helps to discover which spiritual path fits you. Your soul challenges may lead you down the path that will heal your soul. Some people reach God through their rituals, through emotional prayers and devotion, or through self-knowledge and intellect. The difference between you and me in our spiritual practice may be that we have different karmas, different destiny, and different lessons to learn on Earth, different astrology, or different environments.

Everyone Has a Spiritual Path

Spiritual path is unique for each individual since we each have a unique soul, astrology, (religious engagement and personality to unlock the divine plan within ourselves). Are you focusing your attention only on your body, ego-mind, or on the wholeness of your soul and alignment of your soul to your spirit? Swami Sivananda described the spiritual path to me about 40 years ago, when I first read *"Bliss Divine"*. He says the *"Spiritual path may in the beginning appear to be very hard, thorny, precipitous and slippery. Renunciation of objects gives pain at the outset. If you struggle hard to tread the path, if you once make a strong determination and firm resolve then it becomes very easy. You get interest and joy. Your heart expands. You have a broad outlook on life. You have a new, wide, vision. You get help from the invisible hands of the Indweller of your heart. Your doubts are cleared by themselves, by getting answers from within. You can hear the shrill, sweet voice of God. There is an indescribable thrill of divine ecstasy from within. This joy is irrespective of one's religion, Jewish, Christian, Muslim, Buddhism, Hindu and so on."*

In most religions, there are several different paths to spirituality and a relationship with God. However, one can have more than one spiritual path, depending on the individual and his circumstances. According to Maharishi Mahesh Yogi in the *"Maharishi Mahesh Yogi on Bhagavad Gita"*, the four spiritual paths are as follows;

(1)   Through the process of feelings (path of emotional devotion).

(2)   Through the process of understanding (path of knowledge).

(3)   Through the process of action (path of service).

(4)   Through the process of perception (path of meditation and contemplation).

Path of Love and Devotion to God

One of the paths of spiritual practice is the *Path of Love and Devotion to God*. This path involves being humble, emotional, and devoting oneself to God, offering prayers and rituals to God, or praying to the reality of God abiding in you as you abide in Him. Yoga practitioners call this path Bhakti Yoga.

According to Maharishi, *"the emotional approach to God realization will generally suit those whose qualities of the heart are highly developed."* This path is sustained by love, emotion, kindness, devotion, surrender, and worship.

Path of Spiritual Knowledge

Another path is the *Path of Spiritual Knowledge* for those who are intellectual, where the practitioner is a seeker of knowledge and experience of the Higher Self and disseminating knowledge of that self to others. This path involves knowledge of what is real and unreal. Ignorance is no excuse to blind faith. This involves study of scripture, learning from enlightened souls, and the application of one's spiritual knowledge to reach a higher consciousness.

According to Maharishi, *"the intellectual approach to God realization will suit all those who are cultured intellectually, those whose intellectual capacity is high."* This path will involve the application of logic and intellect to know and understand God.

In the parable of the sower where the seeds were planted on good soil, those seeds sown on good soil signify seekers who hear the Word, receive it, and bear good fruit. As the Kingdom of God is within you, the seeker of spiritual knowledge looks at himself as identifying with the spirit within himself, through enlightenment.

Path of Selfless Service

A third path of spiritual practice is the *Path of Selfless Service*, where the individual loves and cares for the children of God, including the poor, the sick, and the one in despair or sorrow. This path is for those who are energetic and very active. The seeker looks at God as the One who is in everyone and everything. This path is known as Karma Yoga in Yoga teachings.

Path of Meditation and Contemplation

Another path of spiritual practice is the *Path of Meditation and Contemplation* for those who reflect on the inner essence. The seeker of this path meditates or contemplates day and night to quiet his mind and receive inspiration from God. This seeker looks at God as the One who dwells within him and his spirit is joined to the spirit of the Lord (2 Corinth 5:21).

The path of meditation and contemplation is supported by the Bible saying, *"Be still and know that I am God"* (Psalm 46:10). According to Maharishi Mahesh Yogi in *"The Science of Being and Art of Living"*, *"the process of perception starts from pure consciousness (spirit) and it is carried on through the instrumentality of the mind and the nervous system to the manifested field of gross creation."*

> *"If however, the perception of pure consciousness is sought it will be necessary that the above-mentioned process be reversed. The consciousness must then be gathered from the outward gross field and directed inward. The perception of pure being, therefore necessitates stopping the activity in the gross and appreciate successively less activity until the least activity can be appreciated and transcended. This gives rise to the state of pure consciousness or the perception of transcendental being."*

There are other paths, such as the path of mysticism, the

path of healing of souls, the path of priesthood and monks, the path of ministry, the path of renunciation, and the mystical path. Mystics pray and long to be closer to God and strive to be in union with Him. Whatever spiritual path you take, you go through stages of growth in consciousness to heal the mind and soul.

Your Level of Spiritual Consciousness

In his book, *"Power vs. Force"*, David Hawkins described *"pure consciousness as the cessation of the ordinary flow of thought or feeling – a condition of infinite power, compassion, gentleness, and love."*

Spiritual maturity involves moving from a level of low consciousness to one of higher consciousness. When one reaches the level of wholeness, there is unity in the individual self with thoughts, desires, and action, and all are aligned with the need of the spirit to awaken from slumber. As Gurdjieff says, *"If there is no unity in the self, there exist several 'I's, without a central command for right thinking, right intentions and right actions."*

Your body's consciousness is different and the spirit, soul, and mind are characterized by a higher consciousness than the body. Thus, if you have too much focus on the desires of the flesh, you will have a low spiritual consciousness. If you purify the ego and move towards wholeness, you expand your spiritual consciousness. If you change from a life of destructive habits to one of good habits, you move towards wholeness.

According to the ancient wisdom of Yoga in the Bhagavad Gita, each seeker grows spiritually from low to high levels of consciousness. The lowest levels of spiritual consciousness belong to those who focus on the body and not the spirit. The highest level of spiritual development involve transcending the ego-mind and personality into a wholeness of the soul, holiness of body, renewal of the mind, and the spirit becoming closer to unity with God. Jesus is the one who said *"Father and*

I are one," implying that he had reached the highest or transcendent level of consciousness, where one's consciousness is God consciousness.

Evolution of Spiritual Consciousness

According to David Hawkins, in his book, *"Power vs. Force: The Hidden Determinants of Human Behavior",* we evolve from low to high consciousness. He writes that our behavior can also be graded on the vibrational scale so that guilt and shame have the lowest score of consciousness while love, joy, peace, and enlightenment have the highest score. In the highest spiritual state, there is unity between the enlightened person and God. Love or enlightenment is the state of God and God is love. He proposed that Jesus and Buddha reached the highest level of human consciousness based on the qualities used for scoring human behavior.

According to Gurdjieff, your salvation rests in the knowledge of your real self and knowledge of the path to supreme consciousness. He emphasized that we can evolve into higher levels or states of consciousness if we do the work required. This work requires daily self-observation, self-remembering, and self-knowledge. He made the observation that we have multiple personalities within us and that it is difficult for us to be whole. The way we practice spirituality depends on the type of person we are.

So, where are you on the level of spiritual consciousness? In his book *"The Integral Vision",* Ken Wilber talks about the seven types of spirituality.

> *Archaic Spirituality* – is for egocentric individuals in the earlier stages of evolution, who are concerned with the instinct for food, sex, and water for survival.
>
> *Magical Spirituality* – involves paganism, egocentrism, black magic, and voodoo.
>
> *Mythic Spirituality* – is more traditional, fundamentalist,

power-focused, ethnocentric, and prone to take a very literal interpretation of scripture.

Rational Spirituality – uses scientific knowledge and logic to separate the truth from false teachings.

Pluralistic Spirituality – of the post-modern world is multi-cultural and world-centric, with a belief that there is a place for all religions to help the individual to grow spiritually and worship God.

Integral Spirituality – is based on a well-integrated self, a whole self, or wholeness of the soul.

Transcendent Spirituality – is the practice where the individual lives outside of the material world and is in closer to unity with God. This is the spirituality of those who have reached enlightenment or unity with God. They are free from sins, attachments and desires, duality, and karma. I understand from Swami Sivananda that Avatars have Christ Consciousness or Divine Consciousness, as these spiritual realms are not easily available to humans.

Ken Wilber has written extensively about the stages and states of spiritual consciousness. He says that one can achieve high states of consciousness at any of the stages of spirituality described above, whether it is archaic or primitive spirituality, magical spirituality, as in voodoo practice, or mythic spirituality in fundamental or cultish Christianity.

Most religions have shown that one does not have to be at the highest level of consciousness to have a life-changing spiritual experience. One can have a state of spiritual experience at any of the levels of consciousness, just as everyone can go into the dream state. Many people have given accounts of incredible experiences of overcoming challenges where there was no hope nor anyone to come to their rescue. And yet, the spiritual solution came through to solve the problem.

My spiritual experience is what keeps me going and keeps me continuing to trust in God. Whether it was a stranger who gave me the right message that I was looking for, getting the right job at the right time, meeting the right person at the right time, or finding the right partner, spiritual solutions are always amazing and attest to the presence of God in each one of us.

CHAPTER SIXTEEN

Consciousness, Ego and
Renewal of the Mind

What is Consciousness?

Most of the spiritual teachers that I have included in the reference section have written extensively about consciousness. This includes Gurdjieff, Ouspensky, Swami Sivananda, Maharishi Mahesh Yogi, Thomas Merton, Deepak Chopra, Gary Zukav, Eckhart Tolle, David Hawkins, and Dane Rudhyar. Consciousness is the state of being aware of what is outside you and what is internally within you. Consciousness is having thoughts, feelings, and perceptions. Your brain plays an important role in producing consciousness of your external and internal conditions. Self-consciousness is having a sense of awareness of selfhood. Our mind is capable of having a wide range of consciousness, ranging from the waking state to high spiritual consciousness.

Our consciousness is the quality of our awareness. It is impossible to change our bad behaviors and habits without changing our thoughts. When we change our thoughts we are changing our consciousness of our thoughts. Consciousness is intentional and directive. Consciousness and attention are linked. Whatever you pay attention to, you become more conscious of. Attention focuses on consciousness and one gains more consciousness by self-observation, mindfulness, and right awareness. Being highly creative requires an expansion of your consciousness so that you becomes a co-creator with the Creator of the Universe and the laws of the universe. Pure consciousness is the silent consciousness that gives birth to visionary ideas, creative solutions to problems, incredible power of the mind, and the beauty of love.

Wikipedia defines Consciousness as the *"quality of state of being aware of external objects (objective), events or something within oneself (internal). It is the ability to experience wakefulness and feel the executive control system of the mind."* Consciousness may be interchangeable with the word Awareness. Spiritual awakening is like being born again. It is connecting with your higher self (spiritual self), instead of your lower self (ego-mind), to transform your consciousness.

We have body consciousness, awareness of the mind or mind consciousness, or 'feeling' the spirit (spirit consciousness). The Spirit of God is pure consciousness, without thoughts or ego. Transcendental or pure consciousness is our spiritual essence when our spirit is aligned or in union with the Spirit of God. Wisdom, silence, love, and pure joy are attributes of pure consciousness or divine consciousness. The key to mastery over the mind and ego is to attain higher consciousness for wholeness. Gurdjieff, a spiritual teacher in the early 1920s, taught that in order to expand one's consciousness, one has to pay attention to oneself, one's thoughts, emotions, and actions and to be constantly aware of who you are (self-remembering).

In his book called *"Maharishi Mahesh Yogi on the Bhagavad Gita",* the founder of Transcendental Meditation explained that meditation infuses divine consciousness into the mind to purify the mind from wrong behavior of the ego and allows one to live a life free from suffering. When one achieves silence in meditation, the mind is highly alert, full of love, and imbued with a sense of righteousness for right thinking, right intention, and right actions.

Consciousness is also light or illumination. The illumined or enlightened mind has a very high consciousness. This enlightened person can see beyond the obvious with his light or consciousness. In his book, *"Power vs. Force: The Hidden Dimension of Human Behavior"*, David Hawkins talks about levels of human consciousness and the emotional correlates of the different levels of consciousness. Fear is one of the emotions that limits the personal and spiritual growth of individuals. Desire is another emotional energy that can motivate us to higher levels of achievement, but it can also prevent us from achieving our spiritual goals because of the propensity for attachments and selfishness. True spiritual states occur with the emotional energy of love, joy, peace, and enlightenment.

According to Maharishi in *"The Science of Being and Art of Living"*, Being (spirit) lies beyond the subtlest stratum of creation in the transcendental field of absolute existence. Therefore, *"in order to experience this transcendental reality, it is necessary to direct our attention to be led in a concrete manner through all the subtlest strata of creation. Then arriving at the subtlest level, it must transcend the experience to know God."* He goes on to add that *"in order to experience God, it is necessary to improve the faculty of experience. If we could improve our faculty of experience through any of the senses, or improve our ability to experience thought before it comes to the conscious level of the mind, then having transcended the source of thought, it would be possible to reach the transcendental state of Being."*

Thomas Merton describes in *"The Ascent to Truth"*, how God draws us into deep silence and solitude during meditation and contemplation. He says *"The deep self which lies too deep for reflection and analysis, falls free and plummets into the abyss of God's freedom and of His peace. Now there is no more adherence to what goes on within us, still less to what happens around us. We are too far below the surfaces where reflection was once possible. Sunken in God, the soul knows Him alone."*

As we undergo spiritual growth, we are drawn to contemplation, meditation, service to others, mentoring less-evolved souls, and so on. Spiritual awakening involves great internal change as we move to higher consciousness. Sometimes suffering is the gateway to spiritual awakening. Other times it is self-knowledge and the reading of Holy Scriptures that wakes us up to make a life-changing renewal of mind and consciousness.

Renewal of the Mind

The Bible says, in Eph. 4:23-24, *"And be constantly renewed in the spirit of your mind. And put on the new nature created in God's image."* Renewal of the mind is a continuous process. The battle of the soul with the ego-mind is one that requires constant reading of scriptures, strengthening of one's faith, and the renewal of the mind. Everything you do starts in the mind, including thoughts, decisions, choices, and actions. Thus, your life improves when you condition your mind to operate through expanded awareness. Transformation of the mind lies in the power of attention, awareness, perceptions, attitudes, and perspectives.

How do we renew our mind? We renew our mind through prayers, meditation, love and service. In his books on Transcendental Meditation and Bhavagad Gita, Maharishi explained that when your mind is restless, diffused and confused by the senses, it wanders aimlessly. When you renew your mind in meditation, your mind becomes more focused, content and resolute to move in the direction of your purpose. He said that, through meditation, *"the attention is brought from gross experience to subtle fields of experience until the subtlest experience is transcended and the state of transcendental meditation is gained."* He adds that *"once the mind reaches transcendental consciousness it no longer remains a conscious mind. It gains the status of absolute being (divine consciousness)."*

This state represents *"complete infusion of cosmic consciousness into the individual mind. After the infusion, the mind comes out again into the field of relativity, then being once more the individual mind, it acts while established in being (divine consciousness)."* This also shows how we achieve union with the God consciousness when the soul attains wholeness. He asserts that when the conscious mind is highly energized or strong, the action you take after meditation will be effective and successful. This is because, *"when the deeper levels of the oceans of mind are activated during meditation, the level of attention and alertness increase. When alertness and consciousness increases one has greater power of awareness."*

Gurdjieff talks about renewing one's mind through knowledge, awareness, self-observation, experience, self-remembering, and silencing one's thoughts. Therefore, renewal of the mind involves a process of going from a highly fragmented self to a unified whole self. One transforms oneself by raising one's level of consciousness to be able to know yourself, your purpose, and the world around you, perceiving with clarity when one is being tested or tempted, understanding yourself and others for better relationships, making better decisions with a well-integrated or whole self.

It is not easy to renew one's mind, as Proverbs 23:7 says, *"for as a man thinks within himself, so is he."* Gurdjieff says man is a fragmented individual with different I's and no central I or integrated 'I' in charge. When the self is not well integrated, everything happens in a disorderly manner. You may have good intentions and intelligence to do what is right in a certain situation, and yet your Ego may run opposite to what you intend and cause you to regret doing something out of your character. *"Egoism is the greatest sin. It is our sinful nature,"* Swami Sivananda says in his book, *"Bliss Divine".*

Spiritual Combat with Our Ego

Swami Sivananda in, *"Mind, its Mysteries and Control"* shows us how to recognize the ego and its operation. He indicates that our mind is made up of conscious mind, ego, intellect, emotions, and subconscious mind. Sivananda says that *"the wall that stands between you and God is the mind."* Pay attention. Most of the problems we struggle with are related to the egocentric thinking in our minds. The ego is not who you are. However, the ego appears to be the controller of your conscious actions.

'Ego', in Latin, means 'I'. It is the ego, our self-image, which we ordinarily think of as our 'self'.

Our true self is the soul, the self that can be aware of what is going on in our body, mind, and spirit, if it pays attention to these aspects of our selves. When we tune out of ourselves and become like zombies, unscrupulous folks can take advantage of us in the areas of religion, psychic knowledge, and so on. In the book titled, *"A New Earth: Awakening to Your Life's Purpose"*, Eckhart Tolle tells us that *"most people are so completely identified with the voice in the head. The incessant stream of involuntary and compulsive thinking and the emotions that accompany it, that they may be described as being possessed by their mind."* As long as you are completely unaware of this you take the thinker to be who you are. This is the egoism mind.

Without the ego, we may not survive. Our ego compels us to act in order to survive. The ego is the part of the self that protects itself against attacks, such as pain, conflict, and aggression. The ego also helps us to be motivated and succeed in life. If you humble your ego, you can use your consciousness to meet your goals for wholeness.

The scriptures say we can change our thoughts and change our circumstances or behavior. The Bible tells us to renew our minds by the spirit of ourselves. Jesus taught his followers the path for being born again so they can enter the kingdom of heaven, which is joy, peace, love, and connection with God.

We have to choose whether we will live a life of humility or one driven by our ego. The egoistic mind wants to control others, tell them they are wrong, blow up in anger, walk around arrogantly, judge others harshly for how they look or behave, lose self-control, feel superior, demand attention to issues only they care about and become sensitive to any criticism of dysfunctional behavior.

As the personality approaches perfection, as Jesus showed, it becomes aware of its spiritual purpose and closeness to unity with God. As the personality comes closer to experiencing the joy and happiness of the spirit, as Buddha experienced it, it becomes aware of the cause of its suffering and the path to liberation from the ego.

According to Maharishi Mahesh Yogi in his book, *"Transcendental Meditation"*, perfection in life would mean the senses are perfect, mind is perfect, and intellect, ego, and personality are perfect. Between the highest stage of evolution, where life is perfect, and the lowest stage of evolution, where life begins to be, lies the whole range of creation.

CHAPTER SEVENTEEN

Know Your Spirit
Through Meditation

Purpose of Meditation

In his book, *"Silence and Stillness in Every Season"*, Father John Main, the founder of the World Community of Christian Meditation (WCCM) wrote that the purpose of meditation is to *"allow God's mysterious and silent presence within us to become more and more not only a reality but the reality in our lives; to let it become that reality which gives meaning, shape, purpose to everything we do, everything we are."* Meditation is therefore a spiritual practice for centering yourself on your inner life, quieting the mind, and expanding your spiritual consciousness. Electroencephalogram (EEG) studies have shown that meditation produces lower frequency alpha and theta waves. This results in a spiritual state of relaxation, attentiveness, and alertness.

Scientists have shown that there is increased activity in the frontal lobes and decreased activity in the parietal lobe during meditation. The increased activity in the frontal lobe increases one's alertness upon coming out of meditation. The benefits of meditation include stress reduction, lowering of the blood pressure, relaxation, high alertness or concentration, and a reduction of depression. Some people ask me why I meditate every day. Meditation provides a heightened consciousness of the spirit within oneself that humbles one's ego, increases one's self-awareness, and enhance one's internal joy and peace of mind.

Continuous practice is necessary for me to focus on the spirit and not the ego. There are several goals for meditators to achieve, including humbling the ego. The fruits of meditation include joy and peace of the spirit. The Bible says in Psalm 16:11, *"You make known to me the path of life; your presence is fullness of joy and the pleasures of living with you forever."* When the spirit is felt within yourself, it brings peace, joy, love, self-control, faithfulness, and other fruits of the spirit. Peace and joy are important in our lives. Romans 14:17 also says that the kingdom of God is not eating and drinking, but righteousness, peace, and joy. The joy of God is the awakened spirit of God within us, as John 15:11 says: *"These things I have spoken to you that My Joy may be in you and your joy may be made full."*

Meditation has become a popular spiritual practice, although it has been part of the world's religious traditions, including Christianity, Hinduism, Islam, Judaism, and Buddhism, for centuries. We all contemplate and meditate in life. A synonym for meditation is contemplation. Some meditate on the Biblical words so that the word of God can work within them. Others meditate in silence without conscious thought to reach that stillness within the mind and soul. Mystics believe and experience union with God through meditation and contemplation. Regular practice of meditation once or twice a day creates a good habit and the discipline needed to pray and meditate even if one is busy.

When your mind is silenced through prayers, meditation, and contemplation, attention can be directed to the spirit. You become aware of the presence of the silent witness of your thoughts, and the sensations in the body during meditation and when you are in a meditative mood. As you meditate regularly, you know the presence of the spirit through peace and joy within you. The ultimate goal of meditation is to merge your inner 'I' consciousness with God consciousness.

I started to practice spiritual meditation in 1976 when I was studying at the University of Science and Technology in Kumasi, Ghana. According to Maharishi Mahesh Yogi who came up with the system of transcendental meditation, the ultimate goal of meditation is to merge your inner spirit with the Spirit of God and expand your consciousness for personal and spiritual growth.

When I found that Catholics were practicing group meditation I was thrilled. I joined a group of Catholic meditators who meditated twice a week, following the practice of Father John Main (1926-1982), a Catholic monk, who founded the World Community for Christian Meditation (WCCM). The Christian meditation was inspired by Father John Cassain and the Desert Fathers in the fourth century.

Father John Main has written extensively about Christian meditation, the nature of spirit and consciousness, and the difference between prayer and meditation. He wrote that the most important thing about meditation is how to meditate. Meditation is the way we respond to Jesus' call to leave the self behind. By silencing the mind and spirit, we lose ourselves by merging with the cosmic Christ consciousness.

Father Lawrence Freeman has now taken up the leadership mantle of WCCM and is spreading the word on Christian meditation. He has written several books, including the book called "Light Within – The Inner Path of Meditation". In this book, he talks about meditation leading to poverty of spirit and purity of heart. Poverty of spirit means that one is filled with the spirit that does not need anything material. The meditator's life is simple, joyful, and self-sufficient.

I usually meditate for 20-30 minutes each time twice a day, in the morning and evening. To begin meditation, sit still in a chair or in any comfortable position. Close your eyes. Sit relaxed but alert. Take a deep breath and then begin to breathe naturally during the meditation session. Sit quietly and do not dwell on any problems or ideas that come in your mind. You may focus on your breath or silently count from 1 to 10 several times in your mind, for about 3 minutes, to distract your thoughts and put you in a quiet mode.

Begin to say your mantra – a single word – silently in your mind without stopping, until the session ends. Initially, your internal thoughts can be distracting to your meditation as you continue to say your mantra. Therefore, consciously avoid chasing any thought that pops into your mind. Be mindful of your body's sensation and thoughts, but pay them no attention. Focus on the silence of the mind, say your mantra, and listen to the sound of the mantra. As time goes on, your mind becomes disconnected from your senses but not from your ego or the voice in your mind. Continue to say your mantra and your internal thoughts or ego thinking is reduced as you begin to experience the silence that comes when the ego is no longer the focus of your mind. You may pray before and after meditation.

Catholic Father John Main is one of my favorite spiritual teachers. He recommends using the four syllable mantra, *Maranatha.* Maranatha is an Aramaic word from Jesus' time meaning *"Come Lord"*. According to Father Laurence Freeman, the mantra is like good soil for planting a seed. It anchors you to the ground and helps you to be in the present moment.

In the focused stillness of silence, you experience a sense of peace and joy that comes from the spirit awakening in your being. In the Bible, it is the expression, *"Be still and know that I am God."* If the ego thinking returns to the mind, just continue to say your mantra internally. When the session ends, you tend to feel alert, have peace of mind, and experience joy.

We need spiritual consciousness within us in order to perceive God and be drawn to God. We have our body self, our mental self, and our soul-spiritual self. Some individuals identify the self only with the physical body or the mind. Some who are obsessed with their minds identify with their mental self. You want to identify yourself with a well-integrated higher self, aligning your body, mind, and soul with your spirit. When you die, the Bible says your spirit and soul will go back to where it came from, the source of Creation.

In meditation, your spiritual-soul self is connected internally to your God consciousness within you. God consciousness is Christ consciousness if you are a Christian, as Christ consciousness is in union with God consciousness. It is Brahman consciousness if you are Hindu. It is Allah consciousness if you are a Moslem. It is Buddha consciousness if you are a Buddhist.

David Hawking explains in the *"Force vs. Power"* that individual consciousness can expand from one level of consciousness to another. For example, from a state of grief to desire, from desire to courage, and then to higher states of consciousness, such as compassion, unconditional love, joy, peace, and identification of self with divinity. Meditation elevates our consciousness and at the highest level of consciousness, which is Christ consciousness or cosmic consciousness, your spiritual self is purified or your heart is purified to see God, as described by Jesus in the Sermon of the Mount. *"Blessed are they who are pure at heart for they shall see God."*

PART SEVEN

Know Your Religious Faiths and Beliefs

CHAPTER EIGHTEEN

Know the Religion
that Fits You

Quest for the Creator of the Universe

All cultures seek God in one way or another. In the book entitled, *"The History of God"*, Karen Armstrong described how the quest for God has been going on for about 4,000 years. The Creator of the universe was called by different names in Africa, the Middle East, Asia, Europe, and the Americas. In Africa, it was the Sky God for a lot of tribes. Idols were worshipped in ancient times. Now, we have a better understanding of the nature of the soul, spirit, and the spirit of God.

Different religions have different belief systems that can influence who you are. And so different personalities pursue different spiritual paths and religious beliefs. Regardless of religious affiliation, we all need religious and spiritual values and laws to help shape our behavior and attitudes as we travel on our journey to wholeness of mind and soul. Religion comes from the Latin word, *religare*, which means to bind. Thus, religion is an organization of people that are bound together by faith, beliefs, doctrine, dogma, rituals, cultural traditions, experience and theology to seek and have relationship with the Creator of the Universe. Religion provides moral code, virtues and values in the culture or society that it is *imbedded.*

Religion provides us with a moral code of conduct, such as the 10 commandments of Judaism. The Bhagavad Gita aptly says in 16:24, *"Let the Scriptures be therefore the authority as to what is right and what is not right. Know the words of the scripture and do in this life the work to be done."* In his book, *"Essential Ken Wilber"*, Ken categories the four stages of religion as: belief, faith, direct experience, and permanent adaptation. Permanent adaptation is constant access to what is acquired through spiritual practice. These are what he describes as stages that believers go through to evolve into higher levels of spirituality. He explains that *"one can have a belief in spirit (God, for example), have faith in spirit, have a direct experience of spirit and you can become spirit."*

What is Your Religion?

I know my religion. I am a liberal Catholic in the Christian Religion and I pursue my personal philosophy regarding religion and spirituality. I was raised as a traditional Catholic by my staunch Catholic mother. I am satisfied with my Catholic faith and I admire the Catholic Church, not only for continuing to keep the Church strong and spiritually relevant over the years, but also for their openness to new knowledge and changes in the way people practice their religion and spirituality. One of the changes that I have experienced is that some Catholics now practice Christian meditation daily, in addition to leading prayerful and contemplative religious lives.

I read my Bible regularly and attend mass as often as I can make it. I practice meditation at home and attend Christian meditation weekly with other Catholics. This type of meditation was organized by Father John Main, a Catholic monk who learned about meditation while in India. Meditation helps me align my body-mind-soul with my spirit, which is awakened by the Spirit of God.

In my adult years, I have remained committed to my Catholic faith, but I am selective about which beliefs and doctrines I accept, based on my knowledge of science, body, mind, soul, spirit, and an understanding of the messages in the Bible and other religious scriptures. I have difficulty understanding the doctrine of the Trinity and the Nicene Creed. One of the Catholic priests explained that the Trinity is a mystery, so I leave it as a mystery. It is heartening to see that the Catholic Church is promoting regular reading of the Bible nowadays by members.

Religious Paths

There is not one religion or spiritual practice that works for everyone. There is not one religion that encompasses the whole truth about God and nothing but the truth. Choosing a religion and spiritual path depends on your personality type, culture, and upbringing. I understand the fear that we all have that one religion will try to take over the world and dominate the other religions.

Everyone wants to practice their religion without fear to seek out the truth that they want to live by. We pray that there is respect for each other's religion in this world.

No Organized Religion is Perfect

It is not easy to understand the beliefs of other religions, so we all need the help of experts to show us similarities and differences in religions. Once I learned about the beliefs and practices of various religions, I realized that no religion is perfect. There is always some belief or practice that will turn unbelievers away.

Each religion has its strengths and weaknesses when it comes to beliefs. Strange beliefs, love of money, lavish lifestyles, pride, arrogance, greed, violence, racism, fraud, sexual immorality, lies, ignorance, and cultish behavior can detract from religions.

Jesus said the path to wholeness is narrow, but broad is the path for destructive behavior. In Matthew 7:13-14, he says, *"Enter through the narrow gate, for the gate is wide and the way is broad that leads to destruction and there are many who enter through it. For the gate is small and the way is narrow that leads to life and there are few who find it."*

What is preventing many people from being objective and seeking a clear understanding of the teachings of Holy

Scriptures in different religions is dogma taught by some churches and religious organizations. Dogma is a belief system, principle or authoritative doctrine that is hard to reconcile with reason and realities of life, but we have to accept as truth by faith. Examples of Christianity dogma or doctrines are the Nicene Creed, and Trinity.

Some of the chief problems in religion involve racism and religious conflicts. Religious people can sometimes treat other people of different races or religions in a terrible way that goes against the spiritual teachings in the Bible and other scriptures.

When I read Pastor Frederick K. C. Price's book, *"Race, Religion, and Racism"*, could not believe how it liberated me from misinterpretation of Bible texts on race and the ancestors of the human race. In the Old Testament, Cush ancestry was supposed to be cursed to the present day. Was this a story that was interpreted literally or applied to the wrong people? We have to beware of wrong information coming from people who are either ignorant of the meaning of texts in the scriptures or who are trying to use the scriptures to promote their racist views. It is heartening that Jesus and his disciples emphasized that God is impartial and does not play favorites by putting one group ahead of another group. Thank God, we are created by the Creator who is God of Justice, Impartiality, and Love.

Good Faith and Good Works

Some say they do not belong to any religion, and yet they have faith that things will go right for them and they have faith in themselves. In religion, faith is belief in God. In science, faith is called theory. In psychic astrology readings, faith is a sixth sense. Religion is more than belonging to a church and going to church service or mass every Sunday. It involves serving others, worshipping God, demonstrating good morals, obeying God's spiritual laws, offering prayers, studying the scriptures daily, and securing the understanding that will guide you to wholeness of your soul.

Swami Sivananda says in his book, *"Bliss Divine"*, that, *"A religious life is the greatest of all blessings. It lifts a man from the mire of worldliness, impurity, and infidelity. Intellect is vain if it is not illuminated by religion. Religion does what philosophy can never do. If you live in accordance with the rules of your religion, you will attain wisdom, immortality, everlasting peace and eternal bliss."* The Yoga guru asserts that *"religion is the foundation of society, the source of all goodness and happiness, the basis of virtue and prosperity of the individual and through individuals, of the nation, civilization, order, morality."*

Sivananda expressed powerfully that *"All prophets are messengers of God. They are great Yogins and realized souls, who have had divine, intuitive perception of God. Their words are infallible and sacred. The Koran or the Zend-Avesta or the Bible is as much a sacred book as the Bhagavad Gita. All contain the essence of divine wisdom. Ahuramazda, Iswara, Allah and Jehovah are different names of the one God. The ultimate source of religion is God. The fundamentals or essentials of all religions are the same. They are as old as the human race. It is the religion of truth and love. It is the religion of the heart. It is the religion of service, sacrifice and renunciation. It is the religion of goodness, kindness and tolerance."*

Are All Religions Alike?

There is only one God, but several ways to worship the Supreme God of this world. The Bhagavad Gita says about God, *"Whatever way men approach Me, I reward them. Men everywhere follow my path."* Human beings came up with religions that fitted the culture of the community in which they lived. Through the inspiration and wisdom of their founders, these religions came up with ways to worship the Creator of the universe and seek salvation and enlightenment. In all aspects, religious people are expected to love God, love everyone, be kind to all people, seek the truth about God, read the religious scriptures, be generous, obey spiritual laws of God and follow the path to wholeness of the soul.

In my review of spiritual teachings and scriptures, I looked for consistencies or overlap between the teachings of

Western religions (Christianity, Judaism, Islam) and Eastern religions (Buddhism, Hinduism and Taoism) with regard to the soul, spirit, individual self, spiritual practices, suffering from desires of the flesh, mind-soul-spirit relationships, and spiritual laws. I found out there is great similarity in the essential beliefs about God in most of the major religions.

Over the years, I have been motivated to learn more about myself and follow spiritual laws through the personality, spirituality, life, and commandments of Christ Jesus, through the nature of the one God in Judaism, Christianity, Islam and Hinduism, through the eightfold paths of Buddha, and the daily spiritual practices of meditation. The thoughts, beliefs and spiritual experiences from different religions have shaped my understanding of God, religion, spiritual paths, and practices.

The major religions reassure me that we worship the same, awesome God in different cultures. From what the spiritual icons of six major religions went through in their spiritual journey on Earth; Moses in Judaism, Jesus in Christianity, Buddha in Buddhism, Krishna in Hinduism, Mohammed in Islam, and Lao Tzu in Taoism, I believe there are many paths to salvation of the soul and enlightenment. There is one God, a unified knowledge of the soul and spirit from the scriptures, and diverse spiritual paths to serve and worship God. If one can follow the spiritual laws of God, put in the necessary work for one's soul to heal and become whole and renew the mind and spirit, one can enter into the Kingdom of God. As the Bible indicates, the Kingdom of God is within you and it is a Kingdom of peace, joy, love, blessings, and constant communication with God.

Religious Beliefs

The Catholic faith was very important in my family and education. My religious beliefs were imparted during my youth in Catholic elementary school and Catholic high school. I had to go through Catholic doctrine and catechism before being confirmed.

It is a great idea to know and understand your religious beliefs and compare them to those of other religions. Your religious beliefs play a key role in shaping what you consider to be religious truths, which you accept, and non-truths, which you reject. Individuals who hold on to bad or destructive beliefs can regress on the path to wholeness. Some of these destructive beliefs include cults and some charismatic churches.

When I was young person, Swami Sivananda's book, *"Bliss Divine"*, helped me to get a good perspective and objective view of the religious beliefs of Hinduism, Buddhism, Islam, Taoism, and Judaism for comparison to the beliefs of my Christian faith. I also tried to understand the faith and practices of various religions in books, such as Robert Pollock's *"The World Religions"*, and the *"Religions Book – Big Ideas Simply Explained"*.

Religious Beliefs of Christianity

Christianity is the faith based on the life and teachings of Christ Jesus and his disciples. The central beliefs include belief in one God, the divinity of Jesus and the Holy Trinity of God, Jesus, and the Holy Spirit. His followers preach salvation through Christ and a life of righteousness, peace, and love for God and for each other. Their beliefs are based on the Bible, including the creation of the world by God in Genesis. Jesus not only said, *"The Father and I are one,"* but he also said, *"Abide in me as I abide in you."* (John 14:23).

Jesus was incarnated on Earth to save us from our sins and save those who are lost. One of the things that Jesus did was to reduce the 10 commandments in Judaism to two commandments; love thy God and love thy neighbor as thyself. Christians, especially Catholics, recite the Nicene or Apostle Creed to capture their essential beliefs. The Church of Jehovah's Witness is different from other Christian churches in their belief that Jesus Christ is an agent of God who will reconcile man to God.

Christians practice their religion through intimacy with a personal God. We can talk to the personal God in our lives. God can also talk back to us, and some evangelical pastors say that they can hear God talk to them. The personal God of Christians can be either the God within you, Jesus, Holy Mother Mary, and the Holy Spirit. Christians believe in life after death and in the eternal soul and spirit. Officially, they do not believe in karma, but they believe in a sinful nature, punishment for sins, and forgiveness of sins.

Christians also believe in resurrection of the body as compared to reincarnation of individual souls as is the belief in Hinduism and Buddhism. The resurrection of the body is different from being born again through reincarnation. Jesus said that one has to be born again by water and spirit in one's existence on Earth. Spiritual rebirth is key in saving oneself from the trap of our sinful nature.

To achieve wholeness, the Christian has to follow the 10 commandments and live a life of integrity, love, charity, compassion, righteousness and holiness. This is the mission given to Christians who want to follow Christ to achieve wholeness of their soul.

The New Testament says in Rom. 12:9-18; *"Let love be without hypocrisy. Abhor what is evil. Cling to what is good. Be kindly affectionate to one another with brotherly love, in honor giving preferences to one another, not lagging in diligence, fervent in spirit, serving the Lord, rejoicing in hope, patient in tribulation, continuing steadfast in prayer, distributing to the needs of the saints, given to hospitality."*

> *"Bless those who persecute you, bless and do not curse. Rejoice with those who rejoice, and weep with those who weep. Be of the same mind towards one another. Do not set your mind on high things, but associate with the humble. Do not be wise in your own opinion. Repay no evil for evil. Have regard for good things in the sight of all men. If it is possible, as much as depends on you, live peaceably with all men."*

Religious Beliefs of Judaism

Judaism is the religion of the Jewish people. The belief in one God as the ultimate authority is the central theme in Judaism. They also believe in the eternal soul. It is one of the oldest religions, like Hinduism. Abraham is the father of Judaism. Their teachings of law, love, goodness, righteousness, and justice are based on the Hebrew Bible. Practitioners of Judaism seek righteousness by obeying the commandments or spiritual laws. They believe that God revealed the 10 commandments to Moses. The Torah is based on the first five books of Moses, which are also included in the Christian Bible. Judaism does not accept Jesus as God, as they believe in one God, the almighty God the Father.

In terms of wholeness and righteousness, Isaiah 11:4-9 says about the coming of the Messiah, *"But with righteousness and justice he shall judge the poor and decide with fairness for the meek, the poor, and the downtrodden of the earth and he shall smite the earth and the oppressor with the rod of his mouth and with the breath of his lips he shall slay the wicked. And righteousness shall be the girdle of his waist and faithfulness the girdle of his loins."*

Religious Beliefs of Islam

Islam is the faith of Muslims. Their beliefs are based on the Koran, the spiritual teachings of the prophet Mohammed. They believe that there is only one God, Allah, who created the world and sustains it. They do not believe in having more than one God, as do Judaism and Christianity. However, they do not subscribe to the mystery of the Trinity of God.

Muslims seek a life of devotion to God, a life of inner peace, submission to the will of God, and acceptance of God's providence. They believe in life after death. God loves those who do good deeds and all actions on Earth are recorded. The five pillars of spiritual practices involve praying five times per day, reciting the Creed of Allah, giving to charity, fasting, and making a pilgrimage to Mecca at least once in one's lifetime.

In terms of the way to wholeness, the Koran Sarah 1 says, *"All praise belongs to Allah, Lord of all worlds, the Compassionate, the Merciful, Ruler of Judgment day. It is you that we worship and to you that we appeal for help. Show us the Way of those you have graced, not of those on whom is your wrath, not of those who wander astray."*

Religious Beliefs of Hinduism

Hinduism is the faith based on Brahman (God) as the ultimate reality. They see divinity in everyone as they believe that all is in God and God is in all, which is a type of pantheism. This belief is interesting if one follows the logic from the Christian belief that God is omnipresent. Hindus seek a path to union with God by right living (dharma). They believe in reincarnation, the law of karma, salvation (moksha), and spiritual unity with Brahman. Their faith is based on the Holy Scriptures, such as Upanishads and Bhagavad Gita.

These scriptures provide the real nature of ultimate reality, where Brahman is the Universal Spirit, and Atman is the spirit of the individual self. Atman in you is the same as the atman in every person. The individual soul, Jiva, is immortal and has to go through reincarnation. To achieve unity with God, the individual must be born again and purified. Atman in the individual unites with Brahman upon attaining unity with Brahman. The cycle of birth-death-birth is called reincarnation.

A life of wholeness and righteousness is believed and practiced in Hinduism. In Bhagavad Gita 16:1-3, believers are instructed to show:

> *"Freedom from fear, purity of heart, constancy in sacred adorations and contemplation, generosity, self-harmony, adoration, study of the scriptures, austerity, and righteousness. Nonviolence, truth, freedom from anger, renunciation, serenity, aversion to faultfinding, sympathy for all beings, peace from greedy cravings, gentleness, modesty, steadfastness. Energy, forgiveness, fortitude, purity, a good will, freedom from pride: these are the treasure of the man who is born of heaven."*

Religious Beliefs of Buddhism

Buddhism is the faith based on the teachings of Buddha, the enlightened or awakened teacher, who taught that the path to spiritual enlightenment (nirvana) or liberation from suffering was through understanding the noble truths and following the eight noble paths.

The four noble truths show us the Way to enlightenment:

(1)   Life is full of suffering or dissatisfaction.

(2)   The cause of suffering is desire or attachment.

(3)   The way to overcome suffering is to refrain from desire.

(4)   The way to escape from suffering and attain enlightenment (nirvana) is to follow the eightfold path.

Buddha urged his followers not to be involved in any discussions of whether God exists or not. They should empty themselves to be free from desires. They believe in the law of karma and rebirth as in Hinduism. The law of karma requires a cosmic intelligence that keeps a record of our actions. The eightfold path to happiness and the end of suffering is to lead a moral life, cultivate wisdom, and develop mindful awareness. High moral conduct means right speech, right action and right livelihood. Wisdom comes by seeking right understanding and right intentions (motives). Mindful awareness is obtained by right thinking, right mindfulness, and right concentration (meditation).

Religious Beliefs of Taoism

Taoism is based on the principles of the eternal Tao which means The Way, Wisdom, or Goodness. Their faith is based on the *"Tao Te Ching"* (Way of Power), written by their spiritual teacher and founder, Lao Tzu. There is no personal God. Taoism preaches the Middle Way, one that is balanced, moderate and without extreme behaviors. Taoists seek knowledge, detachment, peace, and harmony, a life of simplicity, humility, peace, and wisdom. They practice meditation, as in Buddhism, Hinduism, and Christianity.

In terms of wholeness, the Tao Te Ching v. 39 says, *"In ancient times, all entities arose from one integrity: The sky was clear and endless. The earth was calm and firm. The spirit was whole and strong. The wells were clean and whole. The 10,000 creatures were healthy and whole. Leaders were elected to plan the work and defend the community. These are in the virtue of wholeness."*

The Comforts of Religion, Science, and Astrology

Religion, science and astrology are each searching for certain truths in the universe. They all provide comfort to us. Religion is a comforter, especially to poor people. The Holy Spirit is described as the Great Comforter. Religion seeks the truth of God and man. Religion tends to base its moral precepts, understanding of human nature, the universe, and spiritual truths on inspirations and revelations in the Holy Scriptures and from religious experiences.

Science is a comforter, especially when it discovers laws, medicine, and technologies that make our lives better. Science relies on development of its theory, objective approaches, methods, experiments, technological tools, non-biased observations and applications to come closer to the truth of the laws of the body, mind, human nature, and universe.

In his book *"Power vs. Force; Hidden Determinants of Human Behavior"*, David Hawkins writes that *"It isn't unheard of from very advanced scientists who are thoroughly entrained by the influence of their level of Reason to have sudden breakthroughs and emerge into the realm of global wholeness."*

Astrology is also a comforter, especially for those who cannot make sense of the evolution of the soul to wholeness and the hidden knowledge of cosmic vibrations. Astrology seems to rely on the universe, planetary motions, calculations, and charts for understanding the vibrations in the universe, the worldly forecast, the human soul, and its evolution. Some astrologers speak of the Age of Pisces or Age of Aquarius.

God is impartial. Rom. 2:11 says *"For God shows no partiality."* Impartiality and objectivity are a code of conduct in search of truth. When individuals are willing to twist the truth for their own benefits, then their religious beliefs, scientific investigations, and astrological interpretations will run into problems. Showing favoritism, racism, tribalism, and corruption is against the spiritual code of impartiality (James 2:1-4).

Carl Jung coined the term 'collective unconscious' to describe that part of unconscious of the human mind that is common to all individuals as a reservoir of what we have been taught in our culture and tribe. This collective unconscious leads to the creation of stereotypes for people of each race, national origin, religion, and region. Stereotyping groups reflects the lack of wholeness of the person being stereotyped and the person who is doing the stereotyping.

When a human being with a fragmented mind meets another human being who is different, due to race, skin color, tribe, attire, accent, language, education, attitude, poverty, or religion, there is a tendency for the fragmented person to react differently without any solid justification, except for stereotypical discomfort from past conditioning. They may feel fear and suspicion at meeting somebody who is different. A highly conscious and evolved person will be able to override this stereotypical reaction and choose an action that is more healing in the path towards wholeness.

Beliefs in Organized Religions

Most religions believe in one God, but they may differ in their belief systems. There is no ideal or perfect religion. Every religion has issues with their belief system that may not meet standards of reason, science, and reality. Because humans fight over issues of religion, it is best to find common beliefs in one God who is all love, all-powerful, omnipotent, and omniscient.

I look for consistencies among religious scriptures in their beliefs, knowledge, spiritual laws, and worship of God. We can all believe that the universe was created by God and that humans are spirits who have a soul and live in a body. God is omnipresent and so He is present in everything and everyone. The egotism of ordinary consciousness and our desires of the flesh cause us to be separated from God. A change from ordinary consciousness to consciousness of mindful awareness is therefore necessary for the practice of selflessness and ego control. Love of God and love of neighbor are two of the greatest commandments. They align your soul and spirit with the Spirit of God within you.

Socrates advised people to find the truth within themselves and do the work that is needed to transform themselves. Knowing yourself will help you to decide which religion and belief systems you feel will be compatible with your soul's purpose, aspirations, intelligence, and faith. Sometimes, the differences between religions may be due more to cultural differences than to belief in God, Creator of the Universe. The differences in belief systems should not be a hindrance for loving God and loving others as oneself.

Many believe that Christ came to Earth to save mankind. Swami Sivananda describes in his book, *"Bliss Divine"*, Christ Jesus as an example of *"descent of God on earth for the ascent of man."* People of the Hindu faith believe in Avatars or God incarnations on Earth. They believe that God incarnates, like Jesus, are not individual souls, but souls who are in union with God. This is supported by Jesus when He said, *"The Father and I are one".*

If Judaism has issues with the Christian belief that Jesus is God, practitioners of Judaism can still worship God, the Creator of the Universe. If Christians believe that their God is different from Allah, God of Islam, and from Brahman, God of the Hindus, the Christian belief does not prevent practitioners of Hinduism and Islam from worshipping the Creator of the Universe.

Chris Febry has written a book that describes people who are 'ineffective Christians' because they have inexcusably bad habits and they do not toe the line of dogma and literal interpretation of the Bible. I struggle with a few bad habits on the list, as I want to be a good Christian. My bad habits include tolerating the sins of others and living a homogenized faith, where I only keep the faith messages that resonate with me. I also fail to tell people that Jesus Christ is the only way to heaven.

I am sensitive to the religious faith of others such that I respect their spiritual leaders, be it Abraham or Moses in the Jewish Faith, Christ in Christianity, Krishna in Hinduism, Buddha in Buddhism, Muhammad in Islam, and Lao Tzu in Taoism. I would rather tell them that God is the way to Heaven, as Jesus said, *"the kingdom of God is within everyone"*. Another bad habit of 'ineffective Christians' is the use of self-help books. As a seeker of self-knowledge, knowledge about God, and a scientist, I understand that it is important to search for the truth and acquire right knowledge and understanding of what is required on the spiritual path to wholeness.

Each religion has to stand up to facts or truth, logic, and scientific scrutiny in their belief systems. Even within the same religion, there are challenges from having hundreds of denominations. Some Christians would rather form their own church than accept the type of Christianity that other Christian churches may practice. Because the scriptures can sometimes be interpreted in more than one way, this can result in different belief systems within the same religion. Whatever the differences, the motivation to know your spiritual path remains, with the goal of seeking to improve ourselves, renew our minds, and transform our souls through spiritual development.

Personal God and Impersonal God

God is both a personal and impersonal God. The Bible says, *"For all who are led by the spirit are the sons of God."* Should we pray to a personal God or an impersonal God? We pray to a personal God. Should we meditate on the spirit of a personal God or on an impersonal God? I meditate in the mysterious silence of the impersonal God. We are individual persons as well as spiritual beings. In terms of a Personal God, Jesus Christ said in the Bible that *"I am the Way, Truth and Life, no one comes to the Father except through me."* In terms of an impersonal God, the Bhavagad Gita (4:11) says about knowing and approaching God, *"the man who sees me in everything and everything within me will not be lost to me, nor will I be l lost in him."*

Hindus and Buddhists talk about Saguna Brahman, which is Personal God with qualities and attributes or the manifested Divine presence. God without form, qualities, and attributes is referred to as Nirguna Brahman (Impersonal God). Both Personal God (Saguna Brahman) and Impersonal God (Nirguna Brahman) are eternal and transcendent.

Human beings have always struggled with the idea of a personal God versus an impersonal God. In the ancient times, pagans worshipped idols as God because idols provided individuals with a personal god that they could see, talk to and revere. Even these days, the physical wooden cross of Jesus is revered and addressed personally.

At the other extreme, we have religions that have worshipped different images of God. We also have cultures and non-denominational Churches, especially in West Africa, that worship charismatic pastors and human leaders as if they are representatives of Sons of God, like Jesus. These charismatic pastors may be talented in communication and understanding of the scriptures; however, everyone has to be aware of the need for self-knowledge and wholeness. Otherwise, they spend several hours a day listening to preaching and don't spend enough time to implement their plans for a life of wholeness and purpose.

How do you contact God? As a Christian who prays and performs meditation, I have settled on my personal God and impersonal God and have read the views of spiritual teachers and religions on this subject. Christ said, *"Abide in me as I abide in you"* (John 15:4). So, I pray to Jesus as a personal God and to the Holy Spirit as a personal God within me. I meditate on an impersonal God, pure consciousness or the Creator of the Universe, God the Father, who is eternal, infinite, omnipotent and omniscient.

It is not obvious but intuitive that Christianity has a personal God and an impersonal God. Christians have two choices of a Personal God; Christ Jesus or God the Father. The personal God and impersonal God of Judaism is God the Father or Yahweh. Islam has a personal and impersonal God. The personal God of Muslims is Allah, the Merciful one. Hindus have a personal and impersonal God. They have several choices of a personal God, including Krishna, Vishnu, and Siva. Buddhism has a personal and impersonal God. The personal God of Buddhism is Buddha, as you see statues of Buddha in both households and holy places.

Most of the major religions, Christianity, Islam, Hinduism, Buddhism, and Judaism agree that the impersonal God is eternal, absolute, and everywhere. The impersonal God or Ultimate Reality in Christianity, Judaism, Islam, Buddhism, Taoism, and Hinduism is the God who is everywhere (omnipresent), omniscient (knows everything) and omnipotent (almighty and all-powerful).

If God is present in everything, including every form or formless substance, then it makes sense that God can be present as both form and formless nature. The God who is present within matter or form is the personal God. The God who is present as pure consciousness is the impersonal or formless God.

Most religions agree that the personal God has to be omnipotent and omniscient. The personal God can incarnate as a human being or in a different form. The Bible says we were created in the image of God, with a spiritual consciousness (impersonal) and a material body (personal).

The dual nature of human beings, as body and spirit, is a paradox. Other types of paradox in life include the particle-wave duality in quantum mechanics area of physics, where all particles exhibit both particle and wave properties.

God exists as an invisible, formless spirit and as a visible incarnate. Colossians 1:15 tells us, *"The Son is the image of the invisible God, the firstborn over all creation."* The Holy Spirit of God is not a person, but it has human qualities. In John 14:16-21, the

Bible says, *"And I will ask my Father and He will give you another advocate to help you and be with you forever – The Spirit of Truth. The world cannot accept Him because it neither sees nor knows Him... You will realize that I am in my Father, you are in me and I am in you. Whoever has my commands and keeps them is the one who loves me and will be loved by my Father and I too will love them and show myself to them."*

The Bhagavad Gita clarifies the paradox of God existing as Impersonal and Personal God. The Gita says in 7:24, *"The unwise think I am that form of my lower nature which is seen by mortal; they know not my higher nature, imperishable and supreme. Both spirit and matter are in me."* The impersonal or formless God is a spiritual state or consciousness that can be reached by meditation and other spiritual practices.

We pray to the Personal God. God is love. The personal God communicates to your thoughts with love or as the voice of another person showing love to you. How do you know that the person who said something to you that was helpful when you needed it or helped you in your time of need is not God personified? Our physical brain is created to communicate through the mind of our brain to the Mind of the personal God. The brain is the path through which we pray to God and the same path that God uses to communicate with us.

People of other religious faiths have to let their faith and experience guide them to understand that Jesus of Nazareth could have been God incarnate on earth. The Bible says in John 10:34-36, *"Jesus answered, is it not written in your law that you are Gods, men to whom God's message came – and the scriptures cannot be set aside or cancelled or annulled. Do you say of the one whom the Father consecrated and dedicated and set apart for Himself and sent into the world: You are blaspheming because I said. "I am the Son of God."* It is the nature of God as Creator to create and oversee this amazing world and incarnate as different persona to guide the world to godliness.

In meditation, I seek to connect to the pure consciousness of God by achieving silence of my mind. The Bible says,

"Be still and know that I am God." If there are no thoughts in the mind, only silence, then what remains in the mind is spirit or pure consciousness. The individual 'I' consciousness then merges with God consciousness.

Maharishi Mahesh Yogi says in his book, *"Transcendental Meditation"*, that God has two aspects, *"The impersonal, omnipotent, absolute Being and the personal supreme being – we have seen that realization of God could mean realization of the impersonal God or the personal God."* He adds that, *"The realization of the personal God, then by necessity, will be on the level of human perception, on the level of secondary experience. Realization of the personal God means that the eyes should be able to see the supreme Person and the heart should be able to feel the qualities of that Supreme Person. The realization of personal God has to be in the relative field of life. Thus the realization of the impersonal God is in transcendental consciousness and the realization of the personal God is in the level of consciousness of the waking state."*

Maharishi explains further that *"while dealing with the nature of the impersonal God, we have seen that it is absolute bliss consciousness of transcendental nature. In order to realize it, our conscious mind should transcend all the limits of experience in the relative field, beyond relative existence, where the conscious mind would be left to remain conscious all by itself."*

In this analysis, the life of Jesus resulted in a realization of a personal God that Christians choose to worship, in addition to their worship of the omnipresent God. Similarly, Hindus choose to worship a personal God such as Krishna or Rama and the impersonal God, Brahman. In contrast, Buddhists prefer to practice a religion based on Buddha's personality and an impersonal God.

The Mystical Body of Christ and God

The mystical body of God refers to the interconnectedness of all living things in one body of the impersonal God. The Spirit of God is present in all human beings, but we differ in how we awaken the inner spirit in order to exert our will and power.

We suffer when we lose sight of our spiritual nature and separate ourselves from the body of God or source of all creation.

On the other hand, Christianity places a strong emphasis on the personal Christ. According to the New Testament, the human Christ left the earth and the Church is now the new, mystical body of Christ. In 1 Cor. 6:15, the Bible tells us, *"Your bodies are members of Christ."* Members of the Christian church have thus become part of the mystical body of the personal Christ. Christians are united to Christ as members of his body. Christ is still the head of the mystical body as he is the head of the Church. Thus, the mystical body of Christ is kept alive through the worship of God and Christ in church.

The teachings of Christ Jesus are remarkable and reveal his supernormal consciousness, which is described by the Bible as a consciousness that is in unity with God consciousness. Christ's teachings are not based on theology. Instead, Christ uses parables, symbols and allegory to show us the way of the life of wholeness and godliness.

The Bible says in Cor. 12:12, *"For just as the body is a unity and yet has many parts, and all the parts, though many, form one body; so it is with the body of Christ."* If we are part of the invisible body of Christ, we are also part of the universal body of God. It says in Eph. 3: 17-19, *"May Christ through your faith dwell in your hearts. May you be rooted deep in love and founded securely on love. That you may have the power and be strong to apprehend and grasp with all the saints what is the breath, height and depth (of God's love for us); to know the love of Christ which far surpasses mere knowledge, that you may be filled with the fullness of God."*

In the mystical body of Christ, we are all united in love, purpose, power and faith in God (Eph. 3:11-12). In a similar way, in the mystical body of God, we find that Hinduism shows that we are all part of Atman (universal soul) and Brahman (Spirit of God).

CHAPTER NINETEEN

Know Your Spiritual Laws
for Spiritual Renewal

Spiritual Laws

When you follow the spiritual laws of God, you become a better person as you follow the right path to wholeness. Spirituality is an experience, a journey of faith, trust, and reliance on God to sustain us by the Power of his Word and Spiritual Laws. The universe is governed by a system of laws, including scientific and spiritual laws. Each culture or religion has its moral code of conduct that the members value. Those who believe in God want to obey God's spiritual laws in their lives. Those who do not believe in God may have their own personal code of conduct or rely on their conscience, which may tell them what is right and wrong. The scriptures and spiritual teachers tell us to observe the code of moral conduct, for God knows everything we do.

As God is perfect (Psalm 19:7), the spiritual laws of God have to be spiritual truths. They have to be consistent with the Creative Intelligence of the Universe. We depend on the wisdom of Holy Scriptures and spiritually advanced teachers to provide us with Spiritual laws of God. Here are some of the spiritual laws that can guide us to know ourselves and follow the path to wholeness of mind and soul in alignment with awakened Spirit within us.

The Bible says in Psalm 1:1-3, *"Blessed is the man who walks and lives not in the counsel of the ungodly ... But his delight and desire are in the law of the Lord and on His law he habitually meditates by day and night. And he shall be like a tree firmly planted by the streams of water, ready to bring forth its fruit in its season; its leaf shall not fade or wither and everything he does shall prosper."*

Law of Love

The most important spiritual law in Christianity is the one from Jesus. He described love of God and neighbor as the two greatest commandments. He said, *"Love the Lord thy God with all thy heart, soul, mind and strength. And love thy neighbor as thyself"* (Matthew 12: 29-31). If you love God, you should love others and "do unto others as you would have them do unto you. Whoever does not love does not know God" (1 John 4:8).

The one who loves fulfills the old law. The most important commandment is love. The law of love supplants the old Law or old Commandments. The New Testament says in Rom. 13:8-10:

"Keep out of debt and owe no man anything except to love one another. For he who loves his neighbor has fulfilled the Law."

The commandments; *you shall not commit adultery, you shall not kill, you shall not steal, you shall not covet,* and all other commandments, are summed up in the single commandment; *you shall love your neighbor as yourself.*

They say rightly that love is the most powerful aspect of human nature. Love is the vehicle that transforms our life into a higher consciousness by bonding us with God or connecting us with our fellow man, who has the spirit of God within him. The power of love unleashes joy in our lives. To love God is to be spiritually awake, follow His spiritual laws, and do what is right in the eyes of God.

To love thour neighbor is to be awake, to live in harmony and service with your neighbor. Love of man overcomes fear and hate. Embrace differences in nature, including racial and skin color differences. The universe uses diversity to express the beauty of creation. The Bible says in 1 Thess. 3:12, *"And may the Lord make you increase and excel and overflow to love one another and all people."* We are known by the love we show for all people, regardless of race, tribe, gender, and religion. Be willing to show kindness, compassion, and mercy. Be willing to sacrifice if you have to take care of a stranger who needs your help to survive.

Law of the One God

In Judaism, there is belief in one God. Islam's Koran says that, *"And your God is one God. There is no God but the One, the Compassionate, and the Merciful".* Christians believe in one God, the Creator of the Universe. *"There is one Body and one Spirit"* (Eph. 4:4). God is everywhere (omnipresent), knows everything (omniscient), and is all-powerful (omnipotent). God knows the thoughts and deeds of every human being.

God is love and he created humans and the universe out of divine love. *"Whoever lives in love lives in God, and God in Him."* (John 4:16). God is just and impartial. God is holy, wholeness, and perfect. God is eternal, infinite, and unchangeable. God is absolute existence, as he is the cause of everything except Himself. God is pure consciousness without thought. The concept of human individuals reaching transcendence and uniting with God is considered more understandable than the Trinity of God.

Law of Spirituality and Spiritual Rebirth

God is a spirit (John 4:24). You and I are spirit made in the image of God. The Spirit of God is within each one of us. Spirituality is based on your spirit becoming part of God and on moral conduct by one spirit to another in the body of God, which is the world. The Bible says, *"Blessed are the poor in spirit for theirs is the kingdom of heaven"* (Matt 5:3). We are led by the spirit but we tend to be unaware of it at every moment. Be aware of the presence of God in you and be aware of the silent witness within you. Know and remember that you are a spirit with a soul. You are not your body.

When Jesus said in the Sermon of the Mount, *"Blessed are the poor in spirit for they shall inherit the kingdom of God,"* he wanted us to have the spirit awakened in us in the midst of poverty and attain the best reward, which is the Kingdom of God. We need to realize or awaken the Kingdom of God that is within you and me. A life of wealth without an awakened spirit is not a bad life, as one acquires material possessions. However, a life of wealth that complements the awakened spirit within you is a better life than the spiritless one.

Spirituality is a way of life that leads to attainment of one's goals in life. The Holy Scriptures tell us that real happiness is in the spiritual life. We are not our body. To attain the spiritual life, you can practice Eastern spirituality, Christian spirituality, Indian spirituality, African spirituality, Native American spirituality, Chinese spirituality, Muslim spirituality, Buddhist spirituality, Judaism spirituality or other types of spirituality. Whatever spirituality you practice, spiritual life entails following the law of spirituality and experiencing love, wisdom and consciousness of God.

All religions are alike in terms of the essence of the spirituality that they practice. What can elevate each type of spirituality is the need for each tradition of wisdom to learn from each other and integrate good spiritual practices from the other religions into their own.

The spirit must be renewed when you are on the wrong path. Jesus said in John 3: 3-5, *"I assure you, most solemnly, that unless a person is born again, he cannot ever experience the kingdom of God. Nicodemus said to Him, how can a man be born when he is old? Can he enter his mother's womb again and be born? Jesus answered, I assure you, most solemnly I tell you, unless a man is born of water and the spirit, he cannot enter the kingdom of God."* The first birth is the birth from the womb of the mother. The second birth is the birth from awakening of the Spirit of God within us.

True happiness is not achieved by satisfying our physical body. The fruits of the spirit provide peace and joy. For our soul to be unified or aligned with our spirit or Spirit of God, we have to be spiritually-minded and walk in the spirit. Your spirit prompts your soul to seek wholeness and the body tells your soul what it desires. This is the basis of the battle between the body and the spirit for partnership with the soul.

The Bible says in Rom. 8:4-5, *"So that the righteous and just requirement of the Law might be fully met in us who live and move not in the ways of the flesh but in the ways of the Spirit. For those who live according to the flesh and are controlled by its unholy desires set their minds on and pursue those things which gratify the flesh, but those who live according to the Spirit and are controlled by the desires of the Spirit set their minds on and seek those things which gratify the Spirit."*

The Bible says, *"God is Spirit and those who worship Him must worship him in spirit and in truth"* (John 4:24)

1   Tim 6:1 says, *"If someone who is caught in sin, you who live by the Spirit should restore them gently. But watch yourselves or you may be tempted."*

2   Tim 1:7 says,*"For God gave us a spirit not of fear but of power and love and self-control."*

3   Gal 6:7 says, *"Do not be deceived. God cannot be mocked. Whatever a man sows, so shall he reap. Whoever sows to please their flesh will reap destruction. Whoever sows to please the spirit will reap eternal life."*

Law of Divine Potentialities of Man

We are all born with talents, gifts, and potential abilities from God. Our creative energies are unleashed when our mind and soul are consistent with our spirit. Everyone has a spark of the divine within them, which makes us more than what we think we are.

Deepak Chopra, a renowned spiritual teacher, calls this law, the Law of Pure Potentiality. In his acclaimed book, *"The*

Seven Spiritual Laws of Success". Deepak wrote that the *"source of creation is pure consciousness, pure potentiality seeking expression from the manifest to the manifest. And when we realize that our true self is one of pure potentiality we align with the power that manifests everything in the Universe."*

Each of us has to develop the potential within us. Humans are not aware of the divinity of their spirit and the potential they have to be, do, and have whatever they put their mind on. We are all sons and daughters of God. Swami Sivananda writes in the *"Mind, Mysteries and its Control",* that *"each man with a mind is a power unto himself." Jesus said, "I am the bread of life".* You have access to whatever you need, if you are in alignment with the spirit of God.

Law of Unity in Diversity

God is One, but in multiple forms because we all have the spirit of God within us. The world is unity in diversity because God is one in a world of diversity of non-living substances, plants, animals, and humans. The universe is one body of God. All spiritual laws work for everyone, regardless of your religion or distrust of religion. Individually, we have problems with identity, unity, and purpose in life. Only after establishing unity and wholeness within oneself, among the mind, soul, and spirit, can one reach unity with God.

All Christians need to know who they are in order to align their souls with the spirit of God. Paul said, *"I am united with God and I am one spirit with Him"* (I Corinth 6:17). Coming into union with God signifies that your body is a temple of God, your mind in the mind of God, your soul has attained wholeness, and your spirit is aligned or in union with the Spirit of God.

The unity of life is clarified more in Hinduism and Buddhism. The subject and the object become one. In Christianity, the Bible expresses the unity of the body and the union of the individual spirit with the Spirit of God. The Bible says in 1 Cor. 12:12-15 that *"For just as the body is a unity and yet has many parts, and all the parts though many form one body, so it is with*

Christ. For by one Spirit we were all, whether Jews or Greeks, slaves or free, baptized into one body, and all made to drink of one Spirit."

"For the body does not consist of one limb or organ but of many. If the foot should say, because I am not the hand, I do not belong to the body, would it be therefore not of the body?"

One needs to expand one's consciousness to understand that all is in the one God and the One God is in all. Our lives runs smoothly when we stay in contact with God at all times. The law of unity requires us to live in harmony with each other and with the Universe.

Nature brings us unity and diversity. Unity allows one to achieve wholeness, such as unity of body, mind, soul, and spirit. Unity of mankind also means unity of all people on Earth based on our collective humanity. Diversity, on the other hand, brings to us the beauty of creation and variety in culture and habitat, such as the diversity of the races, and the diversity of animals and birds. Diversity also tests our ability to refrain from racism and tribalism, and be tolerant of each other in the journey to wholeness.

Human beings try to live a life separate from their source; God. This leads to dysfunctional behavior and pain resulting from satisfying the desires of the body. Achieving unity moves one from being individualistic and separate into communion with others and union with God. It is better to have an awareness of being one with the universe, as God is omnipresent. You move away from separateness when you get closer to God by seeing yourself united with God. Unity is achievable because Christ said, *"Abide in me as I abide in you."*

However we recognize that we are different individuals, races, genders, nationalities, and cultures in the diversity of life. To live a life that is not self-centered, we seek friendship, collaboration, and relationships with others in order to purify our souls for wholeness.

Gurdjieff calls the problem of lack of unity within each

individual the cause of our inability to become whole and integrated to perform right actions and behavior. The lack of unity comes from not having an integrated 'I', but rather, having multiple 'I' or personalities, because of the ego self and all the roles we play in life. The goal is to achieve unity in mind, soul, and spirit. Gary Zukav also talks about the authentic power that we receive when there is alignment between the personality and the soul.

Abraham Maslow used the term 'peak experience' in spiritual practice to describe moments when we experience a mystical feeling, or when we experience a sense of purpose, unity, and integration in ourselves. Unlike Gurdjieff, who says that man cannot do what he intends to do because of lack of unity, Maslow also describes self-actualizing people as those who do not listen to defenses from the ego but use their unified being to get their needs met.

Meister Eckhart says, in one of his books, *"that what hinders the union between the union of the soul"* (your true self) and God is that firstly, *"the soul is too much divided, too fragmented and broken,"* instead of being simple and pure. Secondly, *"the soul is attached to temporary things,"* and thirdly, *"the soul being fond of the body will prevent union with God."*

Law of Duality

This law empowers us to deal effectively with the uncertainties, opposites, competing forces, and ups and downs of life. Life presents us with opposing qualities, such as matter and spirit, pleasure and pain, good and evil, strengths and weaknesses, sadness and happiness, growth and decline, joy and sorrow, life and death, light and dark, hot and cold, love and hate, and friends and enemies. We have to be able to deal effectively with the presence of duality in the realm of the unity consciousness of God and the interconnectedness of all beings, things and phenomena.

The Gita says in 2:15, *"For the wise man, whom these things disturbs not and whose soul is one, to whom pain and pleasure are the same is worthy of life in immortality."*

ANDREW BENEDICT ACHEAMPONG

Our nature and personality are not fixed and so we go through the flux of life, consistent with symbolism of the effect of planetary motions on our astrological personalities. A person with a high consciousness of enlightenment will transcend the law of duality, where the individual lives a life of unity, unified with God.

Spirit transcends duality, so this law does not refer to unity of spirit within, but the duality of qualities of the experience of the mind and soul. The Spirit of God makes the sun rise on both good and evil. The mind can be powerful for good or evil. The universe provides both rain for plants to grow and lightning that can be harmful.

There is male and female, day and night, black and white, and yin and yang energy. Each quality of the pair has its role to play. The Lord said, *"I created the light and the darkness. I make peace and create upheaval"* (Isiah 45: 7). Our joy in life goes up and down. Lao Tzu, the great Chinese spiritual teacher, said, *"Sometimes things are ahead, sometimes they are behind. Sometimes breathing is hard, sometimes it comes easily. Sometimes there is strength, sometimes weakness. Sometimes one is up and sometimes one is down. Therefore, the sage avoids extremes, excesses and complacency."*

Law of Non-Attachment to Possessions and Ego

The individual receives peace by attachment to heavenly things or the righteousness of God, not by setting his or her heart on material possessions. Desires of the mind lead to attachment to the things desired. Non-attachment to possessions is one of the most difficult rules for the well-to-do to comply with. It requires mastery of the selfish desires and replacement of them with attention on the spirit within to yield the fruits of the spirit, which includes joy, peace, and self-control. In this situation, joy, peace, and self-control overcome desires. Meister Eckhart says the cause of suffering is the desire for or worry about things that are not permanent.

Attachment is not just attachment to possessions. Gurdjieff calls attachment to things as identification with things. When one is identified with something, one becomes lost in the thing and less conscious of oneself. Lack of consciousness can lead to errors in making right decisions and judgments. There is also identification or attachment by human beings to negative emotions, such as hatred, irritability, and anger.

Our ego-mind wants to be in charge of our life, rather than our spirit or higher self. Trust in God rather than in your ego helps to motivate you to a sense of security and fear. Huge ego is a hindrance for the soul's transformation and spiritual growth. The Bible says in 1 Timothy 6:17, *"Command those who are rich in this present age not to be haughty nor to trust in uncertain riches but in the living God who gives us all richly things to enjoy."* Peace comes from meditation on the spirit and not on our desires of material possessions or attachment to the ego.

The Bible says, *"Blessed is the poor in spirit for he will inherit the kingdom of heaven."* Thus, individuals who are in the spirit, but have little ego because they live in poverty, get the biggest prize of the kingdom of heaven. The egos of individuals who are rich often compete with the spirit. If someone has enough material possessions, sees his brother in need and yet has no pity on him, then how can the spirit of God dwell in him? (1John 3:17).

Law of Consciousness

Swami Sivananda writes that, *"consciousness is common to all and pure consciousness is one or unified. The mind is different in every individual."* Spirit is pure consciousness. Know thyself and thy God and you will know the mysteries of God and the Universe.

We have body consciousness, mind consciousness, soul consciousness, and spiritual consciousness. Whatever you pay attention to will grow or become important in your life. Spiritual teachers talk about enhancing the present moment consciousness of your body, mind, soul, and spirit to increase your overall consciousness of who you are, your purpose, your actions, your destiny or destination and your faith in God.

On the journey to wholeness, we move from lower consciousness characterized by ego, self-centeredness, or negative emotions to higher consciousness, characterized by increased awareness, living in the present moment, love, and wholeness.

Mindfulness enhances your mind consciousness. Religious and spiritual practices, such as meditation, are used to enhance your consciousness of your spirit self and align your body and soul with your spirit.

Law of Sin and Forgiveness

Sin means missing the mark, leading to unwholesome behavior. Knowing what is right and doing the wrong thing is sin. Sin comes from desires and weaknesses. Do what is right even if your body desires the wrong thing. The Bible says, *"We know that the Law is spiritual but I am a creature of the flesh"* (Rom 7:14). The Bible says in James 5:16, *"Confess your trespasses to one another, and pray for one another that you may be healed. The effective fervent prayer of a righteous man avails much."* If we forgive others of wrongdoing against us, we also have the opportunity to have our sins forgiven.

The Bible says in 1 John 3:7-18 that *"one who does do what is right is righteous, and the one does what is evil is a devil."* Sin is falling short of the perfection of God. Since humans have a good nature and sinful nature, as Paul says in the Bible, we are imperfect and are prone to sin. The Bible say that Christ Jesus came to save those who are lost and to redeem us from evil so that we will do what is right (Titus 2:12-14). If you forgive others of their sin against you, your sins will be forgiven. The Bible says, *"If you forgive men, your heavenly Father will also forgive you"* (Matt 6:14).

When I first read Swami Sivananda's teaching on sin about 40 years ago, I felt convinced that sin is not about going to hell – a misunderstanding that I felt some pastors took advantage of to put themselves into a superior position. He described *"Sin as an evil deed. Sin is willful violation of the laws of morality and religion. It is transgression of the law of God. Vice issues as sins and crimes".* He adds that sin originates from *"anger, lust, sorrow, loss of judgment, an inclination to hurt others, jealousy, malice, pride, envy, slander, incapacity to see the good of others, unkindness and fear."*

Swami Sivananda goes on to say that *"Egoism is the greatest sin. The wrong notion that I am the body is the real, original sin."* The one thought – the 'I' thought – has wrought all mischiefs. This one 'I' thought has multiplied into thousand-fold thoughts. This one thought separated man from God. This self-arrogating Ego is the real, hereditary sin of human nature. According to Swami Sivananda, the following are all sins; hating others, separating oneself from God, falsehood, ignorance, selfishness, robbing others, and mischief.

Law of Sinful Nature

Humans tend to live at the level of the flesh. Living at the flesh level invites temptations of the flesh and the sinful nature to operate. Ephesians 2:1-3 says, *"And you when you were dead by transgressions and sins, in which at any time you walked. You were following the course and fashion of the world, following the prince of the power of the air spirit that will constantly work in the sons of disobedience. Among these we as well as you once lived and conducted yourself in the passions of our flesh, obeying the impulses of the flesh and the thoughts of the mind. We were then by nature, children of God's wrath and heirs of His indignation."*

The sinful nature comes about because, as spiritual beings, we are not to live as bodies but as spirits. As spiritual beings, we are destined for a life of dignity, salvation, wholeness, holiness, and unity with God.

There is major sin and minor sin (venal sin). Venal sin does not need confession. Major sin needs contrition and confession to reduce the effect of the karma. According to Swami Sivananda in the *"Mind, its Mysteries and Control", "You can attain knowledge of the self (Jnana) if you are free from sensual desires and immoral mental states."*

Law of Mercy and Grace

God shows us mercy because of our suffering in humility. Grace is God's unmerited favor that saves us from troubles. Psalm 56:1 says, *"Be merciful and gracious to me, O God, for man would trample me or devour me, all day long the adversary oppresses me."* The description of a Merciful God exists in most religions, including Islam, Christianity, and Judaism. God shows benevolence and kindness to everyone in need of mercy. In Islam, God is described as the *"Most Merciful."*

Psalm 57:1 says, *"Be merciful and gracious to me, O God. Be merciful and gracious to me for my soul takes refuge and finds shelter and confidence in you, yes, in the shadow of your wings will I take refuge and be confident until calamities are passed."*

Grace comes to those who have a humble heart. We also experience grace because of the love of God. Grace helps us get ourselves out of a jam that we put ourselves into through our defiance, stubbornness, or self-righteousness. Through the Grace of God, we have been shown the way of righteousness and right living in the life of Christ and the life of Buddha. Ephesians 2:7-8 says God *"did this that He might clearly demonstrate through the ages to come the immeasurable kindness and goodness of heart towards us in Christ Jesus. For it is by free grace that you are saved through your faith. And the salvation is not of yourselves but it is a gift of God."*

Law of Evolution into Wholeness

We evolve from fragmentation of mind or soul to wholeness, from low to high stages of consciousness, and from a life of sin to one of holiness. Jesus said in the Bible that the *"Father and I are one"*. The most evolved person transcends normal consciousness and becomes one with God, as Jesus became one with God.

According to Maharishi Mahesh Yogi, in *"The Science of Being and Art of Living"*, the aim of life is God realization and the expansion of happiness, and evolution is the process through which it is fulfilled. Wholeness is our first destination in this life that we have been given by God.

Wholeness is not living with pomp and pageantry. It is living a life of fullness, surrender, love, and understanding. God wants us to take the bold steps with the love and courage necessary to overcome our faults and weaknesses and not to allow our fears and a sense of inadequacy to stop us from transforming our life into a life of fulfilment and wholeness. God has provided us the ability and strength to become whole, as the spirit of God is within us. He allows our free will to choose between good and bad habits and between bad and good decisions, knowing that we have to learn from our mistakes.

Christ Jesus, Buddha, Lao Tzu and other supernormal minds have showed us the path to wholeness and godliness, but we have to follow through with right actions, according to laws of God and sacred scriptures. James 1:4 says, *"But let endurance and steadfastness and patience have full play and do a thorough work, so that you may be perfectly and fully developed, lacking in nothing."* The Bible also tells us in Deuteronomy 30:12-14 that *"It is not a secret in heaven that you should say who shall go up for us to heaven and bring it to us that we may hear and do it ... But the word is near you, in your mouth and in your mind and in your heart so that you can do it."* We have to do the soul work needed on the path of wholeness in an effortless manner, without bringing our ego to compete with our faith in the healing of the soul.

To change one's bad behavior and addiction can require considerable effort. We have to do the work of doing good deeds, paying attention to our intentions and choices, supporting each other, and overcoming our weaknesses with great effort and love of our souls. People want wholeness to be free from fear and to choose a life of love of neighbor and love of God.

Some people talk the talk of wholeness, but they do not walk the walk into wholeness. It is like preachers who preach about being holy or having faith, but they do not do the good deeds or good works. Some people go as far as to say that good works are not as important as having faith. I think what they mean is that we should not let our ego come in when we do good deeds, but let our spirit and faith guide us into good works. The Bible says in Titus 2:14, *"Who gave himself for us, that he might redeem us from all iniquity and purify unto himself a peculiar people, zealous of good works."*

Good deeds take the focus from ourselves, away from our self-centeredness and ego, and help the soul of oneself and other selves evolve and become selfless. If good deeds are not an indicator of your faith in God, then what faith do you have? Should God do the good works or works of wholeness for us and all we have to do is have faith? The journey to wholeness makes us grow in love and understanding that fills every part of us to achieve self-harmony among our body, mind, soul, and spirit. Even a little progress on this path is a step needed to strengthen our faith.

Law of Faith and Reason

Faith is an act of will to trust God. Faith is confidence in yourself and in God. Faith is not achieved instantaneously, but is a process of demonstration that your soul is linked to the spirit within you and to the Creator of the universe. The more faith you have in your connection to God, the closer the soul moves to the higher self or spiritual self. Faith starts with belief in your own being and the spirit of God and then this leads to conviction through experiences in your life. The Bible says, *"Faith is the substance of things hoped for, the evidence of things not seen"* (Hebrews 11:1).

The Tao Te Ching says in v.14, *"That which we look at but cannot see is the invisible. That which we listen for but cannot hear is the inaudible. That which we reach for but cannot grasp is the intangible. Beyond reason, these three merge contradicting experience."*

Swami Sivananda writes in *"Mind, Its Mysteries and Control"* that *"Belief, reasoning, knowledge and faith are the four important psychic processes."* He explains that it is like a doctor treating a patient. First, you have to believe that the patient will be cured. Then you reason out on the diagnosis and obtain knowledge based on your examination and results. If you had a positive experience where a specific drug cured the disease, you gain faith. So you spread the word about your faith and positive experience with the treatment.

The experience of faith makes us want to always be in the presence of God. The Bhagavad Gita says in 17: 3 that *"the faith of a man follows his nature. Man is made up of faith; as his faith is, so is he."* In 6:47, it tells us *"And the greatest of all yogis is he who with all his soul has faith and he who with his soul loves me."*

The Bible says in Rom. 1:17, *"He who through faith is righteous shall live."* We grow our faith by trusting in God, performing good works, reading the Word of God in Holy Scriptures, going through religious and spiritual experiences, devoting some time to prayer and meditation, and overcoming our fears and challenges. Meister Eckhart says, *"Where there are sins, there is no perfect trust."*

Faith has different meanings for different religions. In Islam, faith is submission to God's will. In Hinduism, faith is based on spiritual knowledge (Jnana) and experience (Karma). In Buddhism faith is conviction and an acceptance of God's will.

The value of reason is to lead us into the right faith and not the wrong faith, just as reason is what allows us to distinguish between true emotions from false emotions. The right faith transcends reason and the experience of a strong faith can overcome mountains of challenges (Matt. 17:20). The Bhagavad Gita says in 2:45, *"Know Him therefore who is above reason and let His peace give thee peace. Be a warrior and kill desire, the enemy of the soul."*

Thomas Merton wrote about faith and reason in his book, *"Ascent of Truth"*. He says, *"Faith, without depending on reason for the slightest shred of justification, never contradicts reason and remains ever reasonable. Faith does not destroy reason, but fulfills it. Nevertheless, there must always remain a delicate balance between the two. Two extremes are to be avoided; credulity and skepticism;*

superstition and rationalism. If this balance is upset, if man relies too much on his five senses and on his reason when faith should be his teacher, then he comes into illusion. Or when in defiance of reason, he gives the ascent of his faith to a fallible authority, then too he falls into illusion. Reason is in fact the path to faith and faith takes over when reason can say no more."

Without the experience of the divine, faith can lead to disillusionment. The Bible says, without God, we can do nothing. We are justified by faith and not by works (Gal 3: 24). Trust in God is essential in order to strengthen one's faith to handle great challenges. Without faith it is impossible to please Him. If we decide to separate ourselves from God and do things by our will, we lose the power of connection to God. Hebrews 11:6 says, *"He who comes to God must believe that He is, and that He is a rewarder of those who diligently seek Him."* Ego hinders people from being grateful for the help they receive from God. We find our faith by developing awareness of the power and might of God in operating within us as a co-creator in our lives.

Law of Prayer and Fasting

Prayer is a way of building a relationship with God and resting in Him. Fasting helps us to shift from our focus on our body to a focus on the spirit, which inspires us to live our lives to our fullest potential. Judaism declares that God does not have a body form. Thus, when people pray to God, they pray as one human spirit praying to the Spirit of God. God is omnipresent, so He is there when you pray. Philip. 4:5-6 says, *"Be anxious for nothing, but in everything by prayer or supplication, with thanksgiving, let your requests be known to God."*

Mahatma Gandhi said that *"prayer is not asking. It is a longing of the soul. It is a daily admission of one's weakness."*

The law of prayer and fasting involves communion with God in petitions, praising, thanksgiving, and forgiveness. Fasting helps in purification of the body and self-control, which is needed to focus the mind on God. The Bible says, *"Pray without ceasing."* Prayer is a way to trust in God at every moment, and express your gratitude when your needs are met. *"Ask and ye shall receive, knock and it shall be opened unto you, seek and you shall find. God provides what we ask for by putting the answer within us since He dwells in us but let him ask in faith with no doubt"* (James 1:6).

Whenever you feel that you are veering from the path of wholeness, pray the prayer of St. Francis of Assisi:

> *"Lord, make me an instrument of your peace, where there is hatred let me sow love; where there is harm, pardon; where there is doubt, faith; where there is despair, hope; where there is darkness, light; where there is sadness, joy. Grant that I may not so much seek to be consoled but to console; To be understood, but to understand; To be loved, but to love For it is in giving that we receive. It is in pardoning that we are pardoned."*

Prayers keeps us in tune with our spirit and not our flesh. Jesus said in Luke 22:46, *"Why are you sleeping? Get up and pray so that you will not fall into temptations."* Prayer allows us to shift our consciousness from our body to our spirit so that you can talk to your spirit or spirit of God. After all, the miracle or present you want from God is a shift in your consciousness that allows you to heal yourself or find the answer to your request.

Fasting is a principle or law that helps us to control our sinful nature or desires of the flesh. Rom. 8:8 says, *"So then those who are living the life of the flesh cannot please or satisfy God or be acceptable to Him."* When we fast, we deprive the flesh from satisfaction and focus on the higher self. When we fast and pray, we do not satisfy the desires of the flesh, but we satisfy the soul's need for alignment with the higher self or spirit within us.

Law of Meditation and Contemplation

Meditation involves stillness and silence, renunciation of self, letting go of your self-interest and desiring nothing but God, so that God consciousness will merge with your consciousness.

The Bible says, *"Be still and know that I am God."* Your spirit is felt in the silence of your body, mind and soul. John 4:24 says, *"God is spirit and his worshippers must worship him in Spirit and in truth."* The practice of meditation leads to increase in peace, joy and increased alertness.

The Bible tells us in Psalm 77:6, *"I call to remember my song in the night, with my heart I meditate and my spirit searches diligently."* In prayers, we communicate with the personal God. In meditation, our spirit searches for the Spirit of God to renew and guide us. The Bhagavad Gita says in 2:66-67, *"There is no wisdom for a man without harmony, and without harmony there is no contemplation. Without contemplation, there cannot be peace and without peace can there be joy. For when the mind becomes bound to a passion of the wandering senses, this passion carries away wisdom, even as the wind drives a vessel on the waves."*

The Bhagavad Gita says in 4:58, *"When in recollection he withdraws all his senses from the attractions of the pleasures of sense, even as a tortoise withdraws all his limbs, then his is a serene wisdom."*

Bhagavad says in 9:18, *"I am the Way and the Master who watches in silence; thy friend and thy shelter and thy abode of peace. I am the beginning, middle and end of all things, their seed of eternity, their treasure supreme."*

In 6:36, the Gita says, *"When the mind is not in harmony, this divine communion is hard to attain, but the man whose mind is in harmony attains it, if he knows and if he strives."*

In 2:26, the Gita says, *"Invisible is He to mortal eyes, beyond thought and beyond change. Know that He is and cease thou from sorrow."*

Meditation is a spiritual practice that requires you to become still, silent and immersed in the silence of the Spirit of God within you. The spirit of the mind tends to be overshadowed by the incessant thoughts in our mind. So when we become still and silent, our thoughts tend to be silenced and the spirit is unveiled by the lack of thoughts overshadowing the spirit of the mind.

Law of Giving and Receiving

The Tao Te Ching says, *"The enlightened never hoard anything. They share their possessions. The more they give, the greater their abundance."* Be aware of yourself and the needs of others. Give with no expectation of reward. The Bible says, *"Let them do good that they will be rich in good works, ready to give, willing to share"* (1 Timothy 6:18). Be grateful for what you have. When you are grateful for what you have received, you are more open to blessings and opportunities. Deepak Chopra wrote poignantly in the *"The Seven Spiritual Laws of Success"* that *"the more you give, the more you will receive because you will keep the abundance of the universe circulating in your life."* He adds that, *"if you want joy, give joy to others, if you want love, give love; if you want attention and appreciation, learn to give attention and appreciation. If you want material affluence, help others to become materially affluent."*

Law of Non-judgmental Being

The Bible says in Matt. 7:1, *"Do not judge others and you will not be judged."* By not judging someone, we free ourselves from guilt, which comes when we do the same thing that we criticized. The Bible also says in Luke 6:37, *"Do not judge and you will not be judged, do not condemn and you will not be condemned. Pardon and you will be pardoned."* By understanding the personalities of others, you focus more on their positives than on their negatives and you help them overcome their mistakes.

The Bible also says, *"Do not discriminate as there is no partiality with God"* (Rom. 2:10-11) This law asks us to refrain from discrimination against others who may be different from us in terms of religion, race, gender, or tribe.

Law of Intention

This law requires us to have the confidence and faith in God such that whatever we intend comes true. Whatever you intend to do can change your situation, just give your intention the attention it deserves to get the job done. Each one of us can change our way of life from brokenness to wholeness through our good intentions. What you are seeking in the spirit of your soul, for your wholeness, is what you intend to work on for your transformation.

Deepak Chopra, in his book, *"The Seven Laws of Spiritual Success"*, wrote that, "Two *qualities are inherent in consciousness, attention and intention. Attention energizes and intention transforms. Whatever you put your attention on will grow strong in life. Whatever you take your attention away from will wither, disintegrate and disappear. Intention on the other hand triggers transformation of energy and information. Intention organizes its own fulfillment."*

I also read Gary Zukav's description of the Law of Intention in his book, *"The Seat of The Soul"*. He writes that *"every experience, every change in your experience reflects an intention. An intention is not only a desire. It is the use of your will. If you do not like the relationship you have with your husband or with your wife, for example, and you would like it to be different, that desire alone will not change your relationship. If you truly desire to change your relationship, the change begins with the intention to change it. How you change depends on the intention that you set."*

Law of Karma

The Law of Karma is the law of cause and effect. Every action that we take will result in a reaction or effect. Karma operates at the level of mind, body, and soul. Create good thoughts to avoid bad karmic influences. Karma yoga is the path of selfless action. This law says that as you sow so shall you reap. It is also rephrased in the Golden Rule in the Bible's Luke 6:31, *"Do to others as you would have them do unto you."* There is the belief in Eastern religions that we struggle with bad habits in life and suffer because we do not know ourselves and our ultimate reality. The law requires us to look within ourselves for the cause of our suffering and correct the bad habits, rather than blame others for our problems. The Bible says in Matt. 7:18, *"A good tree cannot bear bad fruit and a bad tree cannot bear good fruit."* In

Job 5:17, it says, *"Blessed is the one who God corrects."* The law of Karma operates at the level of mind, body, and soul.

Our actions are recorded in mysterious ways. Psalm 139:16 tells us *"You saw me before I was born. Every day of my life was recorded in your book. Every moment was laid out before a single day has passes.* Gal. 6:7 says *"Do not be deceived. God cannot be mocked. Whatever a man sows, so shall he reap. Whoever sows to please their flesh will reap destruction. Whoever sows to please the spirit will reap eternal life."*

Karma is a tendency to act in a certain way, and the individual soul's personality or way of actions and behavior is said to arise from Karma. According to Swami Sivananda, most of man's actions are done more or less automatically without great awareness. We need to be aware of our thoughts, desires, and actions as these provide the seed of consciousness. Deepak Chopra writes in the *"The Seven Spiritual Laws of Success"* that *"There are three ways you can do about past karma. One is to pay your karmic debts."* The *"second thing is to transmute or transform your karma to a more desirable experience,"* The *"third way to deal with karma is to transcend it. To transcend is to become independent of it."* Jesus transcended karma, as the Bible says that Jesus *"knew no sin."*

If others mistreat you, but you treat them well, you create good karma. If you fail to perform right actions, you fail to learn your soul's lessons. You follow your faith in God and make changes in your personality to be in line with your divine nature. This may require you to take up the cross of suffering for not satisfying the desires of your mind and flesh, but to renew your mind and be in a right relationship with God so that you can overcome bad habits and achieve the kingdom of God on Earth which is joy and peace.

Law of Destiny and Predestination

We come to this world to follow our destiny, which is our innermost calling. Your destiny is a predetermined course of events in your life based on your choices and innermost calling. Although humans have free will to choose what they want to do, Muslims believe that everything that happens in life is preordained unless God intervenes. The Bible says, *"With God, all things are possible."*

There are two types of destiny in life. There is human destiny and divine destiny. Human destiny depends on the family you were born, country of residence and the culture you were raised in to start your life. We obtain divine destiny because God destined us in love to be his children (Eph. 1:5). You could be raised in a life of struggle, but by partnering with God, your life can be transformed to wholeness.

You have a destiny, but you will not know, unless you know yourself, what you need to do to lock yourself into your destiny. When everything seems to go right for you, seamlessly and effortlessly, you know you are living according to your destiny.

We do not come on Earth to fool around and satisfy our ego. We have to know ourselves and the purpose God has for us. The Bhagavad Gita says, *"Better to follow one's own dharma, however humble, than to follow another's. Though great, by engaging in the work prescribed by one's own inner being, one does not miss the mark"* (Gita 18:47).

In *"The Astrology of Personality"*, Dane Rudhyar says,*"Destiny is essentially the individual schedule of growth, it is also subject to modifications which are not determined by the individual (his form or his past), but which are the results of the destiny of the greater whole (race, planet, cosmos) of which the individual is a part."*

Predestination is an act of God's will that helps you to move towards your destiny, but you still have to do the work for the wholeness of your soul. Predestination is God's determination of what each person's personality will become on Earth, depending on that person's karma. The Bible says, *"no one can lay hold on anything, unless it is given to him from on high"* (John 3:27).

We are all equal in the eyes of God as God is impartial. However, each person has a purpose, so we all do not start living from equal conditions when we are born. On the other hand, being born in poverty or wealth does not mean one is a person of wholeness. You still have to have your soul aligned to the awakened spirit within you. Purification of the soul is what we come to do on Earth in order to achieve wholeness before we can achieve a union with God. Bhavagad Gita 2:15 says, *"The man whom these cannot move, whose soul is one, beyond pleasure or pain, is worthy of life in eternity."*

CHAPTER TWENTY

Know Your Religious
Scriptures for Wholeness

Interpretation of Holy Scriptures

In *"The Purpose-Driven Life"*, Pastor Rick Warren writes about knowing who we are in Christ. What is the nature of God and Christ? Christ Jesus is the foundation of Christianity. The scriptures tell us that Christ was both man and divine and he was perhaps the greatest spiritual teacher to have lived on Earth. The scriptures provide us knowledge about ourselves and our Creator.

I am not a Biblical scholar. I admire spiritual teachers who do their best to interpret the messages in the Bible. The inspired messages from the Bible provide us information on how we are to behave and do what is pleasing to God. It is important that we read the scriptures ourselves and study them to know who we are according to our creator, and who we are in God. Otherwise we run the risk of others feeding us misinformation or misinterpretation of the word of God.

The challenge we have is whether to interpret the scripture literally or not. Are the stories allegories or do we take them as true history or mythic stories? This creates arguments between literalists and non-literalists, and between fundamentalists and liberals. Language can be used to create figures of speech, parables, allegories, similes, etc. When the disciples asked Jesus why he spoke to them in parables. He answered that the reason was *"because: it is given unto you to know the mysteries of the kingdom of heaven, but to them it is not given."*

Are We All Divine Beings?

In the Bible, Psalm 82:6 says, *"I have said, ye are Gods and all of you are children of the most high."* Jesus also tells us that we are divine. Jesus said, *"Ye are gods?"*(John 10:34). Does that mean that we are sons and daughters of God? Many spiritual teachers write that Jesus could be the best model for us to live our lives by. There has been no one else like Him. He had the perfect personality and the Mind of God. He is the way, the truth, and the path to attaining God consciousness.

No one has seen God, except the most spiritually evolved of human beings. However, we experience God in our lives. In John 10:33-36, Jesus said, *"Is it not written in your law that ye are gods."* He also said *"I am the Son of God."* In John 10:30, he said, *"I and my Father are one."* Some people view Jesus and God as a human being with a body.

Understand Your Religious Scriptures

When we do not understand the religious scriptures or hear the messages well, we choose to bring up the religious doctrines and religious laws. Gal 3:1-2 says, *"You poor and silly and thoughtless and unreflecting and senseless Galatians! Who has fascinated and bewitched or cast a spell over you, unto whom, right before your eyes, Jesus Christ was openly and graphically crucified? Let me ask you a question: Did you receive the Spirit as the result of obeying the law and doing the works, or was it by hearing and believing it (a law of rituals)."*

No religious system should make us so dumb that we accept whatever someone says about interpretation of the scriptures, without using valid reason, logic, or research to see if the statements or values agree with the Spiritual laws of God. My mentor advised me not to take the messages in the Bible literally but to test the truthfulness through research and experience.

It is okay when you are a child to accept things without understanding or experience. However, when you become an adult, you owe it to the wholeness of your soul to know what is logical or verifiable, based on scriptures, science, or experience.

As a Christian, I read the Bible for knowledge, inspiration, and the truth of who I am in God. I search for the meaning of the texts in the Bible that will help me to understand what it will take to transform my soul towards wholeness. I have found several texts that I use to fortify myself and make the right moves in the battle between good and evil, God and demons, purity and impurity, right and wrong, light and darkness, religion and racism, unity and division, peace and war, abstinence and cravings, sobriety and drunkenness, strength and weakness, and joy and pain.

Wholeness is Not Perfection, Jesus is Perfection

There is a difference between perfection and wholeness. Jesus was perfect, as He had a perfect personality based on his cognitive-affective personality type. The Bible also says he was without sin. You and I have a sinful nature, so we are not perfect. Wholeness does not mean a person is pure or sinless.

The experience of Christ is an experience of love, light, and truth. Jesus came to show us how to be human and have the power of divine potentialities. He showed us the way to be a whole person and divine at the same time. He showed that a whole person lives a life of love, peace, joy, kindness, and patience. He showed us his divine qualities by forgiving sins, healing the sick, and performing miracles.

Only God is pure consciousness. Wholeness is defined as fullness, ease, well-being, and maturity. We seek wholeness to indicate that we are fully mature, balanced in personality, and fully grown in spirit and soul to avoid the dumb mistakes of the unwholesome behavior of our past.

Wholeness implies that your body, mind and soul are aligned with your spirit to create a unified soul that is under your self-control to do what is right for wholeness. It is not a divisive self where the body self is doing one thing to satisfy its desires, the mind self is obsessive from its huge ego, the soul is lost, and the spirit is unawake or dormant.

Wholeness manifests in our body, mind, and spiritual behavior, The Bible says that when we are whole, and we are purified, we are well-beloved, kind, humble, gentle, and patient (Col. 3:12-14). The Bible also says that when we are whole we are transformed by the renewal of our mind and made acceptable for communion with God. It says, *"Do not be conformed to this world but be transformed by renewal of your mind so that you may prove what is good and acceptable and perfect will of God, even the thing which is acceptable and perfect"* (Rom. 12:1-2).

Lack of Wholeness from Multiple Personalities without Self-Control

When you have multiple personalities, there is no unity or one 'I' controlling your desires, thoughts, attitude, choices, and decisions. If you are whole, you have faith in God, you are self-controlled, and your attention, intentions, and will are concentrated for your soul to make the right decisions and right behavior.

Romans 7:15-19 says, *"For I do not understand my own actions. I do not practice or accomplish what I wish, but I do the very thing that I loathe. Now if I do what is contrary to my desire I acknowledge and agree that the Law is good and that I take sides with it?"*

> *"However, it is no longer I who do the deed, but the sin which is at home in me and has possession of me. For I know that nothing good dwells within me, that is in my flesh. I can will what is right, but I cannot perform it. For I fail to practice the good deeds that I desire to do, but the evil deeds that I do not desire to do are what I am doing."*

If one is not whole, you end up with multiple personalities within oneself. Each personality tries to pull you one way or the other. When you have wholeness, there is unity in your personality as the body, soul, and mind are aligned with the spirit.

Jesus said in Matt 12:43, *"But when the unclean spirit has gone out of a man, it roams through the dry places in search of rest, but it does not find any. Then it says, I will go back to my house from which I came out. And when it arrives, it finds the place unoccupied, swept, put in order and decorated. Then it goes and brings with it seven other spirits more wicked than itself and they go in and make their home there. And the last condition of that man became worse than the first. So also shall it be with this wicked generation."*

Purification of the Body, Mind, Soul and Spirit

Each person comes to the world with an imperfect personality. The human soul and spirit must be cleansed and made presentable for communion and union with God. The Spirit of God within us purifies our spirit, and our purified spirit renews the spirit of our mind. The soul is the conscious self, the observer and decider, but it cannot control the ego-mind easily. The soul journeys on the path to wholeness for purification and alignment of the body, mind, and soul with the reawakened and purified spirit.

Experience of the purified soul ought to be life-changing with the inward and outward manifestation of a whole person. We purify ourselves in various ways, including:

(a) Purifying The Body

Our body is a temple of God (1 Cor. 6:19) and has to be purified. The religious practice is one of baptism to cleanse the body and avoid desires of the flesh. The Bible says, "I appeal to you therefore, brethren and beg of you in view of the mercies of God to present your bodies as a living sacrifice, holy and well pleasing to God, which is your reasonable service and spiritual worship."

(b) Healing The Mind

We are transformed by the renewal of the spirit of our mind (Rom. 12: 20).

(c)   Purifying The Soul

Your soul is your true self or conscious self. It is the witness or observer with the ability to think and feel. The Bible says all have sinned and come short of the glory of God (Rom. 3:35). To purify our soul, we connect our soul to our awakened spirit and surrender to the will of God, pray and meditate continually for inner discipline, intention, and present-moment awareness, avoid attachments to money and possessions, read the Holy Scriptures, and obey the Spiritual laws. The result of purification fills our soul with joy, love, peace, gentleness, and kindness.

(d)   Purifying The Spirit

There is also spiritual wholeness, which is of a higher consciousness than soul wholeness and body wholeness. Wholeness of spirit is achieved through the renewal of our spirit by the Holy Spirit of God within us. We have to purify our conscience by the alignment of our soul with the wholeness of the spirit

We live a life of sin consciousness and need to change course for wholeness. Purification by baptism renews the mind. Purification by the spirit renews the soul to wholeness. The mind has to be renewed so that the ego is humbled, the human will is strengthened, and the truth is implemented in our lives.

Good Actions Strengthen and Evil Actions Weaken the Soul

Wholeness requires that your actions reveal who you we are. If your actions are good, you are considered a good man. If you change from drunkenness to sobriety, your body and soul change to reflect your change in behavior.

The Bible says in Luke 6:43-45, *"For there is no good tree that bears decayed fruit, nor on the other hand does a decayed tree bear good fruit. For each tree is known and identified by its own fruit; for figs are not gathered from thorn bushes, nor is a cluster of grapes picked from a bramble bush. The upright man out of the good treasure in his heart produces what is upright and the evil man out of the evil storehouse brings forth that which is depraved; for out of the abundance of his heart his mouth speaks."*

The Eye is The Window to Light and Darkness of The Soul

The eye is the window to the soul. It exposes the light or darkness of a soul. The Bible says in Luke 11:34-35, *"Your eye is the lamp of your body. When your eye is sound and fulfilling its office, your whole body is full of light, but when it is not sound and is not fulfilling its office, your body is full of darkness. Be careful therefore that the light that is in you is not darkness."*

Our Problems in the Battle of Life Are Self-inflicted

The Bible says in Rom. 14:17, *"The kingdom of God is not a matter of food and drink, but instead it is righteousness, peace and joy in the Holy Spirit."*

What blocks us from achieving wholeness and the Kingdom of God include the demons of our ego and our weaknesses, especially our weakness for the desires of the flesh. The Bible says in Gal. 5:19-21, *"Now the doings of the flesh are clear: they are immorality, impurity, indecency, idolatry, sorcery, enmity, strife, jealousy, anger, selfishness, divisions, party spirit (factions), envy, drunkenness, carousing and the like. I warn you and beforehand just as I did previously that those who do such things shall not inherit the kingdom of God."*

Choose Wholeness for the Prize is Worth It

Thank God for creating a beautiful world of plants and trees that bear delicious fruits for the body of man to enjoy. Because we make progress towards wholeness of the soul, God provides us fruits of the spirit. The Bible tells us in Gal 5:22-23: *"But the fruit of the spirit is love, joy, peace, patience, kindness, goodness, faithfulness, gentleness, self-control."*

Gal 5:25 says, *"If we live by the Spirit, let us also walk by the spirit. Let us not become vainglorious and self-conceited, competitive and challenging and provoking to one another, envying and being jealous of one another."*

Do what is right even if your body desires the wrong thing. We continue to live on the edge, making too many mistakes and hanging out in the dark side of life. We seem to enjoy our pleasures and pay for our excesses.

Past and Personal Goals

Our past tells us a lot about our character and tendencies. Our goals in life tell us where we are going. Jesus said in John 8:14, *"Even if I do testify on my own behalf, my testimony is true and reliable and valid, for I know where I am coming from and where I am going, but you do not know where I am coming from and where I am going."*

Do you have goals for wholeness? Our personal goals allow us to change our strategy for our personal and spiritual development. Everyone needs to bear witness to who they are in order to achieve self-realization. Self-realization is to know and experience who you truly are. Jesus knew who he truly was. He said, *"The Father and I are one."* His consciousness was in union with the consciousness of God. We have not reached the transcendent level of Jesus. We have opportunity to achieve wholeness of our souls. Wholeness helps us to know who we truly are. We are a spirit that can bear the fruit of love, peace, joy, and self-control.

Know Yourself to Appreciate Yourself

The Bible says a tree is known by its fruit. In Matt. 12:33, it says, *"Either make the tree sound and its fruit sound or make the tree rotten and its fruit rotten; for the tree is known and recognized and judged by its fruit."* If we think well about ourselves, we will try to show our goodness and others will take notice of our results.

Before I knew myself, I worried that I was too serious in disposition. Sometimes, people want to have fun, not to be serious all the time. Once I knew that being serious is a trait of Capricorns, who can be very ambitious, I became light-hearted about it. I accepted the way God made me. I began to look at being serious in a positive way rather than maintaining the negative outlook I had had about it.

The least we can do in the road to wholeness is to think well about who we are and love who we are. If we don't like who we are we will have a tough time in friendships and romantic relationships. If someone likes you but you don't like yourself, it means the two of you are out of sync. In relationships, you want to be in sync with each other to enjoy each other's company and avoid fighting, conflicts, misunderstanding, and tensions.

The Bible says in Matt. 12:30 that *"he who is not with me is against me and he who does not gather with me and for my side scatters."*

Living With Worry and Fear

A person with wholeness of soul is calm, at ease, well balanced, self-controlled, strong, and courageous. Timothy 1:7 tell us that, *"God did not give us a spirit of timidity, but of power and of love and of calm and well balanced mind and discipline and self-control."*

Put your spirit into everything you do. If we can turn our weaknesses into strengths, we will be powerful. We cannot be powerful if we show fear. To conquer our fears, we have to give up control by ego, live with love, and trust in God. The quest for wholeness is to bear the fruit of the spirit. If you are determined to be whole, you do not want to live a life of fear. It is not easy to conquer fear because our body reacts to our thoughts of fear by showing physical and emotional reactions, such as panic, trembling, shaking, and an increased heart rate. Fear leads to worry, anxiety, conflicts with others, and stress.

They say the poor worry about money because that is the one thing they want to have. Jesus says we should not worry if we are poor and serve God, rather serving money. The Bible says in Matt. 6:25-26, *"No one can serve two masters for either he will hate the one and love the other; or he will stand by and be devoted to the one and despise and be against the other. You cannot serve God and mammon. Therefore, I tell you stop being uneasy about your life, what you shall eat or what you shall drink or about your body, what you shall put on. Is not life greater than food, and the body than clothing?"*

Living With a Joyful Spirit or a Broken Spirit

John 15:10-12 tells us, *"But we believe that we are saved by the grace of the Lord."* We all have experienced brokenness of our spirit in one form or another. A good friend may hurt you when you least expected it. A wonderful relationship is cut short by the other partner or your sister makes an unkind and wounding remark that makes you wonder if you are safe from attacks. So we seek healing of the soul to repair the wound and make us whole again.

Live With Love by Leaning on God

We lean on God in the journey to wholeness so that we can have strength, love, joyfulness, and determination to complete the task. We know God's hand at work through love. The Bible says in 1 John 4:10-13, *"In this is love; not that we loved God, but that he loved us and sent his Son to be the propitiation for our sins. Beloved, if God loved us so much, we also ought to love one another. No man has at any time seen God, but if we love one another, God abides in us and His love is brought to completion. By this we come to know that we abide in him and him in us; because He has given to us of His Spirit."* We obtain spiritual gifts if we walk in the spirit. The Bible says in Cor. 12:7-9, *"But to each one is given the manifestation of the Spirit for good and profit. To one is given the Spirit of wisdom and to another a word of knowledge and understanding according to the same Spirit. To another, faith by the same Spirit, to another the extraordinary powers of healing by the one Spirit."*

Change Your Old Nature to Your New Person

Jesus says we have to lose ourselves to gain ourselves. We die to our old selves and are restored as new.

When we go on the path of personal improvement and spiritual development, we have to show that we have changed our old behaviors that limited our ability to develop spiritually. Col. 3:5 says, *"So kill the evil desire lurking in your members in you; sexual vice, impurity, sensual appetites, unholy desires and all greed and covetousness for that is idolatry."*

We also have to renew our mind to change our personalities. Ephesians 4:22-24 says, *"Strip yourself of your former nature which characterized your previous manner of life and becomes corrupt through lusts, and desires that spring from delusion. And be constantly renewed in the spirit of your mind. And put on the new nature in true righteousness and holiness."*

Examine Your Weaknesses

God uses our weakness to help us grow (Job 2:11-37, 24). Self-examination is not easy to do. My experience is that knowing yourself is one of the keys to wholeness. The Bible says in 1 Cor. 11:28-31 that, *"Let a man examine himself and so should he eat of the bread and drink of the cup. For anyone who eats and drink without discrimination and recognizing with due appreciation that body, eats and drinks a sentence upon himself. That is the reason many of you are weak and sickly and quite frankly have fallen into the sleep of death."*

We also show weakness in our faith from time to time. The Bible says in Rom. 14:1-8, *"As for the man who is a weak believer, welcome him but not criticize his opinions or pass judgment on his scruples or perplex him with discussions."*

CONCLUSION

At this point in your life, you want to know yourself and your plan for wholeness; if you have not done so, it is time to get it done for wholeness sake. There is a difference between wholeness and happiness. Money, possessions, a sunny climate, girlfriends, boyfriends, and travel can make people happy. Wholeness gives you a full life, integrity, unconditional love, well-being, and joy. If you understand who you are, you understand different layers of yourself, such as your body self, mental self, psychological personality, religious nature, spiritual path, astrological sign and higher self.

In mapping out your path to wholeness, you want to know the following areas of your life and organize them to achieve wholeness of your body, mind, soul, and spirit. Your wholeness map should cover:

- Your body type and health
- Your mental type and emotional behavior
- Your psychological personality type
- Your soul's purpose and destiny in life
- Your astrological Sun sign and ascendant
- Your Chinese sign
- Your religious beliefs, faith, and scriptures
- Your spiritual path, spiritual laws, and spiritual practices

- Your strengths and weaknesses

- Your needs for wholeness and areas to avoid

- Your action plans for soul and spiritual rebirth

- Your body-mind-soul-spirit alignment

- Your birthday numbers and your challenges to overcome

- Your love life, relationships, and partnerships

- Your degree of compatibility with others in relationships

- Your generational behavior

- Integration of yourself to become a whole person.

The table below shows an example of a wholeness map. Each of us is continuously evolving physically, mentally, emotionally, soulfully, and spiritually. Your experiences and progress will provide the evidence for further revision of your wholeness path. Hopefully, you will come to realize the importance of religion, astrology, and science of psychology in your life, as these disciplines evolve to provide better characterization of the well-integrated human personal.

TABLE 7. WHOLENESS MAP OF AN INDIVIDUAL

Description ofSelf	Type	Strengths	Tendencies	Weakness	Needs for Wholeness	What to Avoid
Body	Kapha-pitta	Gluteal muscles, tall, athletic	Belly fat, tight muscles	Slow walk-ing, knees, bones	Exercise, vitality, relaxation	Self-indulgence, high stress
Energy	Introvert	Calm, inner life	Slower to anger	Low excitement	Spontaneous, having fun	Not patient
Mental	Logical Thinker	Doer, Organized	Judicious, Cautious	Emotion, Imagination	Empathy	Negative emotions
Psychology Personality	Guardian-Inspector	Realistic, logistical	Disciplined, managerial	Too serious, overcautious	Heal emotions, spontaneous	Too judgmental

Soul Purpose	Seek God, mysticism	Knowledge, spirituality	Driven	Narrow mindedness	Emotional, discipline	Spiritualism, closed mind
Birthday Sun Sign	Capricorn	Determined, take charge	Achiever, initiator	Too serious, gloomy	Optimism, sociable, fun	Authoritative, selfishness
Ascendant	Scorpio	Transformer, forceful	Endurance, sensual	Too serious, controlling	Intuitive, Self-control	Secretiveness
Chinese Sign	Horse	Humanitarian, action-oriented	Ambitious, self-reliant, free spirit	Opportunistic, self-centered	Selfless, social skills	Isolationist, private
Religious Beliefs	Christianity	Catholic faith, community, worship	Righteous living, moral code	Dogma	Faith in God, service, ministry	Materialism, tribalism, corruption
Spiritual Path	Spiritual knowledge	Spiritual practice	Meditation	self-centered	Love, high consciousness	Lack of self-control
Birthday number (Soul Lessons)	#6, universal, humanity	Caring, Compassion	Perfectionist, adviser	Snobbish	Loving, responsible	Injustice, dissatisfaction
Career	Research	Creativity, strategic thinking	Logistical, process Integration	Social responsibility	Optimism, Communicate	Incompatible boss, avoid gossiping
Supervisor Style	Conductor	Collaboration	Competitive	Clarifying	Empathy	Bossiness
Leadership Style	Situational Leadership	Directive, coaching, delegating	Strategic leadership	Political skills, wheeling and dealing	Integral visionary leadership	Autocratic leadership
Astrological Elements	Earth, Wood	Down to earth, builder, diligent	Quiet, Inner life	Reserved	Structure, stability	Self-centered, worry
Compatibility	Capricorn, horse	Virgo, Taurus	Cancer	Emotional	Soul mate, Evolution	Incompatible individuals
Partnerships	Fire Sign, Social partners	Increased Energy	Air Sign, spiritual partners	Water sign, emotional partners	Fire Sign, Earth sign	Seriousness

Now that you have completed your wholeness map, you have found a way to learn about yourself, see your strengths, discover your weaknesses, integrate your divided self into your vision of your whole self and practice what you need for wholeness to transform who you are and maximize your potential for wholeness, happiness and godliness.

You have now come to value yourself and your purpose. You want to put in great effort to do your soul work effortlessly for a meaningful life and fulfilment. You know which religious faith is more meaningful and transformative for you. You know how your spiritual path matches your personality; whether it is the path of service, compassion, love and devotion, spiritual knowledge, priesthood or mystic. Watch how, armed with this self-knowledge and map to wholeness, you become assertive, fearless, and confident because you know your roots, strengths, source of power, values, connections, and the parts of you that need development, sprouting, and growth.

It is not easy to correct the deficiencies of your personality, but you can grow and expand in consciousness to make the right changes in behavior, habits, addictions and tendencies. There are various types of consciousness depending on what we focus on. Do you have a high consciousness of your body, mind, or soul most of the time? When your consciousness expands you develop greater self-control and the wisdom to make good decision and solve problems.

A friend once told me that the way to the transformation of your weaknesses into strengths and getting rid of bad habits is not so much about doing something to let people know you are trying, but changing your being. The emphasis is not on the self-help or self-growth, but through wholeness of your being, by increasing your spiritual consciousness of God and aligning your soul with your awakened spirit. Your total self is made up of your true self and your acquired self. What you want to transform are the ten different types of consciousness listed below, making each part whole in itself and integrating them into a whole being.

- Spiritual awareness (Spirit consciousness)

- Psychological type (Mind consciousness)

- Astrological/ Chinese Signs (Soul consciousness)

- Spiritual path (Consciousness of faith in God)

- Purpose in life (Consciousness of your destiny)

- Body type (Body consciousness)

- Energy (Chakra consciousness)

- Genetics (Consciousness of hereditary)

- Gender (Consciousness of gender differences)

- Race (Consciousness of racial stereotypes)

We are also challenged by bad habits, such as overeating, lying, excessive alcohol intake, excessive smoking, drug addictions, emotional outbursts, nagging, and disagreeableness. For most people, the elimination of bad habits becomes more difficult as one moves from youth to mature adult. Therefore, there is such a strong need to understand the importance of wholeness and the joy, peace, and self-control it brings to the individual. Smoking was easy for me to quit because it didn't make sense to have the cigarette control me. The key to wholeness is self-control rather than going to extremes, and thus becoming well-balanced.

We are taught by spiritual teachers, counselors, priests, and pastors to correct our behavior and bad habits by right actions, such as:

- Know your strengths and weaknesses to get rid of bad habits.

- Live in the present moment.

- Use your power of intellect, will and discrimination.

- Be open-mind and show more openness.

- Love everyone regardless of race, religion and gender.

- Avoid negative emotions, such as anger, hatred, and moodiness.

- Cultivate strong friendships with people that you are compatible with.

- Learn to engage with other individuals who are incompatible with you.

- Serve others with a humble ego.

- Read the scriptures, pray, and meditate every day to renew your mind.

- Do the effortless soul work necessary for your attainment of wholeness.

The Tao Te Ching says in v. 48 that an effective way to get things done effortlessly is *"Until all is done without doing. When the ego interferes in the rhythms of progress, there is so much doing. But nothing is done."* Wholeness is a high level of spiritual consciousness, below unity consciousness or enlightenment. As we proceed on our spiritual path, we grow, mature, and attain knowledge, wisdom, and wholeness. We continue to have faith in ourselves and in God when we run into setbacks and temptations. The body, soul, mind, and spirit must be well-integrated, balanced, and harmonious for wholeness.

If the body dominates and has its way, pleasures and the desires of the flesh will take you over. If the emotions and ego of the mind take over the self, selfishness will rule and the soul and spirit will be hidden in subjectivity or imprisoned. If the soul dominates and the personality takes over, the spirit is not awakened. If the spirit is dominant over the body, mind, and soul, you become a recluse or renounce the world because you cannot function on Earth.

The Tao Te Ching says in v.10, *"When embracing the unity of mind, body, emotions and spiritual being can we transcend our fragmentations without being a trace?"* Once we become whole, our thoughts are sane and wholesome. We meditate on the spirit daily and go beyond thoughts, desires, and fears to seek our Creator. The more love we show others, the more humble we become. Our relationships become more harmonious and our actions originate from love rather than ego. We interact easily with others, listen well for what may come from the spirit, and inspire others.

Our decisions come from the silence of our hearts and spirit. They are not impulsive or manipulative. We practice selflessness, not self-centeredness. We do all we can to expand our consciousness so that we go beyond ourselves, focus on others, and tune into God consciousness. We do not perform evil deeds, but if we make mistakes, fall to temptations or fall back on our bad habits, we repent and seek the spirit of God within to purify our minds so that we may return to the road to wholeness.

The Tao Te Ching says in v.7, *"The wise are heard through their silence, always self-full through selflessness."* In all, we want to move from self-centeredness and selfishness to selflessness and an integrated soul and personality.

ABOUT THE AUTHOR

Andrew Benedict Acheampong, PhD is a Christian of Catholic faith, seeker of spiritual knowledge, mystic philosopher, and scientist. He has a life-long pursuit of knowledge of body chemistry, drug safety, spiritual practices, religious faiths, science of personality and astrology of personality with the aim of enhancing interest in power of self-knowledge and overcoming life's challenges to achieve wholeness of body, mind, and soul.

He was born in Ghana and educated in Ghana, Canada and the United States. He joined a leading Pharmaceutical company in the US in 1989 and rose to the level of Scientific Director. He has over 30 years of experience in drug discovery and development and has published over 50 scientific articles.

He holds a BSc in Chemistry from the University of Science and Technology, Kumasi, Ghana and MSc and PhD degrees in Pharmaceutical Sciences from the University of British Columbia, Vancouver, Canada. He obtained his post-graduate training at Howard University, Washington DC and University of Washington, Seattle.

REFERENCES

Albert Einstein, *The World as I See It.* Citadel, New York, 2006.

Bible. *New King James Version.* Thomas Nelson Publishers, New York, 1982.

Bible. *Amplified Version.* Zondervan, Grand Rapids, Michigan, 1987.

Chris Fabry. *The 77 Habits of Highly Ineffective Christians.* InterVarsity Press, Illinois, 1997.

Damian Sharp. *Simple Chinese Astrology.* Conari Press, San Francisco, 2006.

Dane Rudhyar. *The Astrology of Personality.* Aurora Press, Santa Fe, NM, 1991.

David Aaron. *The Secret Life of God: Discovering the Divine Within You.* Shambhala Publishing, Boston, 2004.

David C. Funder and Daniel J. Ozer. *Pieces of the Personality Puzzle.* W. W. Norton Company, New York, 2001.

David Hawkins. *Power vs. Force: The Hidden Determinant of Human Behavior.* Hay House, USA, 1995.

Deepak Chopra. *The Seven Spiritual Laws of Success.* Amber-Allen Publishing, San Rafael, California, 1994.

Eckhart Tolle. *A New Earth: Awakening to Your Life's Purpose.* Penguin Group, New York, 2006.

Frederick K.C. Price. *Race, Religion and Racism*. Faith One Publishers, Los Angeles, 1999.

Hans J. Eysenck. *Dimmensions of Personality*. Transaction Publishers, Piscataway, NJ, 1997.

Gary Zukav. *The Seat of the Soul*. Simon and Schuster, New York 1990.

John Garrison. *The Psychology of The Spirit*. Xlibris Corp., 2001.

Jean Simpson, *Hot Numbers*. Crown Publishers, New York,1986.

John Main. *Silence and Stillness in Every Season*. Edited by Paul Harris. Continuum Publishing, New York, 1997.

John Sandford. *The Kingdom Within. The Inner Meaning of Jesus' Sayings*. Harper San Francisco, 1987.

Juan Mascaro. *The Bhaghavad Gita*. Penguin Books, 1962.

Karen Armstrong. *Buddha*. Penguin Group, New York, 2004.

Karen Armstrong. *The History of God: a 4,000-year Quest of Judaism,Christianity and Islam*. Ballantine Books, 1994.

Kathleen Riordan Speeth. *The Gurdjieff Work*. Penguin-Putnam, New York, 1989.

Ken Wilber. *The Integral Vision*. Shambhala Publishing, Boston 2007.

Lao Tzu. *Tao Te Ching*. Commentary by Ralph Alan Dale. Watkins, London, 2002.

Lawrence Freeman. *Light Within ... Meditation*. Crossroad Publishing Company, New York, 1995.

Linda Goodman. *Linda Goodman's Sun Signs*. Bantam Books, New York, 1971.

Linda Joyce. *The Day You Were Born. A Journey to Wholeness through Astrology and Numerology.* MJF Books, New York, 1998.

Maharishi Mahesh Yogi and the Bhagavad Gita: A New Translation and Commentary. Arkana Penguin Group, 1990.

Maharishi Mahesh Yogi. *The Science of Being and Art of Living.* Penguin Group, New York, 1988.

Maharishi Mahesh Yogi. *Transendental Meditation.* New American Library, New York, 1975.

Meister Eckhart: The Man From Whom God Nothing Hid. Edited by Ursula Fleming. Templegate Publishing, Springfield, Illinois, 1990.

P. D. Ouspensky. *The Fourth Way.* Vintage Book, New York, 1971.

Richard Dawkins. *The Magic of Reality.* Free Press, New York, 2012.

Rick Warren. *The Purpose-Driven Life.* Zondervan, Grand Rapids, Michigan, 2002.

Rita Carter. *The Human Brain Book.* DK, Adult, 2009.

Robert Pollock. *The World Religions.* Fall River Press, 2008.

Saffi Crawford and Geraldine Sullivan. *The Power of Birthdays, Stars and Numbers.* Ballantine Books, 1998.

Shambhala. *The Essential Ken Wilber.* Shambhala Publishing, New York, 1998.

Sally Cragin. *Astrology of the Cusp – Birthdays on the Edge of Two Signs.* Llewellyn Publications, MN, 2012.

Stephen Montgomery. *People Patterns – A Modern Guide to the Four Temperaments.* Prometheus Nemesis Book Company, 2002.

Suzanne White. *Chinese Astrology.* Tuttle Publishing, Vermont, 2000.

Swami Sivananda. *Mind, Its Mysteries & Control.* The Divine Life Society, India, 1974.

Swami Sivananda. *Bliss Divine.* Divine Life Society, India, 1965.

Sydney Omarr's Series. *Aries 1999, Taurus 1999, Gemini 1999, Cancer 1999, Leo 1999, Virgo 1999, Libra 1999, Scorpio 1999, Sagittarius 1999. Capricorn 1999, Aquarius 1999, Pisces 1999.* Signet, 1998.

T. Z. Lavine. *From Socrates to Sartre: The Philosophic Quest.* Bantam Books, New York, 1984.

Thomas Merton. *The Inner Experience.* Edited by William Shannon. Harper Collins, New York, 2004.

Thomas Merton. *No Man is an Island.* Mariner Books, Boston, MA, 2002.

Thomas Merton. *The Ascent to Truth.* Harvest Book, Harcourt, New York, 1979.

Thomas Merton. *Thoughts of Solitude.* Farrar Strauss, Giroux, New York, 1999.

Wayne W. Dyer. *The Power Intention.* Hay House, Carlsbad, CA 2005.

CPSIA information can be obtained at www.ICGtesting.com
Printed in the USA
BVOW05s0421290514

354751BV00010BA/228/P